Second Chance

Also by Herbert B. Livesey

The Professors
Anyone Can Go to College

Second Chance
Blueprints for Life Change

Herbert B. Livesey

J.B. Lippincott Company
Philadelphia and New York

Portions of this book have been excerpted in *Quest*
and in *Travel and Leisure.*

U.S. Library of Congress Cataloging in Publication Data

Livesey, Herbert B
    Second chance.

    Bibliography: p.
    1. Occupational mobility—United States.
    2. Social mobility—United States. 3. Middle age.
    I. Title.
    HN65.L57   301.5'5   77–8571
    ISBN–0–397–01223–3

For Samantha and Alexander,
the reasons

Contents

Second Chance

1
The Other Side

Thus, through our foolish curiosity, do we macerate ourselves, tire our souls, and run headlong through our indiscretion, perverse will, and want of government, into many needless cares and troubles, vain expenses, tedious journeys, painful hours; and, when all is done, to what end?
—Robert Burton, *The Anatomy of Melancholy* (1651)

Americans are the restless children of wanderers. We move, fourteen times in each lifetime, one-fifth of us every year. The descendants of rebels, we are summoned to new revolutions, sexual, spiritual, and technological. We shed partners, two million times a year, in order that we may join with different ones. Or we modify gender, under the knife or by the ways we choose to act. Promised tranquillity or ecstasy or both, we eschew meat, attach wires to our minds, or entwine our limbs while listening to the river. Then we discover there is one more last frontier beyond the one just breached. If dazzled by the panoply of options arrayed before us, we are said to be vacillating and indecisive. If we rush to consume them, we are immature.

Simultaneously, we are invited to despair and urged to leap away. And chastised for both.

Yet life is change, and change is risk. The fault lies not in the quest but the method. A realistic alteration of the ways we live can rejuvenate us and refresh our relationships with others. Even in failure, we gain. Should social observers call us selfish—as they have—or hedonistic or misdirected or self-absorbed, so be it. We are here just this one time, and the responsibility is ours alone.

This is a book of attainable fantasies. While there are no rules for creating a new life, we each bear within us a hidden agenda. By learning from others' experiences and by gleaning advice from professional change agents, we can identify it, and formulate and implement an appropriate design. That is the intent of the pages to follow.

"There are no second acts in American lives," wrote F. Scott Fitzgerald. Perhaps that was true of his generation, an era of fifty-years-and-a-watch. But that was before interstate highways, easy divorce, air conditioning, legal abortion, wide-bodied jets, television. There are means to escape now, and we become discontented with our lot more readily, for we know what we are missing. Motivation is there, certainly. The Department of Health, Education, and Welfare says that 57 percent of all white-collar workers and 64 percent of those in blue-collar positions are unhappy in their jobs and would choose differently if they could start again.

It isn't simply lack of money or privilege, either. Top-level managers are getting more of both than ever, and enjoying them less. John DeLorean, for example, suddenly quit the executive suite of General Motors one spring day in 1974. A promising candidate for the presidency at only forty-eight, he left behind a $550,000 salary and a raft of corporate perquisites because he felt mired in unproductive paperwork and committee meetings. He couldn't plan or innovate, he complained.

The executive drain is a favorite topic of business publications. *The Wall Street Journal* and *Business Week* print a steady flow of articles on boardroom dropouts. *Dun's Review,* in one of their periodic "where-are-they-now?" pieces, told of wealthy young entrepreneur Martin Ackerman's turning London art patron, conglomerateur Robert Kenmore as a Stanford graduate student, and former Bank of America president Rudolph Peterson, now a United Nations administrator.

Stockbrokers seem especially vulnerable to the itch, in keeping with hallowed occupational tradition. Paul Gauguin, after all, was a fixture in Parisian investment circles before he sailed for Tahiti at age forty-five in the cause of Postimpressionism. *New York* magazine, among others, has written of brokers and analysts who switched to landscape architecture, film production, land sales, medical research, and carpet-cushion manufacturing. Another was James Brown, Yale '56. In 1968, the apogee of the go-go sixties, Jim raked in $168,000. He had a thirty-six-foot sailboat, a Cessna 172, a Jaguar XKE, "the prettiest Colonial in Darien," a seat on the Exchange, and a his-and-hers shrink. He left all that, and the Street, for a new wife and a free-lance photography business in Marblehead, Massachusetts.

Nor is it merely a flight from challenge. As often, it is a desire to master new fields. Charles Perry was one of the youngest university presidents in the country, making just one dollar a year less than the governor of Florida. At thirty-seven, Perry abandoned sunshine and his "no-win" job to become publisher of *Family Weekly* in New York.

Many changes are mandated by profession: the defeated politician, the aging athlete, the fading movie star. The transition need not lead to anonymity, ineffectuality, or poverty. It can be done with flair. There is Gene Autry, now presiding over a $70-million empire of five radio and TV stations, a film production center, a national sales firm, the California Angels, a cattle ranch, and his own Palm Springs hotel. Not merely a lucky investor, Autry built it all from scratch, starting in his mid-forties, when his career as a singing cowboy was starting to dim. Politics attracted actor Ronald Reagan but ultimately repelled Harold Hughes, the Iowa businessman–senator–presidential candidate who fled Washington to pursue a religious calling. Karl Hess executed an about-face from Barry Goldwater ideologue to back-to-the-earth anarchist. Ken Dryden, quitting in his prime as a top-ranked goalie for the Montreal Canadiens, swapped the ice for the law, and Cary Middlecoff went from dentist to golfer. Composer Charles Ives was in the insurance business until age fifty-six, Robert McNamara went from the Ford Motor Company to the World Bank via the Cabinet, and John Gardner from professor to foundation president to HEW to Common Cause.

But these are exceptional individuals who could trade on past achievements, contacts, financial resources, and often all three, in choosing new directions. More urgent are the needs of those forced to change through circumstances: the housewife newly divorced or widowed, the career soldier prematurely retired, the middle-level manager unemployed through failure of his company. And more intriguing still is the man or woman firmly established in an outwardly gratifying career and life-style who opts to throw it all over for a seemingly unrelated endeavor of uncertain future and compensation.

For commuters trapped in railroad cars and traffic jams, for women facing one more day of folding laundry and making beds, it would seem an impossible dream. How can people seemingly fulfilled, more successful in their first-chosen vocations than most, simply discard that security and the years which went into building it? Where did they find the emotional wherewithal to wrench away from once-acceptable assumptions? What did it cost—in money, in retraining, in accumulated benefits, in relationships with others?

Then come the wistful fancies: If only I had finished school. If only the kids were older. If only we hadn't taken on this mortgage. If only I hadn't married. If only I hadn't left that other job. Or the reverse of any of these and countless other "if-onlys." Then the telephone rings, the train lurches forward, the horns blare, and the dreamer is nudged back to the moment, vaguely regretting what might have been.

But there are answers to those questions. It can be done. All positive life changers share two qualities: the will to try and the recognition that all of us possess dormant talents awaiting exploitation.

The courage to restructure our lives dramatically when and as we wish is bred out of us as much by our own preconceived notions of what is socially acceptable as by actual external pressures. On only three occasions during our lifetimes are most of us actually *forced* to change: upon entering school, when leaving it, and when retiring. In between, we are encouraged to adhere to the verities of the group in which we find ourselves, which are, in turn, established by those who have gone before and enforced by those who now chart our progress.

In absorbing those values and in benefiting from them, we learn to fear. It is dread of loss that prevents us from suddenly altering our goals. Certainly there is much to be lost: seniority, regularity of income, retirement annuities, the education of children, even our homes and possessions. Change can mean deferred or terminated relationships with those about whom we care. Worse yet, it can diminish our power over others or reverse the balance altogether. For some, it may mean an unwelcome realignment of roles.

Consider this story of a New York advertising account executive. After sixteen years of marriage he wants to take a year off, to write the novel he cannot do so long as he must spend his days stimulating the public to deodorize and depilitate itself. There is enough money to pay basic expenses for that period, but he and his family will have to do without the winter vacation, the customary new car, the golf and beach club . . . unless his wife wants to get into real estate, as she's idly speculated in the past. They discuss it and decide to do it.

The immediate prospects are happy ones. For him, it means no more rising at six thirty to catch the seven thirty-six to the city, a leisurely breakfast while reading the newspaper as thoroughly as he's always wanted, a few hours at the typewriter, the opportunity to be there when his daughters get home from school, to go to the hardware store on a quiet Tuesday rather than on a crowded Saturday, to get to know the town he's only slept in, to escape peevish clients and petty staff. For her, it promises to snap the treadmill of chauffeuring and shopping and washing and cooking, of having to cope with an irritable, moody husband who forgets, after the third vodka Gibson, that she has to get up at six thirty, too. Someone else can deal with the plumber, make lunch, cover overdrafts at the bank, and take the girls to the dentist and basketball games, while she gets a chance to test herself and to be measured in the only way anyone ever does—by the number of dollar bills she can bring home.

He'll miss, of course, those moments of triumph when painfully developed campaigns are embraced by new accounts, the gossip about the failures of other agencies, the annual convention at the Cerromar, the stolen nights with imaginative Nancy. And she'll miss the second cup of coffee with the paper when everyone's gone, her Wednesday tennis when the courts are empty, dinner and a show once a month on his expense account, the secret afternoons with gentle Andy.

But they're going into it with their eyes open. It will work.

It does, for a while. In a spirit of sharing, he volunteers to make the beds, vacuum the floors. He learns to bake bread, as he's always wanted. She captures a position with a local realtor, begins studying for her license. He writes, she sells. They go to PTA meetings together. He drinks less, starts to grow a beard. She loses weight, builds a suitable wardrobe. They go to the movies and hold hands. The girls are openly pleased he is there. She is getting the knack of her new work faster than she thought.

Their new careers go *just as they planned,* and their roles inevitably shift. She is now late for dinner, testy, asking if he picked up the dry cleaning as she asked. She has prospects she must see in the evenings and on weekends. He finds that the household chores he willingly undertook take bigger chunks of each day. Or he neglects them and is distressed with the messy house. Finally at his typewriter, he is interrupted by meter readers, magazine salesmen, and missionaries of religious sects. He must take messages for his wife, and he is no longer charmed by the chance to help with daily teenage disasters. Isolated in the house much of the time, he is dependent upon his wife for conversation and adult companionship, but when she is there, she wants to talk about her day. In response to his news, she offhandedly bestows advice about his clogged drain and which veterinarian he should have used when something wiggled in the litter box.

He has lost the power over others to which he was long accustomed, and only now does he admit to himself that he relished it. It is not just that it was his paycheck she put in the bank, but that he could deflect her household complaints by showing the colors of his more meaningful tasks and accompanying travails. And when, in retaliation, she paid scant attention, there were always people in the city who listened and who understood.

Further, he no longer controls the disbursement of favors and small luxuries. It's not that they couldn't live on what he put aside for this sabbatical, for they could. But it would restrict them to off-brand liquor and jug wine instead of the Glenfiddich and Gevrey-Chambertin they had grown to favor, swimming at the public beach rather than at the club's pool, two weeks in the Berkshires, not a month in Marbella. They still live pretty much as they did, but now the extras are underwritten by *her* income, not his. He doesn't say these things, for to do so would be to admit he wanted those tools of domestic hegemony.

So he finds other things. He liked her hair the way it was before, he tells her. There is, he feels, a briskness in her tone lately. But she's lived with him a long time. She knows the reason for his criticism. She reminds him she did this because *he* wanted to. She was simply being dutifully supportive. Now that they've done it. . . .

And so on. As it happens, these are real people, alive and well, in Weston, Connecticut, not characters in a marital *Admirable Crichton*. But it would require little imagination on the part of anyone contemplating such a change to spin out a similar scenario, adjusting pertinent details. Even those untempted by such a reverie can subconsciously sense the implications.

It is common for many who feel they are approaching important intersections in their lives to fear losing their dominance in personal relationships—but it is by no means universal. There are those in whom the need for such authority is absent or undeveloped or who rarely experience it from either direction. These people are established in careers that do not involve exercising prerogatives over others, or they are independent of parents and are bound to neither spouse nor permanent partner. Seemingly, they are without restriction, free to move in any direction. On the surface, an enviable situation.

Our society is not hospitable to iconoclasts, however, despite our collective protestations to the contrary. Peple who choose to remain unmarried or to forgo having children are suspect. So are those who move on to other jobs when they feel they have contributed, learned, and profited as much as appears likely in a given work experience. They are told they are not loyal or properly grateful. Worse, they are self-indulgent. For their own good, they should stick things out, hone the skills taught them at great expense to their employers. If they do not, they are labeled childish Walter Mittys pursuing adolescent fantasies.

It is a logic few are able to resist much beyond early adulthood. To defy it is to invite immobilizing guilt and, in compensation, to become in fact that which one has been accused of being: irresponsible and rootless. Besides, no matter how adventuresome we may be, we inevitably develop relationships, and the assumptions of those individuals or groups weave their tightening webs. To meet their expectations, we increasingly limit ourselves to those endeavors in which we are most likely to do well—based upon prior evaluations not necessarily our own—and avoid those we have not tried or in which we have failed before. As those skills are sharpened and we are rewarded accordingly, our natural taste for exploration atrophies, along with our capacity for wonder.

Sooner or later, we grow to feel enslaved by the institutions we serve. We become addicted to the work that has provided comforts we cannot enjoy. Visions of liberation intensify, but we brush the moments of imagined escape aside. We no longer have the energy to take on new knowledge or to tolerate fresh stimuli, we say. It's not the right time, we insist. Just one more step on the ladder. There's too much to lose.

It is not simply to protect their stock prices or malefactors that corporations and governmental agencies insist upon the heartiest optimism at all levels of management and public proclamation—where problems become "opportunities," and disasters are "challenges"—it is to mask the fact that pessimism is the primary characteristic of the status quo. "Don't anyone move, or it will all collapse around our ears."

This needn't be. We must push ourselves into fresh perspectives and break the inertia of habit and routine.

Sometimes the incentive is provided us.

2
The Last Straw

They that live in fear are never free; resolute, secure, never merry, but in continual pain.
— Robert Burton, *The Anatomy of Melancholy*

Stillman Drake was born in San Francisco before there were bridges. Nearly all of his first fifty-six years were spent there. His club and his office, where he worked as a municipal bond specialist for an investment banking firm, were at the lower end of Montgomery Street, his apartment at the other, atop Telegraph Hill. His was a good life, in the city millions of Americans would pick as their home had they the chance.

But San Francisco has a crime rate to match that unsurpassed regard. One summer evening, Drake strolled unthinkingly past a doorway of a condemned building and was mugged. Weeks later, he accepted a teaching post at the University of Toronto.

He suffers no homesickness. Returning "would be like going to the funeral of someone you cared for," he says now. "I didn't move because of that incident exactly, but I no longer felt rooted to the place, either. As soon as that happened in that particular area, I realized there'd been a big change, and not in the right direction. It wasn't going to be turned back. All that was brought home very personally. I no longer felt any affection for the place. It was like being betrayed by a friend."

Street crime, bad schools, smog, heaps of garbage, costly and uncertain utilities, urban tension, astronomical rents. These are the most common reasons people give for moving from big cities to smaller ones, from suburbs to country, from the snow belt to the sun belt. (Since 1970, our rural regions have grown faster than our metropolitan areas—which include most suburbs. Ten of the sixteen largest cities—

Boston, Chicago, Detroit, Los Angeles, New York, Newark, Philadelphia, Pittsburgh, Saint Louis, and San Francisco—have actually declined in overall population.) But as often as not, deeper, more personal motivations underlie such surface rationalizations.

Writer Bailey Alexander recognizes this. "At first, we just switched locations, not my job, and the only reason we did that was we weren't saving anything, and investing in a house seemed the only way. We couldn't afford anything in the city, so we moved out. It wasn't the schools. I'm not persuaded our kids are getting a measurably more useful education out here in the slurbs. It wasn't pollution or Con Ed, our Mickey Mouse watch of a power company. We have them here, too. It wasn't even the commuting, which everyone gripes about. I didn't mind that, really. In one sense, it was the only time of the day I had to myself. Actually, I miss the city. Despite the clichés, we had many more friends there than here, and they were a lot more engaging, too. Here you don't step on your neighbor's lawn without a formal invitation. There, our place was full of painters and actors and poets and folksingers almost every day. I get so bloody tired of talking about Joe Namath and drains. It wasn't real change, and it wasn't really for the better."

Alexander was an officer manager for a large educational organization. After seventeen years, he headed a division carrying a million-dollar-plus annual budget and ninety-two staff members. At the time he quit, his salary had just reached $28,000.

"There are an endless variety of irritations in a situation like that, all of them craftily designed to grind your psyche down into indigestible little chunks," he says. "Sooner or later, one of them becomes the tiny stone that breaks your back. And it's not that you punch whoever's responsible in the eye and stamp out. I keep hearing about such things, but I don't know anyone who's done it. No, you get up and hobble on. It's just that nothing is ever the same for you again in that place. The satisfaction is drained from you; you're dead, but you don't lie down.

"I remember that point very well. The details that led up to it are too boring to recount. Just say this. Another man and I were in positions of roughly comparable rank. When he was promoted to his, I made a point of going to him to offer any help I could. Nothing altruistic on my part, just good organizational politics.

"Two years later, he'd run his unit right into the ground. So, naturally, they made him executive vice-president. The Peter Principle lives! One day, he called me in. 'Alexander,' he said, 'I've decided I'm going to let you stay another year.' Then this oily little slug chewed me out for an hour about things no one had ever even mentioned to me before, and I dragged myself out, my mouth still hanging open.

"I staggered back to my office, figuratively clutching my crotch. I straightened my shoulders to walk by the row of desks in my customary imperial manner, and closed the door to my inner sanctum. Then I put my fist through the wall. Or into it, to be precise. Fortunately, it was not the adjacent cinder block.

"I took the train home. Drank my usual drinks, fell asleep in my usual chair. Didn't tell my wife. Didn't tell anyone anything. Now, I may have misled. *That* wasn't the time. But three months later, one Saturday morning, I got up, drank my coffee, read my *Times*, went into my den, sat down at my desk—and cried for twenty minutes. Never did know why. The following Monday, I resigned. I'll be lucky if I make half as much money this year as I did last, and I'm happy as a pig in mud."

That's the way it is for most of us, of course. It takes more than one setback, two indignities, or a series of small humiliations to lead us to that irrevocable break. We may take a geographical hop but find we are living essentially the same lives with the same problems, never mind the palm tree replacing the maple in the front yard. That isn't change, it's movement. Positive life changers restructure themselves and the environments in which they function. They don't merely shift location.

Their traumata need not be emotionally debilitating to inspire their decisions. Charles Lord had it all. Still in his twenties after a glossy, privileged education begun at Buckley, continued at Hotchkiss, and completed at Yale, as well as three years in the air force, Lord was made general operations manager for the Central American holdings of Squibb International. There were servants to run the house, the gardens, the car. At the time, taxes on income earned overseas were virtually nonexistent, and the cost of living was lower than here, much of it covered by the housing and living allowance. Lord, his wife, their twin sons and daughter were comfortable beyond the expectations of all but a few of their countrymen. Then, as in the nature of these arrangements, he was instructed to return to corporate headquarters in New York. It was a promotion. He had proved himself.

He didn't regard it as privation. Both he and his wife were soon caught up in community affairs—such as Robert Redford's Consumer Action Now—with the theater and concerts ("You ever hear of the Panama Symphony?"). They had productive and articulate friends, a weekend house in Connecticut. But there was culture shock, in reverse.

It was that winter of national discontent, 1969. The Lord children, born in Panama and Guatemala, had never seen snow. When the first fall came, Mrs. Lord rushed her children to Central Park for those fleeting, magic hours before the city turned it all to gray slush. They sat on a bench, marveled at the amber halos of street lamps, at the dark turrets of buildings flanking the park, all flickering behind the gently drifting curtain of fat, lazy flakes. It was a moment precious in its rarity. There was a sharp bend in the path. From the other side, a voice drifted back to them.

"Man, you gotta try some of this. It's organic," the unseen teenager was saying. "It makes the snow look purple."

An unremarkable event, but the Lords were new to it ("What have we gotten ourselves into?"). They didn't leave right then, or for five years, but it is the point from which they chart their eventual decision. Charles Lord is now assistant headmaster of a small private school on the outskirts of Toledo.

These men were all past forty when they made their moves. That isn't a coincidence. If comprehensive data were available (they aren't), the typical life changer would almost surely be over forty, married, white, formerly holding a managerial or professional position paying an annual salary in excess of $15,000. There is an uncertain mix of emotional, social, physiological, and vocational reasons for this conclusion. Barring unexpected or unusual events that might push personal reassessment forward in the life cycle, the pattern is easy to trace. Formal education is completed somewhere between eighteen and twenty-five. During that period—or shortly thereafter—a presumably permanent partner is selected. After some exploration, an occupation presents itself, customarily chosen through a combination of circumstance and preconditioning. A promotion. Early enthusiasm. More success. Encouragement from spouse and superiors. Time passes. Children. Furniture. Perhaps a mortgage. More advancement, more responsibility. And satisfaction. Not undiluted joy, but none of us is taught to expect that. Thirty is momentarily distressful, for it is the threshold into full-fledged adulthood. But being no longer young has its advantages and gratifications as well as its regrets. The flesh is still firm—relatively —the step nearly as quick, the vision almost as clear. And authority continues to expand.

Ten years pass. Forty looms. Suddenly, no-longer-young is transformed to nearly-middle-aged. And it happened so quickly.

The headlong rush slows. There is a longer wait between promotions, and perhaps only one or two more are attainable. Younger people nudge impatiently. Gratifications are less frequent, more fleeting. Professional decisions are made automatically, without excitement, based upon long practice and prior experience. The challenge has faded. Further achievement is possible, but its farthest edge is now visible. Children require less time and supervision. There is time for reflection, and it is not warming. The next "graduation" is still ahead, but it will signal an end, not a beginning.

Martin Ackerman, a former publishing wonder, made his own opportunities and so was less dependent upon the esteem of others. Nevertheless, he recognized the impact of diminishing satisfaction coupled with escalating demands. "If I didn't work from 7 A.M. until 11 or 12 P.M.," he reflected for *Dun's Review*, "I had feelings of guilt. I was exhausted and unfit. I had grown too heavy. I had to take a bottle of Gelusil everywhere. My marriage went bad. I had a permanent sore on my ear from the telephone receiver. I looked at myself and saw I was growing old too fast. I had to get off the treadmill."

The midlife crisis is real, well documented by twenty-five years of medical and scientific observations and by a burgeoning popular literature. Yet it cannot be comprehended by those still to encounter it, and is patronizingly dismissed by those who have passed beyond. Because it has no precise point of commencement and its physical manifestations can be assigned to less cosmic origins than menopause or phases of the moon, it is difficult to identify. It is associated with (but not limited by the boundaries of) the climacteric, the currently fashionable and only slightly less ambiguous word for the male and female menopause. It can occur any time from the middle thirties to the early fifties. As in puberty, it is a time of brooding introspection broken by moments of intense exultation. Outsiders are bewildered by the rapidity with which the victim's moods shift and, out of caution, stay at arm's length. There are no obvious brackets, though, no middle-years equivalent of the appearance of pubic hair and onset of ovulation, no clearly evident cessation of acne or physical growth.

But it *is* there. Bailey Alexander remembers his instant of recognition.

"I'd gashed my wrist open with my electric hedge clippers. My doctor was the one who'd taken over thirty years ago when I was passed on by the family pediatrician. While he was sewing me up, I thought to ask him if there was anything he could do about my recent habits of oversleeping in the morning, of flaking out after dinner and staying awake half the night. He was your average, stereotyped, old-style, gruff, matter-of-fact GP.

" 'Aches and pains, too,' he said, 'and irritable, moody.' I nodded. How did he know? 'You're avoiding decisions. You don't like your job anymore,' he said. It wasn't a question. 'You don't know where you're going, and you don't see any alternatives. Your kids are growing up, and the streets suddenly seem filled with nothing but girls with big boobs. Your bald spot is getting bigger, you can't get rid of that belly, your wife is acting funny, screwing isn't as much fun as it used to be, and you drink too much.' He didn't even ask if that was accurate. He knew. No, he couldn't do anything for me except prescribe some diet pills. He got out of it, he said, and I would, too. All I could feel was a sort of quizzical relief. He knew all about it because *everyone* went through it. I wasn't alone! That seemed important. Then I remembered *he* was on his third wife, and my mother used to talk about his drinking problem."

Knowing about the crisis helps. It doesn't solve it, but at least it provides a point of departure. And this phenomenon is probably the preeminent reason men and women in their late thirties and early forties precipitously discard careers and partners for apparently irrational adventures.

But if this is the central cause for life change, it is by no means the only one. People are compelled to reevaluate their aspirations under the pressures of external events as well, and at earlier or later stages. It can be a woman's early hysterectomy, before she has had the opportunity to bear wanted children. It can be unexpected responsibility, as for the children of brothers or sisters killed by accident. More frequently, a closely spaced series of disruptive occurrences conspires to bring on the confrontation.

Jim Martin fit the parameters. In 1973, at thirty, he was a sales representative for a national investment advisory firm, operating out of an office in a suburban Indianapolis shopping center. Again, the accoutrements of the dream: an XKE, a Cadillac, two wardrobes, a summer cabin . . . Then it all crumbled between his fingers.

"I was like the alcoholic who hits bottom before he sees the light," says Martin, his boots propped on the cluttered desk in his new CB radio shop. "It was complete. My marriage broke up, my dad died, business was stinking and getting worse, my stepmother had a mastectomy—and my dog got epilepsy. Takes pills four times a day."

It is one of those litanies of personal tragedy to which the instinctive, helpless response is a choked-off smirk. An epileptic dog? Martin isn't laughing. He just had his gallbladder removed four months ago.

"It all happened at one time. Just about everything that could. At this point, I'm a hardened veteran. But I have the chance now to acquire real independence within ten years. And if I don't make it, I'll still be fulfilling my obligations as a husband and father, and I'm no worse off than being unhappy and underpaid as an employee of an Establishment company."

Whether stimulated by inner turmoil or outside stress, the impulse to change can result in apparently ill-conceived actions. Separating transient unease from bedrock discontent is easy for no one, and resulting actions often seem foolish to others. An advertising man quit Madison Avenue some years ago and, in what may be the ultimate fantasy, set sail in his own boat for Papeete, vowing never to return. He even wrote of his decision for *New York* magazine. In three months, he was back. Many recall television personality Hugh Downs's announcement that he was taking an extended leave from the "Today" show to cruise the oceans with his children. On his return, for reasons of his own, he had shaved all the hair from his head. Extensive transplants were necessary when it did not grow back.

Such incidents provoke the mockery of those who view themselves too sensible and adult to indulge in fancy. Definitions of reality are slippery, however. John DeLorean, the General Motors executive, was quoted in *The New York Times* as claiming that his former organization "has gotten to be a total insulation from the realities of the world." Charles Lord said much the same of his work at the pharmaceuticals company, so he became a schoolmaster. Teachers flee in the other direction in order to test themselves in what they inevitably refer to as the "real world." GM? Squibb? Children? All "unreal"? Obviously an adherence to "reality" is as frequently a pretense to avoid the vulnerabilities of change as the reverse is a justification for departure. The conflict in the two perspectives ensures, if nothing else, that friends, relatives, and colleagues will greet the change either with dismay or ambiguity, perhaps even with envy or contempt. The life changer can expect support and understanding only from those closest to him, but with no guarantees there, either.

Many marriages, for example, cannot bear the burden of change. People take unto themselves partners under conditions of tacit "contract." They are, in effect, agreeing to bind themselves to each other in the belief that they will remain within the boundaries of their original perceptions for the next forty years. She will always be pliant, adoring. He will be always decisive, understanding. Both may be able to allow for the influence of passing time on how they look—she, no more a size eight; he, no longer lean-hipped—but they cannot anticipate the ravages of those same years upon those first conceptions of how they wished to structure their lives.

So it is with friends. Drawn to each other in the first place because they share parts of a similar vision, they are confused and dismayed when one decides on a wholly different course. He'll come to his senses, they assure themselves and the rebel. He won't give up—everything. How can he start all over again? He'll get over it. Michael Kritch didn't, and it is difficult to imagine that he sustained his country-club, white-collar friendships when he became a truck driver.

It may be, then, that the life changer will be alone. But the "mid-course correction"—to use the felicitous phrase from Bernice and Morton Hunt's *Prime Time*—can be a positive force for self-renewal, and the decision is, in the end, left to just one person.

Sooner or later, the time to change one's life arrives. Whether it comes as a sudden jolt—a business opportunity falling through, a divorce, a death—or as a flash point in a more evolutionary, internal process, it can be the best thing that ever happens. It is a chance to terminate relationships grown stale and empty, to test new muscles. Crisis can be converted, through the exercise of individual will, to the inauguration of a time more exuberantly energizing and life-affirming than ever imagined.

3
Dealing

*Men's nature is still desirous of news, variety, delights . . . we
cannot endure one course of life long, one calling long, one
place long.*
> —Robert Burton, *The Anatomy of Melancholy*

For most wage earners, freedom translates as self-employment.
No bosses, no schedules imposed by others, no standards of dress or
behavior mandated under threat of economic reprisal. No more itchy
suits donned for breakfast meetings arranged by executives for staff
members whose biological clocks don't slip into gear until lunch is
digesting. Some people fall easily into the decision to start their own
business; a hobby blossoms into a profitable sideline which then overwhelms the primary moneymaking activity. They're the lucky ones;
their course is charted for them.

Steve Foster is more fortunate still. An unhappy insurance salesman, he was driving to Brazil, Indiana, to see a prospect. He was
praying, as was his custom, when it happened.

God spoke to him.

According to Foster, the exact words were: "Go you into a place
which I will show you. Go you into Louisville, Kentucky. There I will
bring you into your inheritance, according to things of the flesh."

Foster did not question. He spun the wheel of his car and returned
to tell his wife. The next morning, they drove two hours south to
Louisville.

However one may judge the source and manner of Foster's inspiration, it is not possible to argue with his meteoric material achievement.
Virtually penniless in terms of investment capital, Foster and his wife
Anna opened an Oriental rug store six weeks after his critical "conversation." They didn't know if they could pay the next month's rent or

if they could find stock, but in four months they grossed $33,000. In the next twelve months, the figure soared to $140,000.

On a bright Sunday morning in April, the Fosters are welcoming visitors from up North. Louisville is in the lush, full-leafed heart of spring, and they are working in the garden. It is not a chore they relish, and they are relieved by the interruption.

"I was a chicken choker when I was a kid," Steve says, "not a dirt farmer."

The knees of Anna's jeans are loam-soaked. She brushes a strand of hair from her eyes, pins it artlessly back. Cold drinks are offered while Steve excuses himself to go "see whether the Colonel has 'extra crunchy' on the menu." The visitors are two friends from Indianapolis with a small Kuba to sell, and Joe, a rug dealer from New York on one of his periodic forages through the hinterland. They are ushered through the spacious kitchen to the dining room at the front of the house.

The interior of their large, sun-filled Georgian Colonial, is utterly without clutter, despite three children from Anna's first marriage and two from Steve's. There are potted ferns and palms and avocado trees in every corner, and delicate pieces of early Victoriana.

And rugs. Everywhere. Kazaks, Ushaks, Bijars, Kubas, Shirvans, Bergamos, even a large Ardebil on the wall. The hues are vivid and subtle, the patterns bold and discreet. These rugs are as distinct from the worn and gloomy somberness of the carpet in Grandmother's parlor as Mies van der Rohe's Barcelona chair is from Archie Bunker's.

Steve returns with the red-and-white-striped buckets of fried chicken. He directs his guests to the table, forcefully resolving a brief skirmish between the two oldest boys. He's a big man—in the mold of a defensive tackle gone somewhat to seed—with a heavy, pugnacious jaw and a presence that dominates the room. After banishing the children to the kitchen, Steve invokes the tolerance of the Lord, then passes the potatoes.

Once lunch is finished, fingers licked, the small Kuba the other couple brought is rolled out in the vestibule. Everyone stands around it looking down. Anna flips over a corner to examine the back.

"Too purple," says Steve. "Too busy. For down here, anyway. Won't get much for you."

Joe shrugs, offers no opinion. They might be playing five-card draw and someone's bluff has been called. Yet no one is faking or even dealing. These are friends. That's just the way rug people communicate with each other. Oriental rugs are a volatile commodity, as are any objects rare or old or handmade. Fifteen years ago, Tiffany lamps gathered dust in attics, worthless to all but a few foresighted collectors. Five years later, prime examples were bringing $1,500 and more. Then came the shoddy reproductions that soon lit every other ersatz Edwardian singles bar and family room in the country.

So it is with Oriental rugs and carpets. Prices and desirability are determined by avarice and fashion, ignorance and caprice, even region and country. There are no set list or wholesale prices, no certain dealer's cost. The price of a rug of even modest desirability can easily quadruple while passing through the hands of four different owners, even if all transactions take place within a total of four weeks and all persons involved have roughly equal knowledge of the rug's marketability and quality. Settled again in squashy chairs on the sun porch a full sixty feet away from the dining room, Steve and Anna talk about the unpredictable nature of their business.

"Until 1950," Steve is saying, "ninety percent of the top-grade rugs in the world were in the United States. We were the only nation with any money. Even ten years later, you could still buy rugs by the pound. Now the Germans are in a boom, and they like those thick, dark-red Sarouks that used to be in Grandmaw's room. Those don't sell here anymore. And Joe ships almost everything *he* buys back to Iran. Germans and Iranians are stripping the country. I used to think they'd only scratched the surface, but now I'm convinced they've gone pretty deep."

What kinds of rugs *do* sell here?

"All Americans like Caucasians," he says. "The uncluttered, geometric cleanness of the designs appeals to the American taste."

"And they'll compete with the Germans in buying them," Anna interjects, "as they won't for Sarouks."

"In the South," Steve continues, "rugs from the Herez and Ushak areas of Turkey are favored."

"Southerners prefer pastel, light-toned, open-patterned rugs, probably because of the climate. Up in the North, they like the warmth of dark, redder, busy rugs."

Are the figurative pieces—the ones that have stylized representations of dragons and mushrooms and trees—more popular than those with purely abstract motifs?

"Not particularly. People in our market are buying for color," he says.

"People have to be taught to look at rugs in the correct way," she says, "just as with paintings. A collector looks for balance of design, boldness, color—all together. There is a rhapsody in one of these rugs, harmony. It's really a moving thing."

Steve nods agreement. He and Anna enjoy lobbing the conversational ball. They share their life—all aspects of it—more easily than most couples. "A collector looks only for the finest example of weave and quality of a particular region. That's his goal. He doesn't pay that much attention to pattern or superficial condition. Let's say I set a shiny new red Volkswagen out there on the street next to a ten-year-old Mercedes that's dirty and scratched and needs a paint job. You know which car the collector will pick."

Can't the analogy be overdrawn? A threadbare rug won't really sell, will it? Or is Steve talking about the differences between a relatively new Oriental and an antique in basically good condition?

"A really worn rug would have to be awfully rare to be at all valuable," Anna says. "Down in Lexington, dealers tell customers that the more worn out a rug is, the more valuable it is. They'll even go so far as to try to wear them out, by rubbing Calgonite in them or something."

"The opposite is usually more accurate. People think their rugs are in excellent condition when they aren't."

What constitutes an "antique"? Where do they draw the line?

"First, rugs aren't like furniture, they're not as durable," he says. "But it does take twenty-five or thirty years to put enough age on it to give it mellowness and softness. The Oriental rug business is based on 'semiantiques,' which were made between the wars, and 'antiques,' those made before World War One, or even as far back as 1900, according to some people. Anything after World War Two is a different thing."

"The newer ones are really tacky, is what they are. The colors are harsh, they're stiff. Louisville is an old city. People who buy rugs have very old, very lovely furniture. If you put a new rug among all those things, it sticks out like a sore thumb."

How did they learn the business?

"For anyone to go into Oriental rugs, you have to be crazy first. To gain the knowledge you need, you have to go for people's throats. We throw 'em on the floor and jump on 'em and tell 'em we won't let them go until they give us what we need," she says.

She laughs at her joke, and Steve joins her.

"It takes *people*, because you can't learn it from books and no one knows it all," he says. "It's a closemouthed business because it's primarily Jewish-owned."

It is not intended as a slur, but Joe winces almost imperceptibly and Anna rushes to soften the remark. "It's the same way for us. We aren't going to teach an outsider. We'll educate our sons. When we *do* teach collectors, it's not about prices and values."

"Still," Steve persists, "we're the wrong nationality to be rug dealers. They're all Armenians and Persian Jews. Joe here is unique. He's honest in a crooked business. And he helped us. He was the answer to a prayer. He taught us, showed us things. But Joe isn't a typical dealer. He is in trouble with other dealers *because* he's honest. That's his reputation around the country, and, as a consequence, he gets all the rugs."

"His competitors don't like him a lot for that," says Anna. "He'll go into a man's store, and if a price is too low, he'll pay him more. Very few guys do that. Of course, the psychology to it is that that man never calls anyone else but Joe again."

Speaking of psychology, two things. One, why is so much of the business done in cash? And two, why do rug dealers, when buying, so often require the seller to quote an asking price, instead of making a bid themselves?

"Steve and I deal almost ninety percent in checks, actually," says Anna. "But we're retailers working in a particular area. If you're off in some small town in the middle of nowhere, sellers want cash because they don't know you and your check is drawn on a New York bank.

"On the other hand, there is the situation where someone doesn't want to sell a rug and you whip out five hundred-dollar bills, and that has a magical effect. They're thinking how they don't have to report it on their income tax, and there's the money right there in front of them. In our situation, we can't play that game. There are too many ways for the IRS to keep track of us. Now, on the wholesale end. . . ."

Joe, speaking for the first time, says at least 50 percent of his business is cash. "In some areas, like Florida and California, dealers have given bad checks, so people will only take cash."

"As for the other thing," Anna continues, "we never make an offer on a rug, because then we're just giving a free appraisal. They'll never sell it to you if you do. If you make an offer, they'll sell it to someone else for five dollars more. You *never* get a rug you make an offer on."

"Sometimes we do bid," Steve says, "but we make it ridiculously high and tell them it's their only chance. We know they're going to shop around. Then when they call us back because we gave the best price, we tell them the market changed, and get the rug for what we wanted in the first place. It's the only way when they won't give a price."

"We have to do it. People play games with you. They have something they want to sell, but they don't know what it's worth, so they attack our minds. It's like asking a doctor for medical advice without paying for it. Then, if you quote them a price, they take it somewhere else."

"What happens," Anna says, "is that Mrs. Jones wants to sell to her neighbor, Mrs. Smith, but doesn't know what to charge. So she calls up the Fosters to get a price, then turns around and gives it to Mrs. Smith for that amount."

"We provide an appraisal service and charge accordingly," Steve goes on, somewhat indignant with the ignorance of the public. "We appraise at *retail* replacement value, but that's not what we'll pay for the rug."

The Fosters demand only $10 for expenses and $5 per carpet for appraisals, depending upon how far they have to travel. The values they estimate can then be employed by their customers for insurance or tax purposes. Should those clients wish to *sell* the rugs, however, they are unrealistic to expect to realize more than 50 percent of those amounts, and 20 percent might be closer. One recently divorced woman received a $3,900 estimate on six Kazaks from an appraiser. Her intention was to liquidate her household possessions. In the end, she had to settle for $770 from a free-lance dealer who, in turn, restored the rugs and resold them to a wholesaler for $1,500. All six finally sold through a retail outlet for $3,400.

Restoration can play an important role in the rug trade—indeed, in most aspects of the antiques business. A dealer nearly always chooses a carpet with cigar or moth holes in otherwise fine condition over another piece of similar origin and quality with badly worn patches, simply because the first is easier to repair. Often, the dealer does the work himself. Anna Foster still does, although not so much as when they were starting out.

Shortly after their marriage, the Fosters found some pieces of French furniture in a junk shop. Repairs were required, so they studied construction. From working on the tables, they discovered things that weren't apparent from books. Friends saw the renovated furniture and asked the Fosters to fix *their* antiques. Then friends of friends—even the Indianapolis museum was sending pieces. The Fosters found themselves with rare eighteenth-century boulle furniture, complete with marquetry, tortoiseshell, and brass filigree. No one in the area had the skills required to work in such arcane techniques, so Steve and Anna taught themselves. They were making money at all this, but it remained a sideline.

Soon they were exhibiting at antiques shows and serving as middlemen between buyers and sellers. The resultant income began to rival Steve's sales job with Bell & Howell. He quit. When the antiques business proved less profitable on a full-time basis than they had hoped, he had to take the position with the insurance company. His communications with his God intensified, culminating in the directive he received on the way to Brazil, Indiana.

Once in Louisville—they had barely enough money for gas—they went to see their friends in the antiques business. One suggested a store he believed was to become vacant. The proprietor confirmed her desire to leave, but the Fosters had no capital and they needed a $400 deposit. They walked down the street, wondering what to do. Wandering into an antiques shop, they spotted a small Sarouk. They wrote a $300 check against their empty account, then drove back to Indianapolis and sold the rug for $700. They returned to Louisville and paid the deposit. To pay the first month's rent, they found a Caucasian and repeated the process.

Now they had their store but no stock. Not one rug. They picked up a few, continuing the pattern, but also started putting the profits into higher-quality carpets. Still, within one month of their opening, they had only 20 percent of the number they felt they needed to operate even a marginal trade. In a furious three weeks of day-and-night searching, they accumulated the rest, all of it on consignment. Very little was spent on redecoration. Their store is a cavernous space without counters, signs, or displays, a testimony to the plain-pipe-rack school of retailing philosophy.

It worked. In less than two years they had grossed nearly $400,000. Now they are here, in this splendid house, awaiting further direction. They take no credit for their achievement.

"All we did was obey God," says Anna, her plain, open face betraying no uncertainty. "He keeps us from falling over the edge."

Steve nods, smiles. The sun porch grows cool.

Rockport is a tiny, exquisite pearl in the strand of villages and hamlets cast upon the rock-strewn shore of Cape Ann, which knuckles into the Atlantic just north of Boston. It is the prototype New England fishing village, a fact recognized by so many generations of watercolorists that a battered shanty on a pier in the harbor was long ago labeled *Motif Number One*. Gulls dip and wheel over bobbing lobster boats, bleached traps and bright floats lie in heaps by jetties, narrow lanes twist through the spaces between huddled seamen's cottages and somber saltboxes. If Boston is the East Coast's San Francisco, Rockport is its Tiburon.

The main road, such as it is, winds past the harbor, then north to Pigeon Cove. As it rises to the crest of a bluff above the town, it passes a compact, deconsecrated Methodist church. The building is the home of J. D. Russell, Inc., doing business as James Russell Silversmiths. It is painted earth-green, with a wooden sunburst above the door.

The former vestibule, a room no more than sixteen by ten feet, has been converted to a workshop. Seven bearded and/or ponytailed young men and women in jeans and denim shirts idle at their workbenches, passing a plate of raisins and cheese, gently joshing. It is the midmorning break. A small child teeters in the middle of the floor, choosing direction, then lunges determinedly to one of the workers, who sweeps her up in his arms. A well-fed dog of uncertain lineage lifts his head at the intrusion, then collapses with a sigh. The room is tidy, the mood serene.

Up the circular staircase, under the belfry, women are packing boxes of jewelry and display racks. Their dress and demeanor are not of the counterculture—as their colleagues' below—but of Yankee mainstream. Off to the right is a cramped office which contains a desk, three chairs, and two men in their thirties. They dwarf the furniture when they stand to greet the stranger. Both could slip into a snapshot of the Celtics' lineup without attracting notice. They have the slightly stooped and shambling posture of men resigned to communicating with shorter people.

The improbable plutocrat behind the desk is Jim Russell. He leans back, swings his bare feet up to rest on a stack of papers. No suit, no tie. He and Peter, sitting opposite, are fraternal twins, but Jim's features are more symmetrical. His hair is parted in the middle and trimmed more neatly. He is also given to a whimsy that flirts with mockery, not a quality designed to put a visitor at ease. Probably he doesn't care.

Jim Russell seems an unlikely entrepreneur, but his corporation is to gross $670,000 this year. How did this happen?

"Greed," he answers.

No, really.

"It started as a humble sandal shop on Nantucket Island. I was a reject from a mortgage banking firm and decided it would be fun not to wash for a while. I started making sandals. We needed some sparkle in the shop, some of that ineffable zip. So I made jewelry. They were awful, but they sold like hotcakes."

A silversmith comes in to offer the remains of the fruit and cheese. Jim pulls his hand back after examining the plate, wrinkles his face with distaste.

"Richard! What *is* that?"

To get back, do you take a salary, or . . . ?

"I take whatever I can get. We skim it in every possible way."

There is a metallic-blue Mercedes 450SE in the driveway. Is it . . . ?

"That's the company truck. We make every effort to do our bit for the American economy."

Does that get written off?

"Everything gets written off."

You live in back. That, too?

"They're *all* tax write-offs."

Where do your people live?

"I don't know. They never invite me."

Peter volunteers that their staff rent houses in the area and that two more live at Russell's shop in Tilton, New Hampshire.

"Anyway," Jim continues, "the leather business went along fine, but then I ran into some problems with my partner. We split up, and instead of spending the winter in Florida as I had been doing, I stayed on Martha's Vineyard and made jewelry. It went pretty well."

Where did you learn how to make jewelry?

"Bought some books, got some tools. Sat down, tried it."

No formal training or apprenticeship?

"I didn't have time for that. I had to make a living."

The telephone rings. It is the adjustment department at Jordan Marsh. Jim has had trouble obtaining guaranteed repairs on a washing machine. From his end of the conversation, it is obvious that it has been an acrimonious dispute. When he hangs up, he is more serious.

"That's no way to run a business," he says. "We don't do that. We take back anything from any one of our customers that doesn't sell. Anything. At any time, for any reason. If you can't treat your customers as you treat your friends, you shouldn't be in business."

How did yours progress after that winter?

"At that time, I was just selling out of my shop. No wholesale. And I was putting in long hours. The first three or four years, it was eighty-hour weeks, week after week; no vacations, nothing. I didn't have any capital to start with, so it was necessary to build it up. I did that by not hiring people.

"Then things started to smooth out—this was about 1973—and I was able to go into the semiretirement in which you now find me."

Where Russell is, according to him, is in sole ownership of "the largest handwrought jewelry company in the United States and the second-largest employer in Rockport." Not bad for a Cornell B-School dropout and ex-beachnik.

It was not always so, obviously. The Russells did not follow the same road. Peter attended New York University; Jim went to Wesleyan. Peter became a recruiter for the NYU admissions office, worked his way up the administrative ladder. Nothing spectacular, but steady progress. In 1972, he accepted the director of admissions slot at a state college in Westchester County, twenty-five miles out of Manhattan.

"That was my first mistake," Peter says now. "I was working for a bunch of elitist dilettantes who were playing with a campus. Very soft administrators with no vision. No understanding of how to run a major office like admissions or student life. Or maybe it was their *excess* of vision, with nothing to back it up.

"Then there was all that starting up of a brand-new college—the power plays, the establishing of domain, all that. When I first went there, I had a separate division, responsible to the vice-president. I thought I did a super job, considering we didn't even have a course catalog before March of the year we were to enroll our first class. The dorm wasn't even completed.

"Then they brought in this jerk as dean of students. I was moved underneath him, and from the second I met him, I knew my days were numbered. We did not get on at all. It was a constant battle. Finally they told me my contract would not be renewed. That gave me eighteen months. I appealed, and faculty and students signed petitions in my behalf.

"But my associate director had decided he didn't like the way I ran the office, so he gave the dean a list of my 'transgressions,' nine-tenths of which were pure, outright lies. The dean bought it. Three other deans stood by me, but that was the end."

It was a bad time for Peter. He was plagued by a chronic kidney ailment that had nearly taken his life a year before. His wife, Peggy, was bored with her teaching job, and the city they lived in—Ossining, the home of Sing Sing prison—was troubled by severe racial tensions. Other positions in his specialty were available—in a era when admissions directors are blamed as readily for falling enrollments as are football coaches for losing teams—and he could have found something easily. But Peter had had enough.

"I'm glad it happened. Jim had talked to me for years about joining him. This gave me the push to do it." It meant a cut in salary from $18,000 to $9,000, but he and Peggy sold their house at a $15,000 profit, and Peter drew some extra income from the state university pension fund. Property taxes in Rockport were about half what they were in Ossining, but the cost of living was slightly higher. Peggy worked as a waitress to help get them through the first six months.

Peter has no difficulty working for his brother. "I'm the vice-president," he says, drawing himself up, then laughing. "Of course, the guy out there on the first bench is the 'purchasing director' and the one next to him is the 'quality-control agent'—everyone has a title."

Jim leaves the office, and Peter is free to confide, "We get along very well, really. We didn't when we were younger. Now, though, there's a real feeling of love that's developed. No problem with him being boss. He lets me do pretty much what I want. And we both have our special strengths. I think I deal better with people than he does, and he has the good business sense.

"Jim has a *super* mind, actually. Could do *anything*. He makes harpsichords, for example, probably some of the best ones in America. From just scrap wood, not kits."

Jim returns, invites Peter and their visitor into his quarters at the rear of the building. He has not stinted. The rooms are generously proportioned; the ceiling of the living room reaches to the roof. All are comfortably and tastefully decorated, without allegiance to any particular style. There is a broad, plant-filled shelf beneath the windows overlooking the ocean, a large sun deck just beyond. At the entranceway from the office, one wall is hung with religious artifacts of ambiguous origin. These are not related to Jim's own spiritual beliefs—he and most of his workers are followers of an Indian master, Kirpal Singh—he just "put them up to give the place some ecclesiastical flavor."

The brothers settle into chairs, bringing mugs of coffee. The visitor wonders aloud if Jim has always had a flair for merchandising or was it discovered as he became involved with jewelry?

"Always had it, starting with selling Christmas wreaths when I was thirteen. I've always found it easy to make money."

Jim's lighthearted approach is evident in his promotional brochures. On one occasion, the company sent a letter to customers over the signatures of the "humble overworked workers." It read:

Dear friends:

You have been keeping us so busy that it is killing us. Jim needs a vacation. He has had to put in almost two days a week. The rest of us, of course, can barely stagger home at night. We're so tired. Jim doesn't know we're sending this letter, so don't tell him. The one he wrote we've hidden in the IRS file. We need a break. The enclosed fliers should be put into your catalogue. Do Not Look At Them! They have been selling so well that we are being driven crazy. Please be kind. Don't look at the enclosed fliers. You don't need the extra sales; we don't want the extra work.

Russell's "incensed" response followed the next day:

> I was going through my IRS file and to my shock found a flier
> prepared by my well-paid, underworked employees. I hope you
> didn't take that too seriously. These people are so lazy they think
> sleeping is work. Besides, as you know, our business is nearly a
> philanthropic one; our main concern is to see that you make more
> money than we do. To prove this point, we've come out with 15
> inch liquid silver chains that sell for a low, low $30 a dozen.
> . . . Please don't worry about overworking us. After all, an idle
> mind is the devil's workshop.

Another of Russell's blandishments was a "two day paid Holiday
for Two in Rockport" for the lucky clients winning a drawing (after
filing orders of $100 or more). Featured were tours of the Pigeon Cove
post office and the new sewage pumping station, chocolate truffles at
Tuck's Pharmacy, and a viewing of the company's baby-picture exhibit,
touted as a moving tribute to the downtrodden workers.

Whatever one may think of this variety of commercial humor, it
works.

"When he first started," says Peter, "Jim was very long-haired,
with a full beard. Everyone who worked for him had that kind of look.
These little bouffant women came in and liked the idea of seeing these
poor struggling silversmiths make some money. They ate it up—spending time with these guys in beards and blue jeans. It was really just a
sales technique! This is eight years ago, remember. He'd send those
fliers out, like 'thank you for all your orders this year, now we can dump
the old Mercedes because of all the junk you bought from us.' It's all
part of our mystique, our identity."

Jim discovered gift shows after his first few years on Martha's
Vineyard. No one had told him there even were such things. Now Peter
travels to ten cities twice a year to participate in such expositions as the
National Boutique Show in New York and to similar events in Atlanta,
Los Angeles, Chicago, San Francisco, and Boston. Virtually all their
sales are now wholesale or direct mail. (Their ads can be seen in the
backs of mass-circulation shelter magazines.) Their customers range
from mom 'n' pop stationers to Pappagallo's, and even include art
museum stores in Chicago and Cleveland.

"A little booth at one of these shows costs three or four hundred
dollars for a week. I just sit around in the booth, people come by, and

I give them my pitch. We joke around a lot, we're not serious at all. We do it for fun. Other people try to sell the same kinds of things we do, but they can't because they try too hard, as if their lives depended on it. In actuality, ours *do,* but we don't let anyone know that."

"When Jim first tried this, he picked up three thousand dollars in orders in three days. Next week, in New York, I'll do at least thirty thousand. I'm just amazed at what can be sold in this world. Anything! A lot of it is schlock, but nice things go even better."

The Russell catalog lists hundreds of items: earrings, bracelets, pendants, rings, necklaces, pins, barrettes. Retail prices start as low as $1.25 and top out at $700 for a few pieces in gold. No one is going to describe any of them as notable achievements of the jeweler's craft, least of all the Russells. The jewelry is, after all, mass-produced, though handmade. Nevertheless, they are carefully fashioned in thin silver wire and tubing—hammered, twisted, spiraled, soldered—and are mod in design. Only 15 percent of the line is cast, and that is done by another firm. Although it's true that any moderately facile person could learn the necessary techniques relatively quickly, the Russell offerings are nevertheless honestly rendered and equitably priced. That's important to Jim.

"It's the way every business should work," he observes. "We don't make compromises. If we don't like a design, we don't make it. Then we say, 'Here it is, it sells, do you want it?' If it doesn't sell, we take it back. That's been our guarantee from the very beginning. Anything we promise, we deliver."

What are the unhappinesses of the business?

"I think sometimes of selling it and retiring, but I get over that. It's a happy shop, but I have to be concerned with bill paying, financing, dunning. Those are worries I don't enjoy. Having to call people and ask why they haven't paid their bill, why they haven't been honest with us; why did they say they'd sent the check when they hadn't?

"Peter takes a lot of that off my back, but I still have to deal with the bank. We have a forty-five-thousand-dollar capital loan with them at the moment. That finances our accounts receivable. I have to go down there every so often and genuflect. Those people are not fun to deal with. They're everything I'm not interested in being involved with."

How about personnel problems? That seems a central difficulty for people in straight, white-collar jobs.

"We don't have any."

None? Aren't they inevitable when you put two or more people together in a common enterprise?

"This is not a democracy. We don't vote. From my analysis, no successful business runs in a democratic manner. It can't. It's gotta be an autocratic situation. One person makes the decision and sticks with it. If that person is wrong, he takes the blame. If someone calls here and has a problem dealing with us, I can't say someone else made the decision. Our way, customers know who they're dealing with, they have a way of finding solutions, they're not put off from one department to another. The buck doesn't pass around here. It works better that way. Everyone makes contributions, but someone has to make the final decision. It's not put up to a vote. This is in no sense a communal operation. It's run as a strict business, with, I hope, a heavy injection of humor and consideration for the employees.

"On the other hand," he admits, "while they're working for me and have one boss, I'm working for them, in a sense, and have thirteen bosses. If it were not for them, I would not have this gentle life I pursue. So I'm attentive to my 'bosses'' needs."

That has included health and pension plans, profit sharing. What now, then? What happens? Expansion? Diversification?

"To really push it," Peter says, "it would mean a lot more traveling. To make eighty thousand a year each,"—Jim draws $30,000, and Peter $18,000—"we'd have to kill ourselves for three or four years. We'd have to borrow more, get more staff, give up a lot of things. I'm not sure it's worth it, and Jim is no longer interested in making a million."

True?

"Why bother making life plans?" Jim answers. "It may be that the Karma of this business is to be in the hands of someone else, or that it is to be dissolved. Who can say? Who *wants* to say? I have no influence over that, although emotionally I may think I do. In point of fact, I don't. My best approach is to let it flow. And it does. People spend so much time planning their futures. Why bother? Why not listen to music?"

Fatalism seems a characteristic of life changers. It also dampens conversation. Peter senses this and invites their guest on a tour of Rockport and environs.

The sunroof of the 450SE hums back into its slot. The seat embraces the body as if it were custom measured. It is the thirty-first car Jim has owned. Peter starts it, backs up, and turns down the hill toward his house. There is small talk, and then the question: Is he glad he did it?

"To come from higher education, with all its ridiculous politicking, to this, where everyone respects each other's strengths and weaknesses without rancor, is a revelation. You bet I'm glad I did it. The pace is much slower. I walk to work or ride my bicycle. I'm really responsible only to myself. My brother gives me a free hand. I don't have all that agony of playing up to people or playing them off each other. These are super people to be with. No petty jealousies. That's because of this Yoga thing most of them are into. It's a disciplined way of living, a blissfulness, and it shows in the way they relate to others."

The car glides to a stop by a gray-green clapboard house on a corner overlooking the harbor. Peter uncoils from his seat, shuts the door.

"This was built about 1820, a fisherman's cabin," he says, walking across the lawn to the garage, ducking under tree branches. "As far as we can find out, we're only the fourth family ever to have lived in it." He stops, peers in the window at the rear of the building. "My tenant isn't in, and I don't have the key. Anyway, I've made this into a studio, and when she leaves, I'll do my painting in here. I'm really enjoying that. Never had the courage to take my drawing really seriously until I got up here. I've even formed a drawing group with a local sculptor. We meet every week to work from models."

Back in the car, he says he is hoping to reduce his workweek to four days so he can devote more time to the painting. "I'm not fully confident in my artistic ability yet, but I'm getting there. Some days I can't do much better than stick figures; other times, I'm Michelangelo."

It looks and sounds an idyllic life. In what ways does it fall short?

"I'm not fond of the repetition of the jewelry making, and I still have to put in four or five hours a day at the bench. The orders have to be turned out, and we try to fill them all within forty-eight hours. I'd prefer mostly administrative work, doing just enough jewelry to keep my hand in.

"I'm much, *much* happier, but this isn't nirvana. I feel I know myself better, but I'm still not fully satisfied with what I'm doing. This is, after all, my brother's thing. I have the desire to do something on my own. Maybe marketing original artworks."

He lets the Mercedes coast down the short slope in neutral. "Perhaps it's my nature never to be fully satisfied with my life," he muses aloud.

He slaps the lever into gear. "I think I'm still growing. I hope I never stop."

For many new-life people, change becomes a continuum, a journey of many stops and no predetermined destination. They confront the unknown eagerly, for, once they have made a first major adjustment in priorities, they are inspired to explore further options. The Fosters and Jim Russell placidly await direction; Peter Russell is actively shaping his.

So is Jim Martin, the former stockbroker, now remarried and a purveyor of CB radios. "We're looking at country property in Brown County. When we find what we want, we'll have to decide what kind of life-style we'll follow. I've been thinking about a truly rural subsistence farm, with a house we build ourselves from lumber cut on our own property.

"It would be a major question as to whether or not we should have electricity or a telephone. It might be kind of a schizophrenic existence with all these radios here in the shop"—he waves his hand in the direction of the stacks of boxes and the bench cluttered with electronic devices in the center of the room—"but I doubt it." He thinks about that a moment. "Or maybe in a secret black room in the middle of this log cabin, there'll be Formica on everything and fluorescent lights and transceivers sputtering and winking, and every now and then I'll skulk in there and pick up a mike and growl, 'Breaker one-nine!' Maybe. But those are things we have to think about—electricity or not, a telephone or not, water that comes out of a well or lake. . . .

"This shop is a means to an end. I'm not particularly interested in becoming Columbus, Indiana's, biggest retail merchant. I'm less interested in selling all the CBs and radios I can this month than I am in stringing it out over a period of time to provide us with a comfortable living at a pace commensurate with my own tranquillity.

"That's one of the most substantial attractions of being in business for yourself," he reflects. "To be able to modulate the pace set so you're not all wrapped up in an ego trip or just making money. The friend who helped me set this up is a child of high technology. He *needs* that private plane of his, even fixes his own radar. I, on the other hand, am just using this as a key to open the door to a *low*-technology life-style."

He would keep this business, then?

"Oh, yes. Don't misunderstand. I'm not against consumption, just *irrational* consumption. That's a whole open-ended discussion, of course. A black person who's never driven a Cadillac may not think that owning one is irrational, it's just something he's been denied. What I'm against is the high price of high technology. I just don't want to pay it. If I could own my land, put up a modest dwelling to keep my taxes down, raise the food we need, and not have to pay expensive electric, telephone, water, and sewer bills—that would be a helluva sweet thing."

He seems to be seeking the highest possible degree of independence, his visitor suggests.

"I think so. Yeah. If I could make enough money to pay for all that and still make my child-support payments and have three hundred dollars a month left over, I'd sell the business and retire.

"That's what I say now," he admits. "Maybe ten years from now I'll be thinking about getting up to a million dollars. That's what happens. But I've seen so many older fellas, stockbrokers, who made a lot of money—and I just remember what the Japanese say about the young man not having it and the old man not enjoying it. So I'm going to try to keep my expectations down. Most people who have a job with someone else can't even think of acquiring independence in ten years. I can, and I'll be only forty-three, young enough to have a grasp on the things that are important to me."

How did he come to this point of view? It wasn't the way it started out for him. Those cars, the two houses, the two wardrobes . . .

"My divorce. I'd fallen into a rut—in terms of behavior, what I wanted, what I was doing. I wasn't really happy with any of my jobs. I don't think most people are. It's just a matter of time before it begins chafing, especially if you're working in a corporate organization. It made me reexamine what I wanted."

The newspaper boy enters. Jim greets him, chides the publisher on his niggardly use of ink. Then he refills his coffee mug, thinking.

"Stocks and equities are the most stressful endeavor a person can pursue," he says finally. "It's feast or famine, which obviously doesn't allow for orderliness or stability. Brokers have a very high rate of alcoholism and divorce. Most of the ones I know who are making money at the moment are just paying off debts from the rotten years which preceded. It's the worst possible job to have had if you want to do something else. A typical broker is really nothing more than a salesman, even though he's usually highly motivated, highly intelligent, and highly moral. And the jobs just aren't there. The banks are swamped with ex-brokers. Their trust departments and investment committees are loaded up to here. An engineer or lawyer who tries teaching, say, can always go back to what he was doing before. Not a broker.

"I know guys in their late forties who used to make a hundred thousand dollars a year when times were good. They went out and joined the country club, put big down payments on expensive houses . . . then the next year they netted twenty-five thousand. That's when the Rothkos and Rauschenbergs went on sale. *That* market's been flooded, too, the last few years. It's no way to live."

But starting his own retail enterprise was no more reliable, was it?

"I think so. Look at the stocks-and-bonds field. At the peak of the market in the late sixties, the broker population was over sixty thousand. Now, it's under twenty-nine thousand. The firms are folding right and left. At one time, there were over five hundred member firms; now, it's more like two hundred. A lot of the 'boutique' houses and the ones which specialized in research have given up the ghost. Reliable technical analysis of the market—charting, graphs, computers—has proved to be mathematically impossible. They talked about the 'random-walk' theory, but you cannot predict tomorrow's prices from yesterday's. Prognostications of more than a year out always miss the mark.

"But even up to that point, even after you've come up with an econometric model that looks good, developed a list of clients you care about—even after all those things, you're still at the mercy of the mob. People will overreact, on the upside and the downside. There's no way to predict that. Sooner or later, no matter how good your recommendations, it begins to wreak havoc with your conscience and self-confidence. The fellas who stay become good because they really don't care, except about commissions, churning, production, and volume. Or else they just muddle through. In either case, I wasn't willing to go along."

Understandable. Yet now Martin has chosen to enter a business as potentially mercurial. CB is booming. At the time Jim is speaking, the FCC is receiving 650,000 applications for licenses every month, and retail sales are expected to top $2 billion—double the year before. Books on CB language are on the best-seller lists, magazines are full of stories about the phenomenon, and country and western singers are being awarded gold records for their laments of the open road. Surely it is a fad, but how long-lived? Some merchants express fears that the bubble will burst and they'll be left overstocked with costly equipment. It happened with pocket calculators.

How does Martin view all this? Is he hedging his bets?

"It was sheer accident," he says. "I had an interest as a kid in electronics. Most of what I can do now is based upon what I'd learned by age twelve. I went another direction, but the knowledge was still there. As it happens, I had a friend who was an avionics technician making a couple hundred bucks a week. He quit that job back in '67, and went into the CB business when it was just a specialty hobby for a few people. He began making money but still worked out of his kitchen. I saw him every now and then.

"About five months ago, he called me. Turns out he's now grossing over a million a year. Has twenty employees. Said this is what I ought to do. 'Any fool can do it.' He gave me fifty thousand dollars' worth of advice, and, just as important, he lets me have stock I pay for *after* it's sold.

"Now, the longevity of this fad may well be measured, although I don't think it will peak for several more years. There is a very substantial need for CB in business communications. The concrete dealer, the oil dealer, the big farmer—they all need it. But CB is AM, and the channels are all jammed. The businessman needs accessibility and reliability, so we sell him FM units. Some truckers are putting two radios in their cabs—one AM, one FM.

"Ten percent of the farmers around here have it. They need it to save gas, coordinate their deliveries, talk to their employees and families, their brokers. Even to get their sons to the dentist or to replace an exhaust hose. And it's not a matter of *if* but *when* the other ninety percent have it. That's one of the reasons I chose Columbus. The other merchants aren't getting to the farmers. I am.

"CB is useless to farmers. It's limited to four watts, about the same power it takes to light a Christmas tree bulb, and it's too crowded. FM can have as many watts as you want. Instead of a four- or five-mile range, you get noiseless, clear transmission as far as fifteen miles. Farmers don't all work contiguous acreage, you know. Often they lease property miles away. They need this, and the market's wide open."

A lean, windburned man in overalls and a yellow International Harvester cap comes into the shop. They greet each other and chat while the man browses among the boxes of a new shipment.

"Jeb, now," says Martin, "has a two-*kilo*watt base station. The local broadcasting station only runs five hundred watts."

To get back for a moment—what does it take, minimum, to start up?

"Let's see," he says, considering. "I'd say that if a guy had ten thousand dollars to roll with and then had some to live off, or had low expenses, he could make it. There are ways to cut that down. We lived in the shop here the first few months, didn't take out any money. Put it all back into inventory. We bought almost all this furniture and the tools at auctions. Purchased used test equipment.

"It helps to have a working wife, too. Mine's a nurse. We live off what she earns. Fortunately, I'd organized my life so I had no debts. Where you live is important, too. Rents aren't bad here, but they could be crippling in a larger city or more expensive town. Our apartment is only eighty-five dollars a month. But obviously you must keep your fixed expenses as low as possible. That's a big factor. And sticking to one thing. That, too.

"Now," he grins, "I can come anytime I want and leave anytime I want, so I get here at seven thirty in the morning and leave at nine thirty at night. I put in ninety hours a week. Never worked harder in my life. But I'm building something. I've been in business four months. The month before last, I turned profitable and earned eight hundred dollars. Last month was better than that. Based on that, I'd say things are looking propitious."

Is there satisfaction beyond making a living?

"Oh, yes. No question. Most new businesses fail, as you know. But at the same time, the small-business population remains amazingly stable. And there's challenge, variety—from accounting to sales to repair to personnel to tax reports—it's just tremendously energizing.

"Not just that. CB is very profound. Really! It's the chance to plug into the global village. You hear the greatest optimism, the worst depression, genius wit, banality, and everything in between. You can plug into the broadest network of naked need and sensibilities the world has ever seen. The possibilities are limitless. For two generations we've been talked at—radio, movies, TV—and now we can talk back, to other human beings. From what was just redneck radio, to truckers, then salesmen. Now everybody. I sell them to corporate execs who say they never use it, that they just listen in on the way to Florida vacations or to their lake cottages in Michigan. But they get out around the corner, whip out the mike, and it's *'Breaker one-nine!* Y'all got your ears on?' How can you lose when you're selling games and fantasy?"

4
Innkeeping

Many and sundry are the means which philosophers and physicians have prescribed to exhilarate a sorrowful heart . . . but, in my judgement, none so present, none so powerful, none so opposite, as a cup of strong drink, mirth, musick, and merry company.
—Robert Burton, *The Anatomy of Melancholy*

For four hours, the car hurtles into the whirling cone of snow. The rear wheels lock in sickening smears, then grab, then sluice away again. The night is blotted out for long moments before the groaning wipers push across the windshield, their paths filling immediately. Interstate 91 is buried, bordered only by winking mile markers. Its traffic is grinding, bleeping plows and an occasional pickup truck with a Sunday night cargo of six-packs. Even Vermonters don't go into a night like this.

The turn, finally. The road is now a one-lane channel with walls ten feet high. Another hour and the car slides under the big oval sign in front of a long porch. The engine sputters, surrenders. There is sleet now, and the stars are lost.

The front room of the inn is deep and high and warm. To the left center, there's a massive fireplace of native stone, the flames within leaping and snapping. Sofas, chairs, and side tables piled with magazines are arranged in a wide circle. At the far end, a bar of amiable proportions and clientele gives onto a dining room filled with the contented hum of patrons undeterred by the weather. They are guided through their meals, firmly but unobtrusively, by the boniface of the Chester Inn, Jim Patterson.

Dressed in black turtleneck, slacks, and a burgundy jacket, Patterson moves with graceful bearing, having adapted his stoutness to his instinctive sense of elegance and propriety. He and one waitress serve thirty customers without flustery impatience. Wines are presented, opened, and poured properly but without ostentation. Salads are mixed and tossed at tableside to ensure freshness. By eight thirty, the guests have finished their meals, and there are only two tables at which guests are lingering over espresso and brandy. A foursome arrives at the entrance. They are guests of the inn, but when Patterson finds that their reservations were for eight o'clock, he turns them away. He is unmoved by their noisily indignant protests.

Later, the room cleared, the breakfast setups completed, the help dismissed, Jim and Audrey Patterson sit down to a light supper of chicken and salad, by candlelight. These are among their few waking moments alone together, so they have chosen a table in the far corner of the room to avoid being hailed by guests. The bartender, Tom, a friendly though laconic sort in powder-blue jump suit and toupee, shields his employers from disturbance. His primary conversational topics are the snow and Morris, the slothful blue-point Siamese who presides over the lounge with stately disdain. Gorgon the Saint Bernard laboriously raises himself from his place by the front door and moves ponderously across the lobby to the dining-room entrance. At the end of his trek, he collapses heavily, with a satisfied groan.

Morris grudgingly relinquishes the wing chair flanking the fire to the latest arrival. The cognac is balm. Featured on the front page of the *Chester Sentinel* is the news that the nationally acclaimed California Cuties are to be challenged Tuesday evening by the Chester All-Stars. The Cuties, it is noted, is a roving team of men who play basketball dressed in women's clothes. With last week's unexpected snowfall, Magic Mountain has reopened and the skiers have returned.

The grandfather clock clunks past the half hour. A log pops. The last glass polished, Tom asks the remaining solitary guest to turn out the lights before he goes to bed.

It is midafternoon the next day before the Pattersons can sit down to talk, with advance apologies for the inevitable interruptions. The interviewer wants to know their methods of dealing with difficult guests, such as those who arrived late for dinner last night. They sigh and look at each other. Audrey answers.

"When we first opened, we were convinced we had to be *so* nice to everybody, that we had to do whatever the customer wanted. We soon realized we didn't, that certain people wouldn't be happy here, no matter what. And why should we break our necks if . . ."

". . . after you show a potential customer a few rooms," Jim interjects, "and they want to look at this again, and that again, and picking things apart, and . . . well, who needs it?"

"Nine out of ten people who walk in the door are just fantastic, and you enjoy being with them," Audrey says.

"And if you can cope with that tenth one, fine. As long as it doesn't upset things for everyone else. Also, you have to give people some time. Maybe they've had a long, hot drive with bad traffic and screaming kids. They're bound to be edgy when they come in the door. We take that into consideration. A certain amount of crankiness is understandable.

"You have to make your judgment at the time, determine whether it's something that will pass or are they going to be irretrievably difficult. Sometimes you get stuck. The best way to handle that kind of trouble is to shut them off at the outset."

"Trouble" for innkeepers—apart from abrasive and demanding personalities—means customers who express their dissatisfaction with tubs "with feet," black-and-white television rather than color, the lack of room service, the absence of bellhops, or the sagging floors and cracked ceilings inevitable in the older, frequently historic buildings which usually house inns. Jim Patterson gets rid of such prospective patrons easily, suggesting they "look further for accommodations."

"There are some," Jim says, "who are just miserable SOBs, not only with you but the world. The best thing to do with those people is to get them out."

How does Jim do that?

"I tell them to go away."

In just those words?

"In just those words."

"We must make it clear," says Audrey, "that those are just a minority. You have to like the 'people business.' That's probably the main ingredient of success in inns. Now, I'm not out front, partly because I'm not as outgoing as Jim, but . . ."

". . . she's not into that part of the business. And I'm sure even I have my surly moments. You do get a little hard-shelled toward people if you're not careful. On the other side, you have to draw the line between friends and customers, and it's a very fine one. We feel warmly toward many of our customers, but we never expect to receive invitations to their homes. After all, we present them with a bill when they stay here."

What background is required of those who would like to run an inn?

"We had no background. None whatsoever," Jim answers. "I did know something about financial management." He was once an international investment banker, stationed in Beirut. It was his distress with home-office politics which led him to consider innkeeping. "That helped. When you're going into business for yourself, you need to know a little bit about how to make things come out right."

Can't you just hand it over to an accountant?

"You can only hand over what you've done. You have to watch and control things as they are happening."

As emphasis, Audrey is summoned to talk to the egg man, and Jim must speak with a disgruntled reservation seeker on the telephone. Audrey returns first. She has a disconcerting habit of looking at a point above and slightly to the left of the visitor's head.

"That's an example. You have to deal with suppliers daily, especially when you're concerned that everything be fresh. One week we used one hundred dozen eggs. Even so, I have no feeling for money, except how to spend it. Jim does that."

But she runs the kitchen. Had she had prior training?

"Only cooking in the home, which is entirely different."

What would she have done differently had she to do it again?

"About the only thing," she says, picking a spot on the ceiling, "is the matter of timesaving techniques. I would like to have known more about the mechanics of food supply—how you buy, what you buy, when you buy, who you buy from. There was a tremendous amount of wasted energy and time on my part at first. I didn't know anything about a commercial kitchen. I would like to have had some sort of training. Oh, I enjoyed it. It was fun, klutzing around with the kitchen, but it would have been easier and we might have made more money if I'd had some guidance."

Jim returns, shushing their very young daughter. "But we have been very lucky in so many respects," he says. "Even with Audrey's learning. We met a chef who used to have a place in this area . . ."

"His name was Maurice Champagne. Isn't that marvelous?"

" . . . who is one of the greatest people who ever lived and a

fabulous chef. He works like this"—Jim snaps his fingers rapidly—
"and, fortunately, he took a liking to us. After we'd been open about
six months, he spent some weeks with Audrey to give her some training.
Most chefs are very selfish about their secrets, and very few male chefs
will work with women, but there was nothing Maurice would not tell
Audrey. He'd answer anything. More important, he'd show her things
she didn't know enough to ask about. Shortcuts. The easy way to do
things she'd been doing the hard way."

"He rearranged the kitchen, too," Audrey says. "I'd managed to
put all the appliances the maximum possible distance from each other."

Wasn't the kitchen already set up when they purchased the inn?

"It was empty. Utterly empty," she replies. "Not even a sink. The
auctioneer stripped it to the walls. Towel racks, medicine cabinets,
everything."

"It wasn't being sold as a hotel," Jim says, "but as a piece of real
estate. The man who owned it had been in the business for fifteen years
and didn't want to continue. When he couldn't get a hundred and ten
thousand dollars for it as a commercial enterprise, he sold off everything
inside and put the building up simply as property. We didn't get
involved until then.

"We had been coming up here every weekend from New York,
to a converted schoolhouse Audrey bought before we were engaged.
Someone mentioned this place. We certainly weren't thinking of opening an inn. We just looked at it as a lark."

Jim gets up, muttering something about "biological urgency."
They are on one of their periodic fasts, going through the day on water
alone. Audrey picks up the story.

"The price was low enough so we could actually think about it,
and its condition was excellent. We had a contractor friend check it
out because we knew we couldn't take it on if it wasn't in good shape.
We eventually bought it for fifty-three thousand dollars. The sprinkler
system alone was worth nearly that. But *before* we committed ourselves, we went around to four what-they-call 'contract' furniture firms.
We didn't know anything, of course—if we had, we probably wouldn't
have gotten into it—we just said we had forty rooms and what did we
need? The supplier told us we'd have to have X number of wastebas-
kets, X number ashtrays, X number hangers. You forget those things.
It really added up. When we knew, we went back to the owner and
said that fifty-three thousand was all we could offer. He took it, to our

surprise. We sold our co-op in New York—for almost exactly that amount, as it happened—and moved up."

"That was November 20, 1968," Jim says, returning again with another glass of water, "and we intended to open by Christmas Eve. Five minutes after the closing, I called the supplier to deliver the furniture. We had less than four weeks."

"We built the reception desk and the paneling . . ."

". . . and the bar . . ."

". . . and shelving. There wasn't that much construction because the structure was sound. It was essentially cosmetic changes. We stripped these center posts, which were boxed in and mirrored . . ."

". . . the lobby was hospital-green . . ."

". . . and everything was pretty well glopped up."

The walls are now deep chocolate, the exterior a rosy beige with blue trim. Shutters were added. To the right of the fireplace is a display of gilt-framed antique mirrors. A tartan-patterned carpet covers the floors of the bar and the dining room. Artifacts from the Pattersons' time in the Middle East and from their vacations in Mexico are placed about the public rooms, shifted and discarded as they try to maintain a measured freshness. The decorating process is still going on. Owners of a private home may stretch the periods between painting, but innkeepers cannot.

"And just to open the place," Jim is saying, "basic furnishings cost forty thousand dollars, which we were paying off on time, naturally."

That's why they set themselves so early a deadline. They had to have money coming in. Fast. The Christmas–New Year business was critical, they felt.

"We hired a very small staff and had a very small menu. At the outset, we did just one entrée a night. It was different each night, but there were no choices."

"I did it on the basis of what I knew how to do at home," Audrey continues, "with helpful hints from the lady who cooked here before. They weren't very helpful hints, as it turned out. She said that when you had a big crowd, the best thing to serve was steak. On Saturday nights, we had as many as seventy or eighty people. Cutting and cooking that many steaks to order is not as easy as it sounds. Rare, medium-rare, seared—what does the customer mean? There isn't that variation in, say, veal or chicken dishes."

"Our first staff member was a housekeeper. Got her from the

Times. Quite a character. She'd been everywhere, done everything, including working in Las Vegas. She was a big help. We'd be doing up plates, and she'd say that wasn't the way to do it, that we needed to dress it up with parsley or a rose radish. For the year she was here, she did everything."

"We hired two waitresses who doubled as chambermaids and kitchen help, two high-school boys to do the physical work, a cooking assistant. Tom was Artur Rubinstein's butler. We all contributed and all learned together."

The Pattersons' youngest daughter is insisting upon attention. As the dinner hour approaches, the tempo is picking up. Audrey is called away to speak with the Armour salesman. A load of snow slides from the roof with a window-rattling thump. Tom asks Jim to check the new, $1,000 espresso machine. It isn't working. Gorgon lumbers to a more isolated corner.

The definition of a true country inn (as opposed to those of the Ramada/Holiday/Sheraton/Hilton stripe) is a highly elastic one. There are inns in the stately homes of turn-of-the-century turpentine and railroad barons, in farmhouses, in hunting lodges. They once served as Colonial taverns, stagecoach stops, twenty-room summer cottages of the pre-Wilson rich, and even as inns. They may be brand-new, very old, or restored. The label is bestowed more often on the basis of ambience than details of construction. By consensus, though, "inns" are those hostelries that serve meals and lodge travelers and in which the managers live. They are otherwise resistant to categorization, for they are the individual and often eccentric expressions of their owners' tastes and preferences. They are both recognizable and unpredictable.

There is, conversely, little agreement on what inspired the boom in country inns. Some trace it to the back-to-the-earth movement of the late sixties, some to a renewed interest in national origins, still others to gasoline shortages, inflation, recession.

It really isn't that complicated. July arrives. We encase ourselves in two tons of Granada or Monte Carlo or their ilk and fling ourselves down thousands of miles of unchanging expressways in order to inhale the exhaust fumes of aluminum campers chugging past Old Faithful. We fall exhausted each night into a room without surprises, pop the paper band on the toilet seat, and try to remember what it was that we did that day. Then we turn around and go back home, marveling at the absence of stoplights between here and there. We do not consider that the only thing the federal highway system has done for us is to connect our traffic jams.

Country inns are the better way. They don't have singles weekends or mambo lessons or Paul Anka. They are places to feel new snow crunch beneath the feet, to trail a doe or creep up to a beaver dam, to sip mulled cider in a cozy inglenook. They sit beside tranquil village greens, or on hilltops among flaming maples, or within sight of waves chasing sandpipers over powdered white sand. They are hideaways to be alone together or to get to know the kids again. And they—or their potential—are in every section of the land.

Wherever they are or may one day be, all inns are in debt to a man who calls himself the Berkshire Traveler. In 1966, Norman Simpson published a slender volume he entitled *Country Inns and Back Roads.* He had situated himself in Stockbridge, Massachusetts, within a day's drive of perhaps half the inns then extant. The book struck a chord. Revised annually ever since, *Country Inns* now lists establishments from Canada to the Carolinas to California, and the guide has sired a cottage industry producing books on cooking, Indian history, and Shaker furniture, and employing a not inconsiderable portion of Stockbridge's women. Simpson spent much of his life as an actor before evolving into independent publisher. Now he knows as much about innkeeping as most owners, and Jim Patterson says Simpson has done more for the business than anyone in the country.

Country Inns is, in effect, an advertising vehicle. Although the fact is not mentioned in the book, every innkeeper pays a fee for his listing. Possibly the fee is the innkeeper's guarantee of exclusivity, for many equally estimable places in the immediate vicinities of those anointed are unlisted. Simpson won't say. Whatever the levy or its restrictions, it also defrays expenses for the activities of the Berkshire Traveler's Innkeepers Association. The organization meets at member establishments twice yearly, usually in October and May. Although Simpson limits attendance, he sometimes allows the participation of people considering innkeeping as a livelihood. An affable and kindly man, he has always tried to respond to pleas for information about the business.

He is rarely encouraging. People are unrealistic about innkeeping, he says. They have not thought it through. While it is quite possible to make a comfortable living, there is "no quick buck to be made." He purposely emphasizes negatives, listing disadvantages which a prospective innkeeper might not otherwise consider. Couples don't know until they do it how they will get along for twenty-four hours of every day, every month. Inn life is difficult for smaller children, who must be restricted in deference to the largely middle-aged and older clientele. Parents cannot give them full attention. Older children find themselves pressed into service shoveling ashes, waiting on tables, and cleaning bathrooms. Simpson has found that wives are distressed to discover that the housewifely roles they had hoped to discard are, on the contrary, reinforced, and that the same is true, albeit to a lesser extent, of husbands. Further, many are underfinanced and often completely unequipped in even a portion of the necessary skills.

Still, the dream persists. And if Simpson is persuaded that an inquiring couple has a reasonable chance, he'll try to bring them together with others wishing to sell. It happens often enough. Among the members of Simpson's association are former airline pilots, accountants, theatrical performers, diplomats, copywriters, corporate executives, architects, artists. So frequently is innkeeping a second career that trained hoteliers and chefs seem the exception, not the rule.

Tom Wells was an interior designer. Rosalind Wells was an opera singer. They call their place Wells Wood.

Yesterday's eighteen-inch snowfall, the heaviest of the winter, has not profited the Wellses. They are friendly with the Pattersons a half-hour's drive away, but their inns are very different in proportion and concept. The Chester Inn is on a main road, in the heart of town, within minutes of five major ski centers. The Pattersons have thirty-two rooms; the Wellses, only four. Wells Wood is isolated from what passes for population centers in central New Hampshire, up a steep hill from the secondary road below, sometimes inaccessible in bad weather. Although both caravansaries emphasize the quality of their cuisine, the Chester Inn's profits are primarily in its lodgings, while the Wellses derive most of their income from their restaurant.

There are distinctions in temperament as well. The Pattersons are restrained, proper, precise. The Wellses are voluble, outgoing, demonstrative, delivering veal and opinions *con brio*. Both couples manifest supreme confidence in all they do, but the Pattersons do so with serenity, the Wellses with overpowering gusto.

"We are creative!" Tom Wells says, waving a huge arm. "We are *imaginative! Eating* in our place is an emotional *experience!* Two nights ago, a man stood up in the middle of the dining room and shouted, *'I have not eaten food like this since the First World War, when they stopped cooking!'* Then he sat down. To applause! People go by the kitchen and pound on the window and cry, 'Take me in!' "

"Our place is an *event!*" Roz laughs, just as exuberant and as amply proportioned as her husband. "I'm a conductor in that kitchen! The meals are *orchestrated!* The garlic butter is right there. The minced clams are ready. I create anything I want. I cook *only* with butter. Only butter! Everything is cooked *to order.* The salad dressings are all homemade, the bread I bake myself from stone-ground flour."

"Roz makes up what she calls 'Jason's Royal Feast,' " Tom says, "which is composed of petite filet mignon and crab Mornay and all kinds of good things from the kitchen. It's *unbelievable!* Takes her longer to set up the plate than it does to cook it. Now, all our plates are heated and covered. One time, when the waitress served it to this customer and took off the cover, the lady said 'Oh, my *goodness!* Take this back!' The girl was *shocked. No one* ever sends back anything. She asked what was the matter, and the lady said she wanted the chef to *sign* it! The girl almost had a heart attack!"

Roz and Tom roar at the recollection. Then she goes to prepare tea while he drives six-year-old Jason to school, giving the visitor a moment to catch his breath.

The Wellses' personal quarters are as joyfully freewheeling as their creators. The living room is a flamboyant phantasmagoria of every furniture and decorative style between Jacobean to Art Deco and beyond. There are samovars and candelabra, peacock feathers and stained glass, South American wood carvings and Flemish oils, bowls of marble eggs, a Seth Thomas clock and a Chinese chest, curving black-leather sofas and marble-topped Victorian tables. It is scrolled and gleaming and polished and thoroughly enchanting.

Roz brings the tea, fragrant but not cloying, and tiny, fat, flaky pastries. Tom bursts back into the room and begins again as if he hadn't stopped.

"We have a very *definite* life-style we enjoy, and we brought it *with* us. This is the way we like to live. We wanted safer, cleaner, saner surroundings, and that's what we found. But we still enjoy cities. We picked this location partly because it's two hours from Boston, three from Montreal, four and a half from New York. We travel quite a bit —to Europe once a year, to California. And we take advantage of New York. We're theater buffs, still interested in opera, the museums. . . . The thing is, we use New York, it doesn't use us."

"A mistake a lot of people make when they come up here," Roz says, "is that they completely change. They become instant New Englanders. They are maple-sugaring and skiing and kayaking as soon as they get here. They throw away all the accoutrements of the activities they once loved. Everything they cared about is discarded."

"We're probably the only inn up here that is European rather than Colonial. Most people go Americana as soon as they cross the border. We're *unique!*" Tom is revving up again after those moments of relative repose. "We had to decide who we are, and we knew we had to be *true* to that! We had *definite* likes and dislikes, and *knew* we wouldn't be comfortable running around in Quaker uniforms and serving on Shaker furniture. That all has its *place,* but it's not to *our* taste.

"When I was looking for a place, they showed me all these inns dating back to 1700—in *original condition!* I'd gone through all that! But when I came up the driveway *here,* I knew this was *it!* I didn't have to see the inside. There was a problem at first. I thought I had this place nailed down. We had sold our house in Chicago before we found out the owner here had changed his mind. So I flew out here and got a big old Victorian. Then we drove back here with two forty-five-foot van loads of furniture behind us, and Roz said, 'It's *lovely!* But don't unpack because I'm not staying.' Encouraging. But we only stayed two months, then this place became available again. This time, she had the same reaction I did."

The cluster of cream-and-brown buildings that is now Wells Wood was once the home of Maxfield Parrish. His critically scorned and immensely popular paintings of extravagantly voluptuous sunsets and gowned wood nymphs were essential in the decorating schemes of middle-class homes in the early decades of this century. Parrish lived far beyond his time, dying in 1966 at age ninety-five. In Tom Wells, he had a suitably respectful yet robust successor. The fifty-acre estate of woodland remains intact. Majestic oaks still shelter the main house and outbuildings. Apart from their private apartment, Wells has been subdued in furnishing and refurbishing the inn, which has a magical whimsy all its own.

The grandly scaled dining room, which served Parrish as a music salon, has a twenty-foot beamed ceiling and Palladian windows nearly as high. On the interior wall is a baronial fireplace, and at the far end a stage with a grand piano watched over by gilded cherubim. The adjoining cocktail lounge is a glassed-in room of more intimate dimensions, but it provides an unhampered view across a twenty-mile, two-hundred-degree sweep of the Connecticut Valley. The river curls past Mount Ascutney, just over the border in Vermont. Tom describes the reflecting pool and formal gardens beneath the snow just beyond the windows.

He mixes a martini for his guest, pours a glass of Chablis for himself, then comes from behind the bar to settle down on the next bar stool. The Wellses do not serve lunch in the winter, and there are no other lodgers today. It is very quiet. They sip. The bough of a tree outside shivers as its icy burden abruptly falls away.

"The house is hard to define," he says. "I can't say what style Parrish did it in. Our decor transcends, yet unifies, what he did. The result, I think, is very comfortable. You can get fully dressed in long gown or dinner jacket, or just a sweater and slacks. Either way, you'll be at ease. We don't have a dress code as such, although we don't allow shorts or dungarees. We want people to be comfortable.

"The chairs are specifically designed with that intent. We want people to spend two hours in our dining room. You can't do that in a Shaker chair, 'cause you get up and it's left an imprint. We didn't go in for crystal stemware and Spode china. That's *offensive* to me. You can have good food without ultraformality. Only in America do they associate the two. High-quality food doesn't need stuffiness.

"Customers are company here. Our waiters and waitresses don't make you feel like you don't belong. Our guys and girls are local. I don't care if they mispronounce the wine, but I want the wine on the table when it's supposed to be. And none of that exaggerated tableside service, either. I want an atmosphere where people can have a good time. Not boisterous, but relaxed, and with the respect you'd show in a friend's home."

On the way back to their apartment, Tom pauses at the library, where guests serve themselves breakfast and pass the evening hours. He demonstrates how to work the windows, which Parrish designed to slide into the walls instead of up and down. Across the lawn from the main building is Parrish's machine shop. He fashioned all of the many brass fittings and much of the paneling himself. "Others are carpenters so they can paint," he once said, "while I paint in order to be a carpenter." Wells has left the machines but now sells antiques there, as catholic an assortment as that which fills his own quarters.

Tom rejoins his wife upstairs. Some of the Pattersons' observations on dealing with difficult customers are related, and the Wellses are asked their own methods.

"Roz has a very good philosophy," Tom says.

"I certainly do," she laughs. "The main idea is to keep *him* away from them."

"I used to go right for the *throat,*" he admits. "I have an emotional stake in this place. When I ran the front, there was always someone with eight-o'clock reservations who'd come in at quarter to nine. We had a digital clock at the front desk, and I used to stand there tapping it meaningfully and glowering."

"Everything in the kitchen is *timed* . . ."

". . . and we're doing our *best* to make things right for them, and it's *unfair* and inconsiderate of them to come downstairs late and expect everybody to *dance* around for them and *screw* everybody else up and *maybesomebodyiswaitingfortheirtable* and I won't *tol*erate it!"

He does get excited, doesn't he?

Tom grins a little sheepishly. "I do, I do. That's why Roz put me in the bar and hired a maitre d' who loves people."

"We try to explain to Tom," says Roz, who hasn't stopped laughing, "that it doesn't matter *what* he thinks, that they're here to have a good time, and his tapping that little finger doesn't mean a damn thing in their lives."

"Roz theorizes that we should let them grump and fuss, get them seated, and then get them something to eat. If they're *still* complaining after they've started eating, ask them to leave! That's it!"

"I don't know that a guy hasn't just had a fight with his wife in the parking lot," Roz says, "that he didn't wait forty-five minutes for her to get dressed, and now she's yelling about whatever it was he did last night. They get here, and they're not ready for the *wonderful* experience we're going to give them. They want to *kill* each other! Tom, in the meantime, is tapping his finger, so he makes a marvelous target. He's glowering, and he's large, and they turn on him.

"After their first bite, if they don't see the difference in the way we handle things—the surroundings, the atmosphere, the service, and *then the food!*" Roz turns solemn. "If they—are—not—ready—for—*my—food,* then I draw the *line!* Give them their check and tell them to come back when they're feeling better."

"We do that," says Tom, calmer. "It's very few, really. The lunatic fringe is not fifteen percent, it's more like two. My reactions are milder now, because I'm more sure of what we're doing. Those few can be *so* insane, though. One said, 'We're in a hurry!' I told him he was in the wrong place. This isn't a Big-Mac-and-fries operation. He was incredibly obnoxious. An hour late, insisted on immediate service, drove the waitresses wild. Then he snapped his *fingers* at me for dessert! His kid said he wanted to go to Dairy Queen. I said they *all* should, that it was much more their style, then gave him his check. Then I told him not to come back. Ever! Another time, though, a guy was bellyaching about waiting for his *escargots*—loudly—and a customer at the next table said, 'Siddown and shut up!' Most people are with you, they're on your side.

"Good food takes time, and a lot of restaurants state that right on the menu. If you want it scooped out of a steam table, go to a place that does that. Food can't be prepared any faster than it can be baked or broiled or sautéed. Someone who doesn't know the difference shouldn't eat at a fine restaurant. Or open one."

Tom, like most innkeepers, finds the need to keep separate his friendships and his business to be a sensitive issue. An acquaintance from college once called long distance, planning to stay at Wells Wood for a week or so. Tom said they'd be glad to see him—and read him the room rates. He had to do it, he maintains. This is their home, but it is also their livelihood. They didn't hear from the man again.

They moved to New Hampshire when both were thirty-one. Tom had already been a designer for ten years. At first they thought they would keep the inn open six months a year, spending the balance in Chicago. Then Jason was born, and they felt he needed continuity of friends and environment.

"We said we would not change our life-style for children," Tom says of their decision. "That works up to a point, but he's a child and deserves certain things. When we were in the city and put him in the backyard, we had to go out every thirty minutes and dust off the soot.

"So we said, 'Let's do it!' We were young enough. If we didn't make it, then we didn't. We could always go back. We aren't afraid to change careers. It was to be a *total* break. After that, some suburb just wasn't far enough away. We needed—this."

Another wave of his arms to encompass their hilltop redoubt.

"Why *here* exactly? We never considered an in-town location. There is nothing appealing to us about medium-size towns. We wanted this isolation because we can just close the gates. At an inn in a town, you can't do that. You're a public service and a community meeting place. The Kiwanis has lunch there every Tuesday. Up here, it doesn't pay to have those kinds of functions, and I'm glad of it. When you're new in a business, you feel you should be there all the time, doing everything. That soon wears very thin."

The Pattersons speak of the necessity of specifying an inviolate day off as well as consistent vacation periods. The Wellses agree. Mondays they are closed. April in northern New England is "mud season," and business slows from the end of the fall foliage weeks until Christmas. Both sets of innkeepers take those weeks to travel. In other regions, different times are appropriate. According to Norman Simpson, though, no inn can be expected to provide a living for a typical family if it is open less than nine months a year.

". . . which doesn't mean there's nothing to do here," Tom is saying. "One of the reasons we chose this area is we're only twenty minutes from Dartmouth and the Hopkins Arts Center. Roz took German last year; I learned pottery. Woodstock is nearby, an exciting and very beautiful town. We've had the Boston Ballet, a Cleo Laine concert—there's always something going on. Art galleries, shows, crafts, and interesting people. We're surrounded by people who are definitely our peers intellectually. There are sculptors and designers and writers tucked away in all these hills. . . ."

And the *dis*advantages?

"It took a long time to get established. We've been here four years, and there are still people in town who don't know we exist. There aren't enough rooms for overnight guests. We're building more. Staff is a problem. Our first chef robbed us blind. Kitchen and service help have to be trained because there's no pool of professional restaurant people around here. And slave labor is gone, except when you work for yourself. We've had floods, fires. Utilities go out. City people don't realize how delicate the plumbing system is. They throw incredible things in the toilets. . . ."

What would it cost—right now—to recreate what they've done here?

"At minimum? With an empty building? We put in everything we had. It's different everywhere, so it's nearly impossible to say. Let's see. Say you buy a house for a hundred thousand dollars. Up here, that would be the smallest house you could get that would be big enough. Then at least fifteen or twenty thousand for kitchen equipment. I'm *appalled* at prices—five thousand dollars for a dishwasher! For tables, chairs, china, silverware, and so on, at *least* ten thousand. And you need enough to live on and pay your help until the money starts.

"The building can be mortgaged, with probably twenty-five to thirty thousand down. The kitchen and maybe the furniture can be financed over three or four years, with about a quarter down."

So a rock-bottom cash fund of about $60,000 would do it?

"And a lot of luck."

What is his advice to someone who wants to try?

"Do it! You can always go back. I know too many people who are fifty and still waiting to decide what they're going to be. You can fail at what you're doing. Why not fail at something you like? *Do it!*"

Outside, water drips from the oak branches, forming puddles in the flattening snow. There is a legend on the license plates of the cars in the parking lot. *Live Free or Die.*

With the exception of farming, there is no owner-operated business more comprehensive in scope than an inn, or where the margin of profit is so slender. Success doesn't necessarily ensure income. Anne Edwards and Stephen Citron vouch for this. They owned and ran Orpheus Ascending, a sophisticated weekend hideaway with Gallic overtones. In their book, *The Inn and Us,* they related that in their first season they were booked to 80 percent capacity. They lost $14,216. But they received good notices and word-of-mouth; Leonard Bernstein and Norman Mailer became regulars, along with other luminaries. Business was brisk. More favorable reviews. The second season, they lost $17,346.

One example: Inns are selling charm, history, romance. For most of their clients, this requisite ambience is symbolized by snuggles by the fire. The guests think nothing of tossing on extra logs for the desired effect, even on a cool night in July. A cord of firewood costs upwards of $60. One Connecticut innkeeper claims to spend $200 a month on firewood alone. And there's still the fuel bill.

Essential foods can double in price in a matter of days. Any home cook can guess what last week's butter increase might mean if he or she were feeding one hundred people two times a day. Commercial discounts are not universally available, either. State law requires the Pattersons to buy all their liquor through package stores, not distributors, and at regular retail prices.

Tom Wells figures that foodstuffs consume one-third of his operating funds, and maintenance, utilities, and debt service another third. The only major expenditure that can be significantly pared is personnel. That's why there are virtually no single owner-managers. There must be at least two people who are able to devote all their waking hours to the running of the inn, with little certain compensation beyond room and board. The Pattersons talk about alternatives.

"One person *could* do it," Audrey says, without conviction. "Obviously, you'd have to hire more help, and you'd be under the strain of having to find key people. When we started, if any help left, we'd just do a little more to cover. If you're alone, you can't."

"Obviously, it's preferable that it be a couple," Jim agrees. "I can see where two men or two women could do it, but only if they had no interest in the other sex. Otherwise, one is going to find someone he or she wants to marry, then what happens to the business? One has to buy the other out, or the new person moves in. Those threesomes can be very dangerous. I've seen a few such combinations, and it just doesn't work."

Foursomes present similar difficulties. "It's not a good idea to go into this business with friends. It looks appealing because costs can be spread out, but then so are profits. Husbands and wives can usually work things out between them; friends often cannot."

To be together so much requires the kind of tolerance and mutual understanding built over many years. Still, it need not be confined to single-couple management. Many inns are family affairs. Everyone participates. The Campbell family of Vermont's Saxtons River Inn is a prime example. With children and spouses, there is a grand total of twenty-one Campbells, all of whom have taken active parts in running the inn at one time or another, some on a permanent, full-time basis. Noteworthy, too, is the Williams family of West Dover, Vermont.

At first, Ione ("Eye-own") Williams did the cooking, and husband Rod was the front man. Son Brill helped in the kitchen, as did his wife, once he married. Brill proved so placidly competent, he is now head chef. Ione oversees staff, housekeeping, the accounts. A grandmother helps, primarily in preparing pies and squeezing juice from fresh tomatoes. Assorted other children and relatives put in time as waiters and hosts in the dining room.

So capable are they all that the Inn at Sawmill Farm remains open twelve months a year, although Rod and Ione vacation in Europe and elsewhere six to eight weeks a year. Rod deflects any credit for the inn's solvency—it grosses between $250,000 and $300,000 a year—to his family.

"The inn is Ione's; its success is hers," he insists. "She was an interior decorator and has a great eye for color and arrangement. She's done it all here. Our books go to the accountants once a year, and that's the only time they see them. She does them. She's meticulous. Wants to know she's on a solid rock before she takes a second step. A really great gal.

"Brill is unflappable. He just has the feel for it, so easy, no confusion. He'll have ten tickets hanging there with five or six meals on each. Never gets excited. Other people, things are flying around, they're yelling. *I* can't do even eight breakfasts. He looks at one ticket at a time, and while that one's in the oven, he's prepping another, putting others on their plates. I don't know how the hell he does it.

"Brill's wife, Lex, is a great girl, too. She does a beautiful job on our French pastry, bakes about half our pies and cakes. Normally, she's the hostess, because I'm often flambéing steaks or cutting lamb chops, and it takes two people to run the door. She jumps around, though. Tonight, she's waiting on tables because my nephew's sick."

Still, the Williamses cannot rely exclusively upon familial ties. At any one time, their staff totals about fourteen. They are paid well by regional standards—waiters make $300 to $350 a week—but the Williamses are demanding. Shirts and blouses must be clean daily, dirndls and pants carefully pressed, hair neat, fingernails immaculate. Grease spots on cuffs and curls of dust under beds are not tolerated. Waiters are expected to know who gets the lamb chops and the sole without asking. Plates are to be delivered with a whisper, not a sliding clatter. Rod Williams is scornful of the ski bums hired by other inns. His staff members are largely college-educated, with an international flavor. Right now, the bartender is Austrian, and there are two young Colombians.

Everything works. The public and sleeping rooms are spotless. Service is both correct and friendly. Fresh flowers and even potted plants are replaced frequently (although, in keeping with Vermont tradition, the Christmas wreaths are still in the windows with Easter approaching). There are delightful extra touches, too. Afternoon tea is served in translucent china, with moist, thick brownies and chocolate-chip cookies. After the dinner entrée, a finger bowl with a slice of lemon is provided.

In 1967, the Williamses had no thought of opening an inn. Rod was president of his father's Atlantic City architecture firm. Ione was a sometime schoolteacher and interior designer. But they were skiers, and they often stayed at a lodge in West Dover. To amuse themselves on one day of stinging snow and sleet, they asked a local realtor to show them some of his listings. To their surprise, the tour included the farmhouse and barns they had admired from the lodge for many years. The property was three times too expensive, but they bought it anyway. Even after the papers were signed, they didn't know what they were going to do with it.

"That," Rod says now, "was when we decided to get out of Atlantic City. "That night, over a couple of martinis, we talked about how dissatisfied we were with things as they were. I'd gone as high as I could professionally. The only next step up was New York or Philadelphia, and I'm just not a big-city guy. Absolutely not. We had all the worthwhile clients in Atlantic City, and that city is going downhill, and they're leaving. It'll never come back. Gambling won't save it. It's scarier to walk along the boardwalk than at midnight on Forty-second Street in New York. It took a year for us to get paid for a job there. Even the big banks and hotels were doing it. So we decided to make ourselves an inn and get out of New Jersey."

The battered structure which now houses the lounge, two dining rooms, kitchen, bar, and several bedrooms was little more than a shell when they bought it. But in six months, the Williams registered their first guests. Rod's modesty about his contribution is unwarranted. His creation is without visible flaw, the embodiment of a vision which possesses half the home buyers east of the Alleghenies: the ultimate converted barn.

The first large space after the entrance is the "living room," paneled with weathered barn siding, filled with squashy sofas and chairs in floral slipcovers. And copper! Gleaming kettles, pans, kitchen utensils, tabletops, pots. Everywhere. Up above, there is a book-lined balcony with a balustrade salvaged from the cattle stalls. And antiques. A century-old grandfather clock, a Davenport secretary, and spoons, candlesticks, trivets, lanterns, plates. The rest of the rooms are similar in feeling, yet different. The more formal dining room is decorated with spidery chairs and tavern tables, ancestral portraits and wrought-iron chandeliers. The bar houses a player piano and Gay Nineties artifacts and posters. "To school well-fed on Grape-Nuts," says one. The patio dining room, overlooking the swimming pool and flowering fruit trees, is festooned with trailing greenery. Other rooms are faintly Colonial, vaguely Swiss, suggestively Victorian, but all somehow crisply. New England. "We want them to know they're in Vermont."

Behind the well-conceived setting is a straightforward philosophy shared by all innkeepers who survive their first tentative years.

"Money means nothing," Rod declares. "The best you can give, that's what counts. There's ten farmers right here, but Ione drives twenty-two miles to buy from a place that charges fifteen percent more but whose vegetables are perfect. We use nothing that's frozen. All our meats are fresh. We butcher our veal ourselves. The chicken is still on the bone and still has its skin until the customer orders. Only then is it prepared. All this attention makes it just that little bit better. It makes the difference."

To prove it, he guides his visitor to a table beneath the ivy. Breakfast is as good a time as dinner to validate his contention. It is soon apparent that he has not exaggerated.

But Rod is distracted. Cater-corner across the room, a scruffy, zit-picking late adolescent in T-shirt and farmers' overalls noisily slurps his shirred eggs with shallots and whole-tomato sauce. Two younger siblings ape him in manner, grooming, and decibels.

Rod fails to disguise his displeasure. "Some children can just ruin a dining room. We get an older crowd most times of the year, especially around events like the Marlboro Music Festival, and it only takes one kid squealing and running around at the pool or the restaurant to disrupt things." He glances at the departing teenagers. "During holidays, we'll take anyone. The rest of the time, no kids."

Most innkeepers seem to agree. Youthful exuberance and impatience do not mesh with the pace of leisurely, made-to-order meals and the restful mood so painstakingly promoted. The patron of country inns is usually white, over forty, and a college graduate who fits in the higher-income groups. He or she works in one of the traditional professions or as an executive, and the combination makes for a person of conservative mien and attitude. Since typical innkeepers fall within those parameters as well (except for the fact that they have left their former occupations), there is little conflict in their mutual perceptions of what constitutes a proper inn.

That image doesn't suffer children easily (except the innkeepers' own, of course). Nor is it tolerant of the recreational predilections of teenagers. Discotheques, for example, nearly always fail as part of an inn, although the more mellow varieties of folksinger and piano player are acceptable. Children are frequently barred altogether or from the dining rooms, and the presence of teenagers is discouraged. At least one inn in New England prohibits anyone under sixteen from registering.

The Wellses, Pattersons, and Williamses are not that rigid. Unlike some of their colleagues, they are not leery of customer couples of ambiguous sexual persuasion or legal sanction, either.

"They're among our most delightful guests, actually," Rod says. "They're marvelous conversationalists. Many of them are in the arts. Heterosexual or otherwise, they're usually nicer than our other guests. They don't fight, and they're considerate of others. One couple came here for three years, *then* got married, right in the inn."

Ione has joined her husband over coffee. "We don't make distinctions," she agrees. "Couples are couples."

"On the other hand," Rod interjects, "we try not to take groups of more than three. You get four or more couples, and they try to run the inn. They take over. They're unwieldy in the dining room and generally difficult to handle."

"They become very possessive," Ione says. "They come into the living room, take their shoes off, lie on the sofa, put their feet on the tables. They begin to feel they can go behind the bar and make their own drinks . . ."

". . . or go into the kitchen to raid the icebox. The same thing is true when a guest stays too long. We discourage people from staying more than five days or so. The longer they're here, the more they think they're entitled to special service."

"Maintaining that balance between warmth and distance is tough. You have to play it by ear, though, because each person is different."

"A few can be very difficult," Rod says, sliding into the incantation of customer intransigence and oafishness that must form the substance of Norman Simpson's annual meetings. "They don't respect or appreciate what we've done here . . ."

". . . candy mashed into the carpet, the bedspread rolled up and thrown in the corner . . ."

". . . their kids throwing billiard balls around . . ."

". . . snapping their fingers at the waitresses. . . ."

The visitor makes a mental note to check the state of the bed-clothes and towels in his room, and changes the subject. What has been the Williamses' experience financially since they purchased the farm, and what would it take to duplicate it now?

"To start from scratch as we did," Rod replies, "you'd have to have a hundred and fifty thousand dollars. In our case, it took a year to get into the black . . ."

". . . and then it was very little, and we put it all back in the business . . ."

". . . and then about *five* years for the repeat business to start catching up with us. Only then did we start seeing old customers and referrals. All our people today are repeaters.

"You don't go into the inn business for money, or you shouldn't. We don't have a thing in the bank. But it's a different world. It used to cost me to live in Atlantic City what it costs me to run this inn. I used to make a hundred and fifty thousand a year, but we eat here, sleep here. That's free. Gasoline, our two cars, even bills at other restaurants and hotels are deductible. The only thing we really have to pay for is clothes."

Jim Patterson even deducts his clothes—as "uniforms." Innkeep-ers customarily write off all their living expenses if they reside on the premises. No one can guarantee the reaction of the IRS should it choose to audit, but the Williamses have avoided that so far.

"I never give any thought to it," Rod says. "We come to work at seven in the morning and work until eleven at night. Christ, we're entitled to something. Of course, I haven't bought a drink in ten years."

Most city restaurants derive substantial income from their bars. Is that true of Sawmill Farm?

"We price our drinks thirty cents higher than any other place in the valley specifically because we don't *want* a bar trade. We don't want drunks knocking over chairs or bumping into tables or getting into fights or automobile accidents in the parking lot. You watch. As soon as the last houseguest leaves the bar, the bartender starts blowing out the candles. That's our invitation to the outside people to leave. We usually close down at eleven. It's a lousy buck, anyway. You sit there until one o'clock and make another ten dollars.

"The off-the-street guest is a problem in other ways, too. In ten years, we've had only two paintings, an ashtray or two, and a few other items stolen. Almost every time, we've traced it to outside people who just came in for a drink or a meal.

"The people who stay here are just great. They respond to what we're doing. There's a feeling, too, I guess, that you might rip off a corporation, like a Holiday Inn, but not an individual. We've only had two bad checks in all this time, and we don't have to bolt our lamps and pictures down."

Innkeepers are a fiercely independent breed with unshakable convictions, so few generalizations about techniques and philosophies of management can be made.

Although professional hoteliers, for instance, say that the most desirable and acceptable division of labor is the man in the kitchen and the woman out front, the Pattersons, the Wellses, and the Williamses do not follow that pattern.

Tom Wells thinks that newcomers to the profession are best advised to purchase an existing inn instead of converting a property originally used for a different purpose. He is persuasive. "If you turn a New York City brownstone into a restaurant, there are *eight million people* who can hear about you! The total population of New Hampshire is less than a million! The biggest drawbacks we had were that we were *not* known and *not* in a central location! With an *established* place, you have a built-in reputation, and you know that it meets *all* legal requirements. Even if you don't *like* the stove, at least it's *there* and can be replaced after some money comes in. Starting from scratch means an enormous capital outlay." Rod Williams doesn't agree. "I wouldn't buy an established inn. If you're successful, you'd never know if it was due to what you did or what *he* did. You have to live with his mistakes and follow his traditions. I would always start from scratch." Jim Patterson isn't sure. "With a new business, you don't have to pay someone for goodwill, but you don't have his client list or records, either. It's a draw."

The Wellses and Audrey Patterson believe that apprenticeship of some kind is a good idea—perhaps working as managers for another owner. Rod says you only learn other peoples' bad habits when you farm yourself out. All of them, though, have varying degrees of contempt for the products of hotel and restaurant schools, and none had any experience as innkeepers.

All three couples seem to concur that people considering innkeeping should:

1. Talk to insiders—a lot. They are a loquacious breed, usually ready to provide guidance, given some notice. Ask about their own experiences, about properties they have heard are available (perhaps their own), about local oddities in food supply and law.

2. Learn the state and local regulations affecting a desirable property. The Wellses were not required to have a sprinkler system; the Pattersons and Williamses were. That can be a difference of tens of thousands of dollars.

3. Determine the extent and limitations of liquor laws, as well as methods of distribution. Brill Williams finds he can't obtain the variety of wines he would like, for example. Local regulations may severely restrict not only the types of alcoholic beverages served but the hours and methods of serving them.

4. Plan to serve only the very best food possible. Whether or not inns draw most of their profits from the bar, the rooms, or the restaurant, the quality of food and service is what sets and sustains a reputation. Patrons who favor inns will tolerate spare rooms without television, but not mediocre food poorly presented.

5. Be certain that personal energy—physical and emotional—is sufficient to withstand the demands.

6. Since New England and the Middle Atlantic States may be reaching the saturation point for inns, explore other regions, even cities.

7. Consider all financing possibilities. In addition to conventional mortgages, the present owner may elect to accept a second mortgage or to lease the property with an option to buy.

8. Do not anticipate profits of any significance for at least two years. In fact, it may take ten before it all starts paying off.

9. Check all references carefully *before* hiring staff, especially key personnel.

10. Be prepared to scrub toilets, wash walls, empty garbage, clip shrubs, wait tables. No task is too lowly for keepers of inns.

11. Keep perspective. Pleasing customers is the business, but the inns which flourish are those which most nearly reflect the personalities and tastes of the owners. A clear identity is critical.

12. Avoid going into it with friends or to save a marriage.

And keep an open mind—about methodology, customers, staff. And the future.

Rod and Ione Williams, in their fifties, expect to stay where they are and pass the inn on to their son. But they are expanding the dining room to make their guests more comfortable, and adding lodging space so that they don't have to rely on outside dinner guests.

Jim and Audrey Patterson had no intention of leaving, but agreed from the outset that everything had a price. Two months after that last spring blizzard, they sold the Chester Inn—for nearly $400,000. They don't know what they're going to do now. A small restaurant, perhaps a store of some kind, somewhere . . .

"We don't say forever about anything," Tom Wells declares. "We want to grow. We're doers. Values change, and they must be respected. Successes and failures are *equally* important. People who don't venture and don't try have wasted their lives! We will *never* say that we have come to an end. Somehow what we are doing will be different ten years from now. We will not stagnate, because that is wrong. *Wrong!*"

5
Feeding

*Everything hath two handles, the one to be held by, the other
not . . . cut thy coat according to thy cloth.*
—Robert Burton, *The Anatomy of Melancholy*

The customary variation on the innkeeping theme—given relative expenditures of energy and capital—is to open a restaurant of one's
very own. It will be warm, friendly, and informal, goes the scenario.
Patrons will be equally comfortable in jeans or three-piece black silk,
and they will be major-league athletes and gay theatrical designers,
tabloid columnists and stateless shipping magnates—all joined in a
happy ecumenical burble. Renowned gourmets will proclaim the birth
of a New World cuisine very nearly worthy of comparison with a
certain class of unassuming Lyons bistro.

The sole will be fresh, from Dover, not frozen flounder from Long
Island Sound. The vegetables will be crunchily undercooked, bought
every morning at the market by the docks. Neither iceberg lettuce nor
margarine will ever cross the threshold. Baking will be done on the
premises. There will be croissants, sweet butter, plum preserves, and
Sazeracs for Sunday brunch. (Copies of *Réalités* and the Sunday *Times*
available.) The salad will be served *after* the entrée. Plants will fill the
windows; fresh flowers, changed daily, will adorn each table. There will
be galatine of duck, never canard à l'orange; baby squab, not Rock
Cornish game hen. Honest martinis, half-pound hamburgers of 100
percent sirloin, and chili and rice will be served at the bar from noon
to closing. And so on, through the thousands of variations wrought by
experience and idiosyncratic preference. Whatever the particular
model, the urge to test individual taste in the marketplace is endemic
to life changers. In few enterprises is success more sweet (or failure

more ordinary) than in the restaurant business, for even mere survival is vindication of one's personal vision.

One city is exemplary of the recent renaissance in gastronomic entrepreneurship. It cannot yet rival San Francisco or New Orleans in numbers of restaurants per capita. In quality and variety, however, it is surpassed only by New York. Its dining places are cosmic-funky retreats, gilded cafés, amiable boites. Most feature eclectic menus and companionable table service by young people temporarily betwixt semesters or artistic appearances. Most fall within the parameters of the kind of establishment outlined above. But however they may be described, nearly all are of the counterfranchise, antichemical vanguard of the food revolution.

The city is Philadelphia. Yes, Philadelphia. Yet it is less startling that this phenomenon happened and continues in a city that is so often dismissed as plodding and unimaginative than that so many refugees of Ho-Jo childhoods have not only made their dreams real but have flourished. Philadelphia has the necessary ingredients, certainly. It is a place of soul-soothing human scale. (A statute of William Penn stands atop City Hall. It is said that no new building may rise above his revered buttocks.) The crime rate is relatively low, as are the costs of buildings suitable for conversion to restaurants. But these things don't explain it.

Jay Guben doesn't really know why, although some people say he started it all. On February 16, 1972, he and a few partners opened Les Amis, a slick and breezy eatery on the ground floor of an office building near Rittenhouse Square. Then, in rapid succession, came Upstairs, Downstairs (Caribbean food), Friday, Saturday, and Sunday (Continental), Morgan's (English pub), Aunt Sylvia's Cheesecake (as it says), and the Restaurant (mostly French). All represented experiments of one kind or another. Morgan's is in a desolate, seedy, riverside location. Friday, Saturday, and Sunday ran against the conviction that a restaurant has to be open at least five days a week to break even. (Accurate, apparently. It's now open five days.) Upstairs, Downstairs was given over to new sets of novice managers every six months or so to mount whatever kind of operation they chose.

The Restaurant represented the biggest test, though, for it is the laboratory of a school very probably unduplicated anywhere else. Basically, the Restaurant School trains people to create and operate restaurants of orchestrated individuality, moderate size, and decided flair.

Beyond that, neither Guben nor his associates are certain of their objectives.

"My five-year image of what the school would be like," says Guben tentatively, "was a circus with a high-wire act. The school was the net. People could do their 'acts' and perfect them while we would be supportive. If they fell off, they could bounce back without being hurt. We encouraged people to do new and different things, with the knowledge that change would do no damage to them."

Guben is sitting at the round conference table on the second floor of the turn-of-the-century row house that serves as school, restaurant, and think tank. He is ebullient and vaguely mystical, with an infectious whinny of a laugh he delivers when he finds himself veering toward solemnity, as now.

"What did I do before this?" He turns to Anita Simon, one of his four partners. "What *did* I do? I had an M.A. in 'conflict management.' I studied by what means the world could be made a better place to live, then worked for agencies trying to tell people how to do it. When they didn't listen to our instructions, I started opening restaurants."

Both in their late thirties, Guben and Simon think of the school as one way to examine the process of change while helping others work through it. Simon was formerly an educational psychologist.

"The restaurant renaissance here is paralleling a reexamination of life-styles among people in general," she says. "The culture now permits people to think about the quality of their lives and what they'd *really* like to do with them. A hundred years ago, this would have been regarded as bizarre. Then, what you had to do was raise your family and make a living. Now, this movement to open 'the-kind-of-restaurant-I-would-like-to-have' is one strain of a much larger cultural movement. We have the free time to consider options. Open career choices, in terms of craft versus corporation, are now possible."

Simon wouldn't start a restaurant, she says. Her mission is to develop models for learning environments that help people bring about whatever metamorphoses they seek for themselves. The specific content is, to an extent, irrelevant to her. What she wants to discover is what it takes to make the "big shift," and what tools are necessary to implement it. So far, she says, they're learning mostly how much they don't know.

"We do know that change requires a support system. It takes someone saying, 'You can do it,' 'These are the skills you have,' and 'What help do you need to get out and try?' There has to be feedback from those who have gone before, too. As we get older, we'll be able to do more of that. Other than that, we're still discovering."

"Beginnings," says Guben, "are very similar in new ventures. The skills necessary to start a restaurant are closely correlated with those required to dig an oil well. We like having problems to solve and the freedom to implement ideas. If we're doing this well, it really has nothing to do with the idea of schools or the idea of restaurants. It has to do with adapting known techniques toward meeting a problem or condition. Restaurants are just the vehicles we've chosen, a tangible way to transfer some of the things we're trying to demonstrate."

Although Guben and Simon intellectualize at length in the tone and jargon of social scientists, the instruction they provide their students is thoroughly pragmatic. The curriculum is no less than a forty-one-week course in restaurant management and operation. At this time, (Guben and Simon reserve the right to wipe it all out and start again), students have 950 hours of classroom study and spend another 1,000 hours working every position in the restaurant, from maitre d' to *sous-chef* to dishwasher. This means five mornings a week in class and three afternoons and evenings in the kitchen and out front. The business-management segment—about one-third of the academic program—covers design and concept, budgeting, bookkeeping, financing, taxes, licensing, supply, staff and customer relations. Another third is devoted to table service, and the rest to food preparation and cooking. Along the way, fifty hours are given to the mixing of cocktails and the selection and presentation of wines.

To an outsider, the cooking portion of the curriculum is the most engaging, especially after observing head instructor Tom Hunter bone two cartons of chickens in twenty minutes with a flashing knife and not a wasted motion. Over eleven months, Hunter takes his students through the making of stocks, sauces, and soups, to combining these with meats and vegetables, and on to total menu planning. While not all the students become master chefs, they have all been exposed to the complete repertoire of international cookery.

No one cuisine is paramount. Students are familiarized with dishes Russian, Greek, Spanish, Italian, Chinese, and French in origin. The objective is to expose them to essential basic skills, not to persuade them to adhere to any one gastronomic banner.

In the basement kitchen, the bartending class is winding up. Hans Bachler, the fourth partner and the manager of London's middling-posh Inigo Jones, is discussing bottle arrangement. ("Use your vermouth to separate the gins and vodkas, because they often have the same brand names, and service can get confused. *All* dry vermouths have a green label, remember, and sweets are red, regardless of country or manufacturer.") As Bachler finishes, today's kitchen staff is finishing lunch. Hunter is ladling stock for paella, his assistant is clearing the preparation counter, a student is arranging hors d'oeuvres.

"Tom is really marvelous," whispers Anita Simon. "A supergood teacher. He can have five different groups cooking and know exactly what's happening in each group. Knows just when to step in and make a teaching point, when to stop everybody to come take a look at something. He's like a fabulous orchestra leader. On top of that, he's probably one of the best food historians in the country. He'll talk about the reasons for the creation of classic dishes, explain that they didn't just happen. He was doing paprika chicken one day and asked if anyone knew why they used so much paprika in the Baltic area. They said, 'For flavor and coloring.' And he said, 'No, for vitamin C. It's an area without many natural sources—except for paprika, which is loaded with it.' Then it made sense for them. And Tom started out as an artist and dancer! None of us are doing what we started out to do."

At one end of the butcher block, a bearded student of near-Falstaffian girth is laboriously filleting a fluke. He has been enrolled less than two weeks. Someone remarks on his ability to shred a formerly recognizable fish. He grins and replies that they should have seen what he did to the veal yesterday.

His name is Jim, he's forty-one, divorced once, married now, and a former salesman of insurance and lighting systems. A textbook life changer. Many of the school's students and graduates are. One was assistant dean of men at the University of Wisconsin. Others were housewives, real-estate agents, executive secretaries, teachers.

Jim steps back, wiping his hands and regarding his handiwork ruefully. "Believe it or not, I've learned a lot in the last ten days," he says. "You can't imagine how much."

Someone asks why he's decided to start a second career at this point in his life.

"It comes down to wanting my own business and having control over the finished product. In other businesses, decisions are made on a wholly different level from where you are. Also, I'd reached the point —in sales and claims—where I'd feel a little unclean at the end of the day. Those jobs meant telling people that they were going to receive benefits as the result of an insurance policy that wouldn't necessarily be received under all circumstances. I knew what the words meant, but when I told the client, the same words meant something quite different. And I *knew* it, but I had to do it to get the sale. It made me feel dirty. I just don't want to do that anymore.

"This wasn't a small step. I still have child-support payments, and my present wife had to stay in St. Paul—we get together every now and then for a conjugal weekend. But I did have relatives in the food business, so I had that exposure, and you can see by the size of me that I like eating. A small, quality restaurant fills my need very well, and there aren't too many places like that back in the Twin Cities area."

Has he had any difficulty adjusting to a learning situation again or relating to his generally younger colleagues?

"In some ways, yes. But my motivation is very high, so it's easy to turn off the TV and open my accounting book. None of these classes are the kind where you doze off, as you might in college. It's much more stimulating and direct. I have a high energy level anyway, and I have the advantage of maturity in that, unlike some of these younger people, I have few internal questions about what I want to do with the rest of my life."

Jim was cautious in reaching his decision to come to the school, and followed a pattern anyone looking for special kinds of training is wise to observe. He read of the school in a magazine. The article mentioned Bill Andrews, the ex-dean of men, who had gone on to open the Country Frenchman in Greeley, Colorado, with his wife and another couple. Jim called Andrews, asked his opinion of the school and his experience there. Andrews was positive. Then he checked with the local better business bureau. No black marks there. He wrote for the application for admission and examined the promotional materials. He was accepted—one of the few who were who had not visited the school. Arriving in Philadelphia, he had dinner in the "laboratory," announcing at the end of the meal that he was to be matriculated the following Monday. The student staff took him through the backstage facilities and introduced him to Tom Hunter. Finally, he observed classes and kitchen activity for a day. *Then* he wrote his check for tuition.

The assistant chef asks if Jim will please fillet fish while he's talking. Jim does, chuckling. His next effort is a decided improvement.

Upstairs, students are changing tablecloths and adjusting silverware and stemware. The Restaurant serves dinner only, and all tips are pooled and shared equally by everyone on duty on any given night. As this is part of the curriculum, though, no one receives a salary. Simon tries to arrange part-time employment at other establishments for students who need the money, and that includes most of them, because the tuition is $3,200 for the full program.

". . . and they learn about lines of sight in arranging the tables," Simon is saying. "If I move this wineglass, one of them will notice it and adjust it. We want them to be able to create a feeling of 'rightness' when the customers come in. Little things like this are important. The customer senses when something is off, even if he can't identify what it is. People always move things around to satisfy their need for psychological space, but they do it with more urgency when the table isn't set properly."

Back at the conference table, Simon talks about différences between the traditional European apprenticeship system and what she and her partners are doing.

"One learns by 'doing' in both situations. But apprenticing in a regular restaurant, you start by chopping vegetables for six months, then you arrange vegetables on plates for a year, then you make stocks and sauces for another year—there's no feedback! You only really start to learn when you get immediate reaction to what you've done. That's built-in here. We have a very tightly structured feedback mechanism. Every student logs his or her questions and experiences each day, and every student gets to play every role, from going to the market at four A.M., to planning the night's menu, to writing checks for salesmen. Everything!"

Guben hangs up the phone and sits down. "Our perception was that all someone has to do if he wants something is to do it. *Anyone* can learn technical skills."

Which is not to imply that restaurants can or should be developed and run by just anyone. Guben inspires, motivates, plans, but he doesn't manage his own places. "I don't have the necessary skills. My life is spurty. I like to do things intensely, then goof off. Managing a restaurant does not afford that luxury or opportunity. You need dedication to run a fine restaurant—evenness, day-to-day caring."

Simon agrees. "There must be joy in the daily accomplishment of the same routine, enough goal orientation not to get whiplashed by personal issues. None of the traditional variables—age, sex, educational background—seems to have any bearing on success in this field."

Although that assessment probably applies to anyone in what has, unfortunately, been labeled the "hospitality industry," Guben and Simon are concerned with a particular subcategory of dining place. Its range in size and profitability is defined by the restaurants Simon has birthed, from the thirty-seat Morgan's, with a total staff of nine and an annual gross of $150,000, to the largest, with nearly a hundred seats and a gross of $500,000 in the same year. They are all moderately expensive—somewhere between $15 and $25 a meal—and can be placed, in ambience and intent, somewhere between mom 'n' pop deli's and the many-branched, portion-controlled feeding plants.

For these last, the founders of the Restaurant School have naught but disdain tinged with contempt, a view shared by innkeepers Patterson, Wells, and Williams.

Of the hotel and restaurant schools serving, and nurtured by, the Bonanza Steak Houses, Marriotts, and Hiltons of our cityscapes, Jay Guben says, "They are very large, very doctrinaire, very dogmatic."

Upon the appearance of the grave and imposing man, the captain of the Escoffier Room bows more deeply than is his custom. Waiters tug at their jackets and touch their ties as the two men pass. The captain escorts the patron to his favorite table and sweeps out a chair, bobbing three times. The customer, Dr. Henry Barbour, regards the table setting for a moment, then sits.

The captain is grateful. Large, leathery menus fairly whistle, they are flourished so rapidly. The tulip glasses are whisked away and replaced by longer-stemmed ones with large, balloon-shaped bowls. Dr. Barbour peers over the tops of his spectacles without speaking. A waiter gasps and fumbles for the wine list. Dr. Barbour accepts it with a small murmur of acknowledgment and selects a 1970 Auxey-Duresses. The young sommelier returns in a minute, carrying the bottle by its neck until Barbour notices the transgression. The boy quickly cradles the bottle in both hands, awaiting approval. Barbour nods. The cork is pulled, a small amount of the wine poured. Barbour grasps the stem of the glass, swirls the alizarin liquid to release its bouquet, puts his lips to the edge, thrusts his nose into the bowl, inhales. Sips. It is all one practiced, flowing gesture, followed by a barely audible grunt.

Dr. Henry Ogden Barbour is a commander of the Chevaliers du Tastevin, the premier Burgundian wine society. In an aside, he opines that the staff of the restaurant may be a little edgy today because they know he has just returned from France and they expect that his taste buds may be more delicately tuned than usual.

Without requesting it, he is brought a bottle of Perrier water. He turns to the menu. The captain hovers, his composure regained. Three waiters shift from foot to foot, hands clasped behind them, faces pale. Their nervousness may be attributed to the fact that the Escoffier Room is a workshop of the Culinary Institute of America: the captain is a faculty member, the waiters and sommelier are students in the last week of their two-year curriculum, and Dr. Henry Barbour is the president.

He consults his guest and orders soup and roast duck for two. When the pale broth arrives, he sips once and replaces the spoon on the plate. He sits back, expressionless, and takes a pen-shaped black cylinder from his breast pocket. He unscrews the top and removes a thermometer, which he then places in the soup. Four pairs of eyes flick to the bowl. Barbour takes his reading, returns the thermometer to his pocket, and pulls out a memo pad. He scribbles a note.

"We've had a small war around here about whether the food is hot enough," he remarks offhandedly. *"This* is not. It's only one hundred and fourteen degrees, which is much too cool. It ought to be one hundred and forty-eight."

A new waiter materializes at Barbour's elbow and offers to bring another bowl.

"Not necessary," says Barbour, "but that's very observant of you."

It is a compliment. The young man smiles and backs away.

The Culinary Institute of America (inevitably known as the "other CIA") is housed in a five-story former Jesuit seminary on seventy acres in Hyde Park, New York, three miles north of Poughkeepsie. It looks like the headquarters of an old-line insurance company. At present, there are 1,420 students, which Barbour says is 112 more than they really want. The majority are young, white males, 1,000 of whom are housed at the institute. They have a faculty of 94. There are 33 kitchens, several dining rooms and banquet halls, a snack shop, 2 *garde-manger* (cold-food preparation) laboratories, 4 bakeshops, 10 classrooms, and 2 lecture halls—all occupying 300,000 square feet. It claims to be the world's largest cooking school and probably is. In philosophy and intent, it is as good an example as any of big education in service to big business, and it satisfies that obligation. The annual operating budget pushes $7 million.

One of the virtues of restaurant schools is the ease with which the quality of their education can be judged. Both the Escoffier Room and the Restaurant are open to the public. Both are representative of their sponsors. The former might as easily be a Stouffer's "Top-of-the-Whatever." Which is to say: unstartling menu choices, competently prepared in advance; correct but distant service; undistinctive but attractive decor; a certain formality; moderate cost—bar-mitzvah–sweet-sixteen–silver-anniversary kinds of places. Upper-middle-middle. The Restaurant is cozier, less intimidating, more stylish; the staff cordial and eager to please; the food selections venturesome, prepared largely to order; erratic in quality, mostly above par, though rarely soaring. Both are what they profess to be, without surprises.

The captain of the Escoffier Room is dismembering the duck, encircled by waiters like five Kildares harkening to Dr. Gillespie in the wards.

"Our mission is to train cooks," Barbour is saying, "but I would like to see a little more emphasis on the dining room as a profession as well as the kitchen. We're starting to move a bit in that direction.

"Restaurant sales have been growing faster than grocery-store sales in the last three years," he points out, "so people are obviously eating out more. A lot of that is in the fast-food establishments, of course, but what we're seeing is the opening of smaller restaurants, replacing those of larger scale. As a result, we're introducing more a la carte work here because our people are going to be increasingly exposed to that sort of operation.

"The differences between an a la carte kitchen and an institutional kitchen are not only in the numbers of people served but in the methods in which food is produced. The one is basically done on order, the other in a quite different time frame—that is, when two hundred portions of something must be ready when the doors open at eleven thirty. So it must be prepared in advance. Two hundred fillets of sole are panned out and placed in the refrigerator at seven o'clock in the morning, or even the night before. You *have* to do it that way. It also means familiarity with quite large pieces of equipment, which aren't found in an a la carte place."

Inevitably, this means some compromise with quality, steam tables being the infernal devices they are. The duck and side dishes having been served, his guest asks Dr. Barbour how he would critique this meal so far. He leans back, hands on the table edge, contemplating the plate of duck, red cabbage, and string beans.

"Too much food here," he intones after a pause. "Not quite hot enough. The duck's a little overdone. The vegetables were very nice, although they also lacked a few degrees of temperature. I personally don't care for sweet sauces on duck, but I don't think this is *too* sweet. High average, all in all."

His guest silently demurs on the vegetables—overcooked—but otherwise agrees. A good meal, really. Not memorable, but fair value. Aloud, he asks what happens to CIA graduates, recalling that some institute detractors have suggested that CIA graduates all wind up making sandwiches in roadside diners.

"One young woman is working in Paris under Michel Guerard, who is the foremost exponent of *cuisine minceur*." (This is the stripped-down version of high French cookery in which very little if any butter and cream are used in preparation, and Guerard is enjoying much attention in the media at the time.) "The night baker at '21' in New York is another woman who graduated last June. And the World Trade Center hired thirty of our people to open their new restaurants." (Some of these wound up in the center's Windows on the World, perhaps the most extravagantly ballyhooed and lavishly praised restaurant to open in the city in twenty years. And Jay Guben might be surprised to learn that Wildflowers, a place very much of the Philadelphia-eclectic mode he favors, is owned by a CIA alumnus.)

Although only 8 percent of the institute's students are over thirty, 40 percent are past the usual college age, with many career switchers among them. In recent years, they have included several thirty-year military men, a woman with a decade as an insurance salesperson, another who was a computer programmer, and a number of onetime schoolteachers and housewives. Barbour observes that mature people have solid advantages over younger grads, especially if they hope to establish themselves in their own restaurants. They are more likely to have had experience in dealing with people, in budgeting, in obtaining financing, in dealing with salesmen and customers. They have developed credit reputations and usually know something about real-estate transactions. Most important, they have lived, and much of what they have seen and done is translatable to their new trade.

"Older people have eaten out much more," says Barbour. "They come to expect certain things in a restaurant and don't even have to think about them when they are doing the serving. A young person may never have seen a wine bottle opened properly and may be less sensitive to such niceties as putting the plate down gently and keeping the glasses full."

Jay Guben agrees. He was astounded to find how many of his students had never dined in a fine restaurant. And although there are special techniques to be learned, anyone who has been concerned that her family be fed with imagination is well ahead of the game, if only because she has had a lot of exposure to cooking terminology. (Braised? Sautéed? Roasted? Pureed? Terrine? Wok? The home cook absorbs an entire vocabulary almost subconsciously.)

If an institute graduate chooses to work for someone else in a fairly large commercial kitchen, his or her progress will proceed approximately this way. First, a station assignment, preparing vegetables or pastry or *garde-manger*. Salary, $756 a month plus meals and uniforms for a forty-four-hour, six-day workweek. After one to two years, a position as section chief, supervising station cooks for $800 to $1,200 a month. Next—within five years—promotion to *sous-chef*, which is, in effect, assistant executive chef, and brings in $1,000 to $1,500. After six to eight years, head chef, at as much as $4,000, but half that being closer to average.

It needn't take that long. *The New York Times* charted for two years the progress of the wife of an out-of-work stockbroker. By the end of that time, she had moved from salads in a suburban steak house to head chef at a fashionable pub near Lincoln Center. She had no formal training.

Education can be a shortcut, nonetheless. Barbour says that the institute is merely a "more efficient" way to compress and absorb knowledge that would consume many more years in a conventional apprenticeship. Advanced placement is easier, too. The average CIA graduate receives 3.6 job offers, usually above the station-cook level and rarely below $200 a week.

But cooking as a livelihood is not likely to appeal to the usual life changer. The hours are long, the work environment somewhat dangerous, and discrimination against women still runs deep. In any event, the point here is not to propose a career over the pots but to emphasize that, according to professionals, success in the restaurant business depends on the owner's awareness of food preparation and supply. The best restaurants, it is said, are those which are chef-owned. That requirement can be met if one of the two partners is experienced in the culinary arts, but a solitary owner-manager must possess skills equal to the tasks on both sides of the swinging doors. Certainly there are those who have plunged in and learned by trial and error. Recall, however, that Audrey Patterson and Rosalind Wells did that, and now think they shouldn't have. With thin capital backup, the waste and false starts of an inexperienced chef can be the margin between survival and disaster.

There are alternatives—less grand, but lower risk. Another former stockbroker, Donn Bruce, discovered one.

The Philly Mignon store on East Eighty-sixth Street in Manhattan is indistinguishable from any of the thousands of stand-up souvlaki, hot-dog, and pizza-by-the-slice stands huddling at every corner in town. It steams and spatters and crackles twenty-four hours a day. On the walls are the usual yellowing photostats of newspaper accolades, hand-lettered signs curling away from dried Scotch tape and popped staples. No more than two arm-spans across and three deep, it has the customary grill at the window, a narrow counter along the opposite wall, a few stools with splitting vinyl seats, a refrigerator, a freezer, a combination broom closet and toilet, a cutting board—and a cash register which never stops ringing.

There are four other Philly Mignons, all equally inconspicuous and unremarkable. Donn Bruce expects to open another fifteen sibling stores over the next two years. Until he and his wife came along, the Eighty-sixth Street location was a four-time loser as a fast-food shop. They made a profit the very first day.

Bruce sells sandwiches of the sort variously labeled "subs," "heroes," "zeps," "grinders," "bombers," or "wedges," depending upon region or neighborhood. Bruce's "Phabulous Philly Hoagie" is a construction of Genoa salami, cooked salami, provolone, capicolla, lettuce, tomato, olive oil, and oregano. It costs $1.60. But Bruce sells only fifty of those a day at each store. His hot item is the "Phantastic Philly Steak" sandwich, available in four versions, steak and cheese being the most popular. Three to four hundred a day. In any twenty-four-hour period, then, Bruce peddles at least 1,750 sandwiches, accompanied by soft drinks and ice cream, the only other items on the menu. That means an annual gross, at a restrained estimate, of $1.4 million.

For five thoroughly ordinary, hole-in-the-wall, quickie sandwich stands.

That is not all they are, to be fair. Bruce does follow the dictum of other businessmen who earn their livelihoods feeding people: Give the best you can for the price you charge. He tested the products of dozens of bakeries to find one capable of consistent production of the Italian bread loaves he wanted. It is softer and lighter than the usual New York wedge. Only imported olive oil is used, and Bruce insists on the Gemma brand, which he feels is superior.

"We go to great trouble and expense," he insists. "The meat in this sandwich is superior in taste and texture to anything sold in New York. We bring most of our ingredients from Philadelphia, where they have better Italian fast food than almost anyplace else. Bassett's ice cream, which is from there, is *clearly* the best ice cream made. There is *nothing* like it anywhere. It's in a class by itself. It's the same with Vernor's ginger ale. *Esquire* magazine rated it as the best in the country. We serve it.

"Quality is *so* important. The Italian fast-food industry in New York has degenerated to the point where it's probably the worst in the country. And it's all the same. As a result, someone who does it well really stands out. Give you an example. Ever been to Ray's Pizza? Sixth Avenue and Eleventh? Now, that pizza is good. I mean really, *really* good. And there's a little guy with low rent on a not-too-good corner, and you cannot get in that store! Any day or night! Lines around the corner! Everyone else not only makes lousy pizza, they make it identical. Even though anyone can go down to Ray's and see how to do it. Ray makes it different. It costs him much more. His food expenses have to be the highest of any pizzeria in the city. Probably costs him another ten cents for each slice. But *he's* doing the business."

Quality, volume, limited inventory, close control, and location. Those are the keys.

"In making money, the prime component is location. My grandfather, for example, built a house in the steel belt—Johnstown, Pennsylvania—for four thousand bucks in the 1880s. Sold it for the *same* four thousand in the 1950s. My friend's grandfather bought timberland in Houston in 1927 for four thousand bucks and sold it for fifteen million a few years ago. And I'll bet you he wasn't one bit smarter than *my* grandfather. It was just a lucky choice of location. All my stores are in perfect places for the kind of business I do. That fancy apartment house over there doesn't send anyone here, but they don't go to McDonald's, either. My customers are young, white, mostly working men, and this block is full of them, at all hours of the night. See that guy with the ambulance corps patch on his jacket? I love to see that. He'll tell all his buddies. Cops, firemen, Con Ed workers, telephone company men —they all tell their friends. Bus drivers double-park outside just to pick up four sandwiches for themselves and the guys at the terminal."

Bruce has opinions about essential personal characteristics, too.

"I've known several people who've gone from riches to rags to riches in the last few years. I include myself. They've all done three things, regardless of what they went into. First, they all worked *extremely* hard. When I say that, I mean that a sixty-hour week for any of us would have been a vacation. Forty hours in a steel mill is easier, and I know because I've done it. Second, we've all taken *enormous* risks. I don't mind telling you that more than once I've owed the sales tax bureau here fifteen or twenty thousand dollars at a time. Delaying payment is kind of a form of credit, but I'm personally liable for that. Other things I've had to do I won't tell you about.

"The third is, we've all done work that most college-educated people just won't do. *Refuse* to do. Such as get behind that counter and stay there for a year. Or mop the floor, or deliver bread.

"Tell you about a friend of mine, as an illustration. My former partner went completely, absolutely broke. Went to Alaska. Leased some land on the North Slope. Traded that up for another lease when they found oil there. Then another lease, and so on. In six months, he ended up in control of the third biggest bank in the state. Now worth easily five million bucks. And that's hard work, high risk, and a willingness to do what nobody else wants to do."

What makes people able to do that—to give up security, to work that hard?

"I can't answer for other people, just for me. I have always felt —and I know this isn't going to sound too good—but I've always thought that I was supposed to be different. That I was meant to do big things."

But where is the kick? Is it in making more and more money, getting bigger and bigger?

"No."

The challenge?

"No. What I want is the time to do what I want to do."

Which is?

"To be a philosopher and a writer. This is the means to that end, but it's self-defeating. The deeper you get, the harder it is to find the time you wanted. When I was broke, at least I could write a couple of chapters a year. Now, I can't write a word.

"However, there is always the hope that you can get big enough and insulated enough from the business, so that you have more time. Perhaps in a year or so, we'll be there. Instead of five stores, we'll have ten by next December. In another year, twenty."

He rises from the stool. "I have to get to the other stores and the commissary. Let's talk in the taxi."

After a few words with his counterman, Bruce goes outside and flags a cab. He is as indifferent to contemporary style in dress and grooming as to the decor of his shops. The clothes might have been the same in which he graduated from Wharton in 1954, with the gray tweed jacket from one suit and the blue chalk-stripe pants from another. He wears a polka-dot bow tie, unfashionable wire-rims, and his hair slicked straight back from his forehead. A tall, somewhat raffish version of a sitcom accountant.

"Once we've saturated New York City," he is saying in the backseat of the battered yellow Plymouth, "we won't move out to the suburbs. We'll go to Houston and open a chain there. Then in Atlanta, Toronto. Places where things are happening. That's the one thing I'd change if I had it to do over again. I'd go to a growth place. It's just so much easier."

The cab bangs into a pothole, then lurches out the other side.

"We are fighting such odds here. For one thing, the older a city is, the more regulations it has. Hundreds of 'em. Houston, for example, has no zoning laws. Want to put up a gas station in your front lawn? Go ahead. That's literally true, y'know. That's one advantage from a business standpoint. No rules. Here, it's the opposite. *Everything* is regulated.

"Another thing is that in the restaurant business you deal with repeat customers. It's hard to get a customer in any business, so once you do, you want to try to keep him. So many of my customers have moved away, though, in just the two and a half years I've been operating. People are moving out of this city, and no one's moving in. Houston gets a thousand new people every week.

"Anyone who's seriously interested in making money—and nothing else!—would go right now to Alaska. Nobody wants to go there, though. Alaska is a horrible place, it's true. Completely barbaric. The people who go there are mostly losers, psychos—terrible! *But,* though the entire state of Alaska has the same number of people as Paterson, New Jersey, its federal spending alone next year will be nine *billion* dollars. Can you imagine what that could do for Paterson? But it's going to Alaska. Then there's all that oil money, and truckloads of people going in there every day. There are fitters on the pipeline pulling down fifty thousand bucks and noplace to spend it."

So why stay in New York?

"I don't really know. Perhaps it's as Steinbeck said, that once you've made New York your home, noplace else is quite good enough. That's really it. Where else is there? You come here because it's the twentieth-century Rome. Young people come here from all over the world—like my wife from Denver and me from Pittsburgh—because this is really where it is. We want to be here regardless of how 'Rome' may treat us. Half the intelligent people in the country live here— probably right on this island. Corporation presidents, intellectuals, artists, musicians. All right here. How else can it be explained?"

The wheels slam into another frost crack, and the driver brakes with a squeal at the curb. Bruce hands him a small preprinted form upon which to enter the fare, date, and signature. It is the responsibility of self-employed persons to keep provable, comprehensive records of every single business-related expense—at least those they want to claim as deductions. On the way down to his subterranean central commissary, Bruce talks about other kinds of expenses.

"The greatest tax shelter in the world is a self-owned business," he says, opening cabinet doors, scanning shelves, ticking off bags of meat and cans of olive oil. "It is. But that's also simplistic. Let's say you're in the pizza business. Say no one stole anything, and the price of pizza was allowed to rise to its real market level. You'd make more money. Pay more taxes, too, but your net would be larger. But that's not the way it is. When people say that about shelters, a lot of them are talking about *il*legitimate tax write-offs.

"Suppose you have a restaurant that does three hundred thousand bucks a year. The net on that should be forty-five thousand. If you don't report the forty-five thousand, you've saved twenty-two thousand in corporate income taxes. If you worked for a company, *they'd* report it *for* you. So you report two hundred and fifty thousand. You're also now ahead four thousand in sales taxes. Now, you're not paying yourself a salary, so you take another fifty thousand. You save thirty thousand in personal income taxes and another eight thousand in sales taxes, plus twenty-five thousand in corporate income tax. That's eighty-five thousand in taxes you *didn't* pay, just by not reporting your original net of forty-five thousand.

"That's what goes on. Really! And there's more to it than that. Restaurant workers aren't like other workers. When you ask a supervisor at General Motors how much he makes, he tells you his total salary. A restaurant employee will tell you what he gets in his pay envelope. The employer must pay the taxes, so the counterman only knows what he takes home. Now, if that man wants to clear two hundred a week and he's in a normal tax bracket, you'd have to be paying him two hundred and seventy to cover the taxes. Give him two hundred *in cash,* and you can pocket the seventy. Multiply that by fifteen employees and fifty-two weeks, and you have quite a piece of change.

"That is *not,* I must add, what everyone in the food-service industry does. Certainly *I* don't, and wouldn't tell you if I did. And those are extremes. But something in between is what's happening in that pizza parlor, because that sort of transaction is often the difference between staying in business and closing the door."

Does he mean to say that someone who plays it completely straight, out of ignorance or honesty, will fail in his own business?

"No, because no one *can* be completely straight."

Meaning, presumably, that everyone fudges in some way, if only by paying bills as late as possible and collecting as early. Bruce drops the subject, for a delivery is being made. He talks with the trucker and an employee in a mixture of English and fractured Spanish. As many of his staff are Hispanic, it's a useful language to know.

While the supplies are being stacked away, he displays an inventory-control sheet, crosshatched and smudged.

"The only way you can do this is with a limited menu and tight controls. Look here. This column lists the units of sale: bread, meat, sodas, ice-cream cones. A running tally is kept on every sale. Yesterday, there were sixty-nine loaves of bread on hand when this particular store opened. Another two hundred and eighty-eight were received during the day. At the opening this morning, there were eighty-six pieces of bread. That means two hundred and seventy-one pieces were used. Below average. Out of the two hundred and seventy-one, we wasted fifteen pieces. They had to be thrown away, or they were dropped on the floor. That's done for everything. Then I multiply unit price and deduct the cost of giveaways—napkins, bags, paper—and I know how much money there should be in the cash register."

The store is filling up as lunch hour approaches. A short, dark, heavy-shouldered man elbows his way to the counter. His clothes are vaguely unlike any others in the polyglot crowd of street people, steamfitters, and junior executives.

"A Gypsy," says Bruce. "They are *something*. Amazing people. The stereotype is really true, more so than any other group. They really *are* musical. They *do* make their livings by stealth and fraud. They haven't changed in centuries. Still move around, only now in a station wagon instead of a covered wagon. Still live ten to a hotel room. Don't work. Can't read or write.

"But if there were such a thing as a Gypsy neighborhood, I'd set up a store there in a minute. There isn't, because the authorities don't allow them to congregate. Gypsies are *the* fast-food experts. They can tell you the best hamburgers in Miami, the best hot dogs in Milwaukee. They say Pat's Steaks in South Philly is the best place anywhere. I agree. They also say I'm the best here, and that I'm going to be rich. Can't argue with that."

Bruce is becoming distracted. The grill man hasn't arrived yet.

By the time the employee does come in, his boss, the proprietor of what will soon become a multimillion-dollar enterprise is flipping steak slices, stirring onions, and splitting bread.

Ideally, the building housing a restaurant is wholly owned by the owner, with a first mortgage from a bank, possibly supplemented by a second mortgage with another lending institution or the previous owner, or various combinations of all three. Obviously, the buyer has to make a substantial investment long before the first stove or wall sconce can be ordered. Even a moderate-size restaurant of the sort Jay Guben assembles can wind up costing $250,000 when total debts and values of equipment bought on time are considered. (This is misleading, however—much the same as saying a house cost $50,000 when a twenty-five-year mortgage is involved.)

There are as many variations in financing as there are businesses. For Donn Bruce's snackeries, housed in less desirable buildings of unpretentious mien (to put the happiest face on them), a lease is quite adequate. He pays as much as $800 a month for the Eighty-sixth Street store, but as little as $250 for the one downtown near SoHo and Little Italy. Most businessmen urge the proprietor to take out the longest possible lease, and Bruce concurs. The main reason is security of location, but another is that costs can then be projected with more certainty. Understandably, the landlord typically insists on an escalator clause in exchange for, say, a ten-year agreement. (Bruce's $800 goes to $1,000 after three years.) Both sides then accept a liability. The restaurateur is legally liable for the rent for the remaining years of the lease, even if he or she goes out of business in six months, at least until a new tenant is found. The landlord, in turn, is stuck with what may become, in the future, a profitless rental or a rate well below rising values.

"You must have a long lease, though," says Bruce, "otherwise your business isn't worth anything in terms of resale. No one wants to take on a thriving restaurant with only a year or so to go on the lease. I have eight years left at the Eighty-sixth Street store. I could sell it to Greek or Chinese immigrants for at least a hundred and fifty thousand, but with a year left on the lease, they wouldn't touch it. In fact, I'm thinking about going back to get a five-year extension right now."

There are other ways to play with this. Sometimes, for example, a landlord will assume a share—often substantial—of the "front-end risk" in exchange for a share of the profits. In one case, at least, the owner of an otherwise undesirable property in a high-crime neighborhood waived rent for five years for 7 percent of the gross profits during that period *and* renovated the building to order, exclusive of fixtures. The restaurateurs were then able to utilize their savings and secured debt for furniture, tableware, appliances, and decoration, with some left over to carry them through the first year.

Any spare cash will be needed. The financial bonus for deciding to take over an established business instead of starting a new one is that amorphous asset known as "goodwill." Bruce, for example, certainly couldn't hit up those hypothetical immigrants for $150,000 merely on the basis of fixtures, and he would be offering, for all practical purposes, no stock. The Pattersons, for another, sold their inn in Chester for substantially more than twice their investment. *That's* goodwill!

Even relative poverty needn't keep one from opening his imagined bistro. Jay Guben doesn't run any of his places; partners do. Along the same lines, it is possible to find "angels" with money to spend who don't want anything more to do with a restaurant than preen with their friends and check the bottom line of the monthly profit-and-loss statements.

Guben has been able to bring some of his graduates together with investors that fit that description. Frequently, the venture capitalist offers the manager a 50 percent "equity position"—meaning full partnership—and even a salary draw against income. This, without putting a dollar in the kitty but having the flexibility, ranging from close cooperation to complete freedom, to create the restaurant of one's dreams. Similarly, Donn Bruce intends to avoid the franchise route in his expansion plans by bartering his expertise for full funding and majority control.

Even after presumably adequate monies are raised for property purchase and renovation, for fixtures and even loss capital, there can be surprises for the unwary. Bill Andrews, one of the Restaurant School's earliest winners, had to pay only $350 for his license to operate in Greeley, Colorado. Back in Philadelphia, it cost Guben $10,000. Local ordinances can be capricious. Some stipulate that only existing businesses may be purchased, in order to limit growth, conserve energy, or reduce pollution. Others severely restrict the locations of specific enterprises, the issuance of liquor licenses, or the interior or exterior architectural style.

After a prospective restaurateur has considered all the financial and legal aspects, he must pin down the kind of business he wants. As Henry Barbour notes, there is a trend not only to smaller, more variegated restaurants, but to those providing a "total experience." In some hands, this translates into tables in railroad dining cars, with punchcard menus, food service by Lionel trains or "conductors," and dioramas rolling past the windows. There are automotive themes, with lovers' lanes and drive-in movie rooms, and steamboats, airplanes, and Wild West saloons—all employing the obvious accoutrements and costumed personnel.

This is painful to the likes of Guben and Bruce, but for different reasons. Bruce, it is safe to say, is not overly concerned with decor, unless the tatty ambience of South Philadelphia can be regarded as a motif. Asked whether a chain should not have a consistent, recognizable, graphic image, Bruce replies casually, "I suppose so, but only because so many people think so. Personally, I don't care for places stamped from a mold, and I don't expect to begin worrying about it."

He keeps the issue open, in any event. The founders of the Restaurant School have stronger convictions. While eschewing the Disneyland varieties of eating place in which decor overwhelms cuisine, they feel that carefully conceived design should carry through from wallpaper to signs to matchbooks to menus to advertisements. Each element, physical or gustatory, should be supportive of the others. Echoing Barbour's concern that younger students are unfamiliar with fine restaurants, the school's founders have included the study of design in their curriculum and expect each potential graduate to produce a proposal for a fully conceived restaurant in lieu of final exams. While doubting that taste can be instilled in fully formed adults, they try to expose their students to the best examples of style and coherence.

It can be discouraging. When an applicant is asked to describe his favorite menu, Guben is appalled at how often it is two-all-beef-patties-special-sauce-lettuce-pickles. . . .

Guben and Simon, with a lot of help from their friends, also participate in a venture-consultant group they call the "Actualizers." Equal parts sound business sense, social science, and touchie-feelie sensitivity, the group provides advice and capital to entrepreneurs who

do not need formal schooling but do require support and encouragement. Similar organizations abound. One can get leads just by calling
the local chamber of commerce or district office of the Small Business
Administration.

The problems of the feeding services are abundant. Street crime,
holdups, Mafia extortion. Drunks, unpaid bills, abusive customers, staff
disputes, strikes. Bureaucrats, licensing, bribery demands, taxes. Most
or all of these are encountered by restaurant owners sooner or later. Gas
shortages, blizzards, and hurricanes can destroy a country inn just as
surely as fire and riot and pilferage can close the doors of a downtown
steak house.

The rewards, on the other hand, are ephemeral and depend more
on the individual than in other endeavors. Few restaurateurs can expect
to do as well as those profiled here. The owner-manager of a single
restaurant can hope—eventually—to draw a salary equal to about 10
percent of the gross. That is, somewhere between $15,000 and $25,000
on the average, assuming one has a distaste for, or fear of, the fiscal
machinations that Donn Bruce outlined. Guben says he thinks of
money as "a way of keeping score"; Bruce, as the basis for personal
freedom.

More important and more likely, the gratification is in having
greater control over one's destiny, in a field where, according to Guben,
"human contact and vision and creativity are as highly valued as
money."

6
Creating

*It is . . . a most delightsome humour to be alone, dwell alone,
walk alone, meditate, lye in bed whole dayes, dreaming awake
as it were, and frame a thousand phantastical imaginations
unto themselves.*
   —Robert Burton, *The Anatomy of Melancholy*

Everyone wants creativity in work. That one need is perhaps
the most pervasive for those stirred to discard old careers. The stimulus
is by no means novel. It is the conviction that "I can do this better.
I can write a better book, paint a prettier picture, throw a more graceful
pot, serve a tastier meal, sing a more moving song. . . ."

It is never too late. Creativity can *be* the work.

John Houseman was an educator. And in his sixties, won an Oscar
for best supporting actor.

Charles Ives and Wallace Stevens were insurance executives. Ives
was also a composer, and Stevens a poet.

William Carlos Williams and Michael Crichton were physicians.
Williams was a poet, and Crichton is a novelist and screenwriter.

T. S. Eliot worked as a teacher, bank clerk, and editor. He also
wrote poetry and plays.

And Paul Gauguin. And Grandma Moses.

And Richard Gill. In some ways, he is the most remarkable of all.
Gill was an economics professor at Harvard from age twenty-one.
Twenty years later, he took some singing lessons. At forty-three, he was
a leading basso profundo for the New York City Center Opera *and* the
Metropolitan Opera. Until then, he estimates he'd seen fifteen operatic
productions in his entire life.

Gill thinks of his new career as a second phase in a life in which
he has "exercised several different sets of muscles," as scholar, teacher,
author, administrator, singer. He has written several books on eco-

nomic development—still does—but in 1954 he won the coveted Atlantic Magazine short story prize. His *Who's Who in America* entry doesn't even mention his singing, for he hasn't gotten around to updating it. When he is too old to play Count Monterone or the King of Cornwall, he thinks he'd like to take up painting.

The Gills have a new white Colonial with black shutters on Possum Trail in Upper Saddle River, New Jersey. It is a late Sunday afternoon in March, just after the opening of *Ariadne*. The slate sky is tinged yellow where it lowers over the city just beyond the treeline.

Gill himself answers the door. He is a man of suitably heroic proportions and must look down to meet the eyes of his six-foot-two visitor. His head is large and mostly bald—no deficiency, as in most of his roles it is bewigged, crowned, or wreathed in laurel. Then, there's his voice. Even "Good afternoon" rolls and rumbles and sloshes the marrow.

He leads the way to the living room, removes the galleys of his latest book from the sofa, and suggests coffee. The room might well be that of an upper-echelon marketing executive—tidy, comfortable, untheatrical. Gill himself might be identified as such, were it not for that voice.

"My ignorance of opera was extreme until four years ago," he says in answer to the first question. The walls seem to shiver. "In the old life, I rarely went to the opera. I have actually seen performed almost none of the roles I've done. My knowledge of the medium was zero. At the very beginning, after I'd signed a contract with the City Center, people would suggest that I do a particular role, and not only wouldn't I know the part, I wouldn't know the opera or the composer, either. It could be very embarrassing.

"The extent of my singing in an operalike situation was when I did a Gilbert and Sullivan role in college, and right after that, the very small part of the gardener in *The Marriage of Figaro* on the Cape. Apart from that, it was only church music or glee clubs. I did have eight months of singing lessons right after college, but it was strictly a side activity, as I was working for my Ph.D. Anyway, my greatest passion at the time was short-story writing.

"For much of that period, I was a full-time administrator at Harvard. I became an assistant dean at age twenty-one." He was the youngest ever in a position most academics are grateful to reach by forty. "With all that, something had to go, so I gave up singing. Reluctantly. It was clear that I'd have to do a great deal of work to get anywhere with my voice, and there simply weren't enough hours in the day. This was despite the fact that I've always had so many interests going at the same time that doing one always seemed a relaxation from the other.

"In any event, it was useful that I could at least read music twenty-odd years later when I entered this new profession, even though I'd done no singing in all that time and had never made a living at it. I hadn't realized just how much music I would have to master in a short time.

"That has not been the problem I expected. In four years I have learned fifty-three roles in six languages, which must be some kind of record. But I can learn music as rapidly as anyone I know, as it turned out. It's the languages that cause me difficulty. I'm very conscious of that right now because I just did Pogner in *Meistersinger* in English at the City Center and have to be first cover for Pogner at the Met in a couple of weeks, but this time in German."

How, for heaven's sake?

"I can navigate in marketplace Italian and kitchen German, so that's a base. Of course, all the operatic languages are extremely poetic and mostly archaic. It's a little like having a comic-book knowledge of Chaucer and trying to do a dissertation on him. There is very little carry-over.

"One does learn how to study in the academic life, however. I keep my tape recorder going when I'm driving, and learn a tremendous amount just by osmosis. Probably fifty percent of my learning is done on that forty-five-minute commute."

Gill picked up a smattering of Italian during a year's sabbatical in Rome. He went to one opera during that time but didn't enjoy it. During 1969 and 1970, he took another leave, this time in England. He and his wife saw three performances that time because he'd recently taken up voice lessons again—"for fun"—and had more interest.

"I did some singing that year at regional theaters on what I would call a 'semipro' basis. They couldn't pay me because I didn't have a labor permit. They gave me things, instead. A full-dress suit, two weeks in a beautiful Elizabethan house in Kent. Quid pro quo. I was reviewed —favorably, to my astonishment—so I started auditioning at higher and higher levels of the British opera world, all the way up to Covent Garden.

"It was suggested at that point that I audition for the New York City Center when I got back. By this time, I was getting the rhythm of the auditioning process. That's an art in itself, and pretty tough. The analogy that comes to mind is not acting but figure skating. You must take risks, do exciting things, execute flawlessly. One stumble and it's all wiped out. In singing, it's one crack in your voice. During the Olympics, all singers empathize with the figure skaters to such a degree that we are emotional wrecks. Disaster is an ever-present possibility, and that factor dominates the audition.

"To get back, though. I wrote the director of the City Center and said I was a bass in England and would like to audition for him. I listed all the roles I'd ever done. It was a *very* short letter." He chuckles at the recollection, rattling the ashtray. "He must have thought it was a selection from many. A few days after we returned to America, I was on the main stage at the City Center. They asked me to come with them for the 1971 spring season.

"No doubt my state of mind was very complex throughout this auditioning spree, but *consciously* I had no thought of leaving Harvard. I persuaded myself that this was merely a way to test my progress. There was no danger of being hired for anything important in England because they knew I'd be going back to Cambridge.

"*Now* someone had said yes, and I had to cope with *that.* We embarked upon a very surrealistic conversation. They gradually found out that I was not a singing teacher but an economics professor. For a while they thought they should make me an administrator, and the discussion got stranger and stranger. I could feel the 'yes' slipping away as they became more and more puzzled.

"I went back to Boston both depressed and elated. I still had this notion I could keep my job at Harvard and sing on the side. They hadn't been optimistic I could do that, and they were right. I later found it simply wasn't possible to commute from Boston to New York on that basis. They call rehearsals on the spur of the moment and produce six different operas a week. They weren't about to have an economics professor dropping in between classes.

"We're not really sure who said it first, but my wife and I were sitting at breakfast one morning, and we decided I had to do it."

A year and a half later, he was invited to audition for the Met. Now he sings for both.

The reviews have been enthusiastic ever since. Alan Rich, music and theater critic for *New York* magazine, describes Gill as a "very fine character singer, artistic, intelligent, a good actor." Gill thinks he may have a career of at least fifteen to twenty more years. Rich agrees.

"The superstars fade faster than the understars," says Gill. "The larger roles are more demanding in length and expose any vocal difficulties due to age. Also, the bass voice has fewer of these 'total' roles, the ones which dominate operas. Many of even the outstanding basses will take smaller roles which are not beneath their station, and so can carry on well into later life."

Being the man he is, Gill is looking to more ambitious roles.

"So far, I do the roles they want me to. In due course, I can wend my way to those of my own choosing. I'm getting more interested in the Russian literature of opera, mainly because of *Boris Godunov*. I've sung Pimen, which is the second-bass role of *Boris*, but I was also the first cover for the lead, which is the greatest of all bass roles. The thought that I might have been thrown out on the stage to do the lead boggled my mind. I probably would have had cardiac arrest. Ultimately, though, that role should be very good for me. If I ever make the breakthrough into world-class singing, it would be by way of *Boris*. Who knows?"

As a measure of the difficulty of that role, Alan Rich says he hopes Gill doesn't attempt it, for "it might take ten years off his career."

Since very few people have any chance of pulling off this particular sort of life transformation, it is more relevant to know *why* Gill did it than *how*. As with many other life changes, it was less a dissatisfaction with his first career than a sense of incompleteness. Certainly it was not a belief that he had reached an end in his progress through academe. Before he left Harvard, he was approached by the presidential search committees of several colleges, and a full deanship was only a matter of time. In fact, if Harvard were one of those colleges which provide free tuition to the children of its faculty, that might have been sufficient to stay his hand. The humbling prospect of nearly $28,000 per baccalaureate for each of three sons would give anyone pause. The fact that the urge to change one's career often occurs at that time in life when the children are ready for college no doubt explains why so many people opt for security over adventure.

It was that close for Richard Gill. Since the $84,000 would come from his own pocket whether he left or stayed, that eased the decision. Still, the contract with the City Center guaranteed only two performances at $75 each, plus options on his services for two years. Although he knew it could be renegotiated if all went well, it was hardly the basis for sanguinity. Why, then?

"Fundamentally, there was a craving in me for music. A life without music was unsatisfactory to me. I wanted to fully explore that world I had only touched as a young man. I imagine the need was under there all the time, otherwise there's no way to explain why this flowered so suddenly. There was this very deep impulse I wanted to express, even though it was submerged a long time."

Gill used to give more facile explanations for his decision—for instance, that he took up singing to repair his lungs after twenty years of insatiable smoking. He now recognizes that opera was simply the element of the environment in which his "impulse" took root. Another reason he would give for the move was the tone of higher education in general and Harvard in particular in the late sixties. In the face of a student idealism which manifested itself in riots, demonstrations, threats, bombings, and burnings, many educators rethought their commitments.

"Harvard was a major target for the radicals," Gill says. "It was a terribly difficult period in many ways, but the basic issue was freedom of expression. Could people of certain persuasions and position come to speak on the campus, or were they to be prohibited by the mob? The Left said no, that they would prevent them from speaking. They seized certain visitors physically, as they did McNamara, or they shouted them down or otherwise endangered them. I invited Lyndon Johnson because it seemed inconceivable to me that the president of the United States could not come to the campus, that freedom of speech was so curtailed. Most of the faculty people I spoke with about it said I was insane, that it was sheer provocation, that it would be a bloodbath. It seemed to me quite a comment on the state to which the university had fallen.

"I had accepted at face value—naively, perhaps—the fundamental tenet of the university, that the free competition of ideas is vital. I completely absorbed that rhetoric, which had been strong at Harvard from the time I first went there as an undergraduate.

"Then, during the late sixties, I found that two-thirds of the faculty didn't really believe that concept at all. They wanted to keep people with unpopular views away, simply to avoid trouble. I now had to confront the realization that these were just ordinary human beings. They were not, as I had always thought, a group of exceptional people whose values were as sharp as their intellects.

"The students became as disillusioned with the character of the faculty as I. When I go back up there now, I am struck with how cynical people are. Morale will never be quite the same as it once was.

"With all that, though, these things were just the background which opened my mind to other possibilities. One never understands one's psychology fully, but I think I was already moving in other directions. I had already started the singing lessons. And anyway, I didn't leave Harvard when things were really difficult, but after this current period of quiescence had set in. Essentially, it was simply an inner impulse that could no longer be denied."

Central to all these partially calculated turnings is the fact that all of us are given several aptitudes. It is circumstance and the inclination to drift with events that cause the development of one talent to the exclusion of the others. This is most evident in people blessed with abilities in the arts. Virtually every artist or performer has several creative dimensions. Whether these latent sensitivities are exploited concurrently or sequentially seems to make no difference in ultimate achievement, for each facet of an art or craft mastered or explored enriches the others. Picasso was also a sculptor, printmaker, and ceramicist; and Michelangelo, an architect and poet. Leonard Bernstein is a composer and pianist as well as a conductor; Robert Shaw, a playwright and author as well as an actor.

Bailey Alexander does not place himself in this fecund company. Nevertheless, his case is illustrative. Armed with two college degrees in graphics and painting, he nevertheless admitted to himself that he was not to be the reincarnation of either Jackson Pollock or Norman Rockwell. He accepted a public-relations position. In the evenings and on weekends, he continued to paint and sculpt.

In the month of his thirtieth birthday, Alexander (1) received a promotion to the job he had held for ten years, (2) mounted his first one-man show of painted constructions in a New York gallery, (3) finished his first book, and (4) sired his first child. The four events were interrelated in a way he did not foresee at the time. He was bathing in these successive waves of ego gratification, he says, and too caught up in self-congratulation to consider the implications. It was that moment of fortuitous confluence which comes at least once to most people, when equal strains of energy, expertise, experience, and knowledge converge and every dream seems attainable.

"Looking back," he says, "I can see that I perceived that period not as one of those infrequent peaks we realize over seventy years of existence, but as simply the beginning of an adulthood which would be one personal triumph after another. Although I had the grace to keep it to myself, I could see a time in the not too distant future when I would be grouped with a select few people heralding the rebirth of the Renaissance man. Really! I was just that entranced with myself!"

Alexander and his wife moved to a larger house to have room for their new daughter. Higher rent, taxes, maintenance. The sculpture exhibition drew several reviews, ranging from "an interesting talent" to "capable enough, but without verve." One piece—the smallest— sold for $175, and that was it. The book, on the other hand, did well. Nothing spectacular, but steady. In the first two years, it brought in $8,000 in royalties. The Alexanders began to think about moving to the suburbs. When their son was born, they did. Alexander found customers for an occasional painting or sculpture, but barely enough to pay for materials. He was sculpting on an increasingly grand scale, and one piece often required $400 in wood and plaster and paint. More, each took weeks to execute. He was making that much in an evening at the typewriter. Now, wood and plaster went into repair of the nineteenth-century house. So did most of his spare time.

"Within five years of my 'debut' in the breathlessly anticipatory art world, I was turning out perhaps three paintings and a sculpture or two a year. In the meantime, I was writing a column for a small newspaper syndicate and had finished two more books. My salary at work began to catch up with our financial needs. When the demands of the job started accumulating along with the income it provided, the writing started to go, too.

"When the day came that I sat down and bawled for no apparent reason, it may well have been in unconscious recognition that I had given up everything I really wanted to do for a job that was merely supposed to underwrite us until I was doing well enough financially in my writing and painting. That may be a protracted sentence, but not so long when you think that it is the summation of twenty years of my life."

Alexander's sudden resignation stunned his friends, causing exclamations of envy mixed with foreboding. His enemies at the company gloated or sighed with relief.

"One of my principal adversaries—whom I had seriously considered assassinating at one time—told someone I should read the critiques of my last book more carefully before I did something so foolish as to try to make it as a free-lance writer. Naturally, the only review he read tore my book to shreds.

"He was only saying, in his endearingly snide way, what everyone else was thinking. The very day I announced my intentions, a story in the *Times* flatly stated that there were only a hundred writers in the country who made a living from their books."

Reading articles in the *Times* can be injurious to the health of a good many fantasies. Alexander remembers an earlier one by the paper's resident art critic. It claimed that there were at least 500,000 practicing artists in the country, and that no more than three hundred in the *world* made a living from their work. PEN, an international writers' association, claimed recently that less than 3 percent of their members survived exclusively on their writing. It is said that out of every twenty-five members of Actors Equity, only one is actually employed. And so on.

However, the testimony of the persons described here is evidence that bare statistics and press pronouncements become meaningless in the face of experience. Few of the people profiled in this book can be considered unusually gifted, with the obvious exception of Richard Gill. Yet all have succeeded within the delineations they have drawn for themselves. There is, too, the question of interpretation.

When "chief cultural correspondent" John Leonard said that only a hundred writers in the country make a living from their books, he was referring not to all writers but to novelists. Although he included "everybody from Gore Vidal to John D. MacDonald" in his favored hundred, he was suggesting that it is difficult to make a living writing novels *exclusively*. Most writers do not confine themselves to a single mode of expression, either because they don't care to or because light magazine pieces, for example, can subsidize their more serious work.

"I do get weary of the bleats of poverty from artists in general and writers in particular," says Alexander. "The angst one must bear in the trade literature about the plight of so-called experimental writing is tedious in the extreme. There is promulgated this idea that society owes them a living. That's a crock. Society doesn't owe artists any more than it does plumbers. Why should there be governmental support for something five hundred and seventy-six people will read? Why should publishers go broke in behalf of such an elitist concept? Anyway, there is no compelling evidence that state subsidization of the arts produces higher achievement. None! Or that painters and poets have a closer grasp on truth, for that matter. Sure, there are inequities—mediocrities making millions, and unrecognized geniuses on welfare. Life is unfair. But a sonnet cannot be valued at the same level as bread and a roof.

"There is no good reason why artists and performers shouldn't compete in the same marketplace as everyone else. If you can't make it as an actor, well, then, don't be an actor, for crissake! Novelists are forever bellyaching how they can't get by on their niggardly royalties. They're inevitably the same ones who take ten years to pull a book together and spend most of that time 'talking' books at writers' conferences and Elaine's. Surely Mr. Leonard himself would not expect the four novels he's written in fifteen years to sustain him.

"The writers who get by are the ones who work at it. *Hard!* They are the ones who are at the typewriter at eight every morning and produce ten pages by noon, and who spend the rest of the day researching or interviewing or polishing. There are thousands of people— maybe *tens* of thousands—paying off the mortgage and sending the kids to camp *exclusively* by writing. Maybe they're not illuminating the dark corners of our souls, and maybe they wouldn't even like to try, but that's not a terrible price to pay for being part of the best profession there is."

Writers are also given to vocal excess, perhaps as a result of spending days on end in their own company. Alexander has been heard to support precisely the view against which he has just railed.

"Conflict is the one essential ingredient of our craft," he agrees, pleased with the ring of conviction he musters. "Naturally, that means you must be able to present all facets of any question you choose to explore. In my case, there may be a carry-over from seventeen years of seeing-all-sides as a manager. Most of the time, however, that *is* the way I feel.

"My basic point is still valid, anyway. It is perfectly possible for someone with discipline—and the knack—to make enough money as a free-lance writer. There are guys who crank out a story a week for the confession magazines, year after year. Each story pays maybe three hundred and fifty to five hundred dollars, meaning they don't get rich, but they're not starving to death, either. One of my editors knows a man who makes thirty thousand a year doing nothing but travel articles, and he's not one of the 'names' in that specialty. Plus his work gives him expense-paid vacations, year-round.

"You need to find your strength and run with it. Just about everyone thinks he has a novel in him, yet there are very capable magazine writers who can't seem to do *anything* more than ten thousand words long. But if they're selling regularly to *Cosmo* or *Harper's*, where's the tragedy? They've found the vehicle in which they are salable. That's the virtue of working at a straight job at first. You can test yourself against various markets, absorbing the rejections until you find the milieu in which you are consistently in demand, where you can get to know the editors who give your stuff sympathetic readings and who come to you for pieces on subjects they know you can handle. Ah, is *that* sweet! When *they* come to *you.* I've done only five magazine articles in the last six months, but on three of them the editors called me first. Two of them had bought pieces when I was still working; the other read my last book. After a while, you gather momentum. One article begets another, which begets a book, then another article. . . .

"This is part of the reason writing is so often a second career. You need the first job to give you the time to establish contacts and analyze your marketability, and you need it to learn how people relate to each other and to build your own store of knowledge and experience.

"That analysis of oneself is critically important, and it takes some time to work it out. To take my own case, since you insist, despite those degrees, I'm not really very well educated, nor am I insatiably curious, nor especially facile. I've had to compensate for those failings. I *am*, on the other hand, an organized sort, a diligent plodder. My work is better when I have the space to tell everything I know about a subject. It's painful to me to have to edit myself down. As a result, I work mostly at book-length projects, and my shorter pieces concern themselves with topics of very narrow scope. I detest the necessity of library research, so I concentrate on things that are best explored on a firsthand, interview basis. Also, I read every periodical and newspaper with a pair of scissors. Any story or paragraph or quickie item that may conceivably be of future use, no matter how remote, I clip and file. There are five filing cabinets upstairs crammed with things I've been saving for twenty years. I'm about to sign a contract for a book based upon some ten-year-old clippings I came across one day, and when I need some obscure bit of data, at least half the time I can find it in my personal morgue. In these ways, and a lot of others, I make up for my intellectual deficiencies and my lack of flash."

He raps his knuckles against every wooden surface in reach. A full-time writer for less than two years, Alexander is aware of the inevitable lean times ahead. Favorite editors change jobs or drop out of sight, publishers alter policies, expected checks are late in arriving, ideas won't come. So far, it has gone well for him. He has contracted to do four books in this time, with enough articles to ensure grocery money.

This isn't so lucrative as it may sound to a public dazzled by tales of million-dollar paperback and movie options, it must be said. The only money of which a writer of books is assured is the advance against projected royalties stipulated in the contract. A survey by the Authors Guild confirmed that most writers receive less than $10,000 in advance payments, and 40 percent are given $5,000 or less. If royalties on sales do not exceed the advance—and at least four out of ten times, they don't—then the writer receives no more money. And the book may have taken two years to complete.

Even if the reprint rights are purchased by a paperback publisher, —the exception, not the rule—the amount is likely to be small and split several ways. Were one of Alexander's books to be bought by a paperback house for $10,000, half would go to his publisher. Of the remainder, 10 percent goes to his agent, leaving him with a pretax $4,500.

That slice off the top to a literary agent is an issue that tantalizes both novices and old hands. Alexander sets one foot on each side of the question, as might be expected.

"I wouldn't be without Hugh," he says, "at least in terms of my books. He knows every editor in town, their idiosyncrasies, when and how to approach them, what kinds of things they're looking for. Once a book proposal attracts interest, he has never failed to get me a far larger advance than I ever could have obtained on my own. At the very worst, he's covered his commission. Beyond that, he hammers out the most advantageous terms on serial rights and royalty schedules he can, he brings me together with people who have stories to tell but not the time or talent to write them, and he gives me good, solid advice on my manuscripts. He hasn't been wrong yet.

"Some writers are hard-nosed and knowledgeable enough to work these things out for themselves. They have the stomach for squeezing every cent out of the publisher. I don't, and I doubt most writers do.

"With an agent, you usually get a reading faster. Your proposal gets past the book publisher's first reader, who is condemned to reading the slush pile of unsolicited manuscripts from bus drivers and gardeners.

"An agent isn't much use in submitting articles to magazines, however, because their fees are pretty standard and unnegotiable unless you're one of the biggies. Apart from a few top-line mags, an agent doesn't really open any doors. If you do attract movie or TV interest, an agent is essential. Those are barracudas out there. My Hugh may be a bastard, but he's my bastard, working to our mutual benefit.

"Finding someone to represent you is another story. If you're unknown, without a track record, the best agents won't touch you. It's that old "to-get-a-job-you-need-experience-but-to-get-experience," etcetera. When I went to Hugh, I had two books and a fistful of published articles. Since he has a pretty big stable, he wouldn't have let me in the door otherwise.

"Then there's plain old greed. You're really grateful to your agent when he swings an advance that's twice what you expected. But three years later, when the royalties are still coming in every six months and he's still lopping off ten percent, you find yourself grumping that you did all the work and all he ever did was swill a few martinis with the editor and make a couple of phone calls.

"On the *other* other hand . . ."

For his four books, Alexander received advances totaling $30,000. Not bad, but that must be spread over two or three years. With about $3,000 each year in royalties from previous efforts, and a similar amount in annual magazine sales, he can continue to work in comfort. With luck, perhaps two books will be reprinted in paperback. If lightning strikes, one might be selected by a book club or a TV producer.

Alexander isn't counting on any of that. If none of his books ever earns more than its advance, he will still be content.

"I set my own schedule," he says, ticking off the advantages. "We go to Europe every year, when we want, for as long as we want. We can live where we choose. All I need is paper, a typewriter, and a dictionary. I am responsible to no one but my family. My wife and I share more, talk more, than we ever have. I spend less on clothes and nothing on commuting. And I'm here when the kids come home after school."

Jim Brown contributed his own story—leading over a rockier course to a similar conclusion—in this letter to the *Yale Alumni Magazine*.

> Went broke in 1970 when firm taken over by Merrill Lynch. Also got divorced the same year. Maintained my seat on the New York Stock Exchange, and worked as a $2 broker until I shattered my leg skiing in February 1974. Left the city in a cast to escape the rat-race, July 1974. Moved to Marblehead with Polly. We got married last April 5, 1975. My family now numbers six kids. Three mine and three hers. Both of us are freelance photographers. Still limping around, but happy as I never have been before.

That last declaration is remarkable only because it seems to be true. Though he is a child of wealth and privilege, Jim Brown's troubles these last few years could blight the lives of a fistful of daytime-serial characters. Nevertheless, he is demonstratively pleased with his lot, although his newsletter story does not reveal how he might be.

"Polly and I both came from a great deal of money," he says, propping his injured leg on a chair. "I never really learned the value of work when I was on the Street. Things were too easy. In 1968, I made a hundred and sixty-eight thousand dollars. Even when things got bad and I thought I was dying, I was still bringing home thirty-five thousand. And *that* was the *low* point.

"I was forced into the brokerage business. I graduated Yale in 1956, and the navy in 1958. *National Geographic* gave me an assignment to do an article and photographs in Africa. I needed fifteen hundred dollars, so I went to my father for it. He wouldn't give it to me. Told me I was 'going to work.' I always did what the old man told me, so I gave up Africa and wound up with Goodbody and Company.

"I bought my seat on the Exchange from my father for a hundred and thirty thousand dollars, payable over a good many years. When I got the offer from Goodbody, my old man said to take it. They had been in business for fifty years and never lost any money. It was the second or third biggest house in the business. They wanted me to work on the floor for them. I did what my father said. He was good at generating business, and the contact end of the business is for shit, so he'd pass on most of my contacts, and I worked on the floor.

"I hated it. You'd walk out of there at the end of the day and think: What have I accomplished? Any jerk with connections could make money back then. We all thought it would go on forever. I saw the value of my seat go to five hundred and fifteen thousand dollars. *Nobody* could lose. We couldn't see any reason why it shouldn't go to three-quarters of a million. But even in good times, those were miserable people down there, and I was one of them. The pressure is incredible, and there was no feeling you were doing anything worthwhile. All that money **meant** nothing.

"In 1967, my first wife told me she was 'seeing' one of my best friends. I hit her. Then we went to a series of shrinks. The analysis got longer and longer and awfully expensive. One of the doctors thought it would be a good idea to buy the old stone house in Darien that she wanted. It *was* nifty. We decided we needed a garage. The fucking thing cost eighteen thousand dollars! A garage! Just as we nailed the last shingle, she handed me the separation papers.

"That was September 1969. I moved out and into the New York Yacht Club in town for a while. First person I called was the gal who lived across the street in Darien. Really nifty gal, great body. I moved into a place on East Seventy-fourth, a sort of crash pad for people in mid-divorce. I wanted to move with a different crowd than I used to. This gal got me into all kinds of things. I started growing my hair. Pants without cuffs. Wide lapels, fat ties. Me! Me, who wore Brooks Brothers underpants! Christ! This gal was helping me bust out of all those old things.

"I was making all kinds of money then. And I was spending it. It was nothing to drop by Mr. Ned's and pick up a couple of custom-made suits. I was doing all those things—El Morocco, weekends on my boat, skiing at Sugarbush, Bermuda and the Caribbean in the winter, East Africa—nothing *really* extravagant, but nothing held back, either.

"But I couldn't really let go with anyone. At a party, I'd always go straight to the best-looking gal there. Even if I got anywhere with her—I usually didn't—I couldn't allow myself to love anybody. Up until the day I met Polly, all I really wanted was for my wife to come back.

"In the summer of 1970, I decided I'd had enough of Goodbody, so I resigned. My agreement stipulated ninety days' notice, so it actually became effective the end of November. On December seventh, Goodbody collapsed. Why? To put it simply, they were in capital violation. Not enough money. They had a ratio of twenty times debt to capital. I got out just in time, I thought.

"At the same time, my divorce came through. I kept doing this singles thing. I played with the idea of taking off for the islands in my boat and tooling around until I got myself together. Instead, I met Polly. With her, I learned I was capable of an open relationship with a woman. My first wife and I were awfully naive. She was a virgin the first three days we were married. To think we had three kids. . . . Anyway, Polly and I moved in together in February 1974. The same month, I flew Pol and her three kids in my Cessna to Vermont for skiing. On the second run down the hill, I went into a tree and telescoped my leg into a thousand pieces. Doctor said it was the second worst he'd ever seen. Hate to think what the first worst was like.

"In the meantime, the thing with Goodbody was dragging along. The board of the Exchange had persuaded Merrill Lynch to take over Goodbody's business by promising to indemnify Merrill up to twenty million dollars in liability. This meant that all the member firms had to kick in. But that wasn't enough. Everyone with a managing or floor partnership at Goodbody—about sixty people—was squeezed dry.

"My resignation was effective November thirtieth, and the merger on December seventh. As a floor partner, I wasn't regarded as part of the management team. Anyway, I'd quit before I even knew anything was wrong. They kept it from us, with little pep rallies to squelch the rumors. I didn't see how I could be held liable, so I refused to sign the authorization agreement.

"This guy on the staff of the Exchange called me in. This was just about the time my ex-wife hauled me into court and I was about to move in with Polly. They called up and asked if I wanted to make a deal. By this point, all but nine of the Goodbody people had come to terms with the Exchange." (Harold Goodbody, who once averaged

$250,000 a year as a managing partner, was severed from an interest in the firm. Four years later, his annual income was cut to less than a tenth of that.) "I said sure, because I naturally wanted to get them off my back.

"I arrived there without counsel. This guy starts off with 'Mr. Brown, you know we have the power to put you into bankruptcy—*and that's exactly what we're going to do!*' There I am, defenseless, and this little worm has two guys with him, and he says that! 'However,' he then says, 'we realize that's a stigma you would not like to bear. Therefore, we propose that you may keep your bank account and your automobile.' My bank account was in arrears, and I'd long since sold the Jaguar. 'We'll take your boat, and you'll pay us a percentage of your income from the seat for the last four years. In addition, you'll pay us five percent of your gross income over twenty thousand dollars for the next five years.' That was the deal. If I agreed, the Exchange would let me off the hook and stop pressing charges.

"I was shocked, of course. When I asked him how he expected me to make a living with my seat gone, he said I could just go out and buy another one. At this point, they were going for about a hundred and forty thousand dollars. Since he intended to take everything I had, I asked how he expected I could do that. He didn't have an answer, and he didn't care.

"As far as I was concerned, they were pissing up a rope. So, I've got them on my back, the IRS says I owe them another eighty thousand, and my dear sweet ex-wife picks this time to wage war on me. She was hauling me into court over and over. She never got anything, but there was this constant drain of legal fees. Still is. My divorce lawyer, my counsel for the Exchange business—still paying, still going to court for six years now, and God knows how much longer.

"Then the skiing accident. That's over two years ago, and I'm still having corrective surgery. A year ago, the Cessna was wrecked. Damn shame. It was such a nifty plane."

Brown's studio is getting busy. Each of his lawyers calls. His ex-wife has a new demand. The Exchange is calling him to a preliminary hearing before a judge. Four of his children come in to ask permission to go to the movie. A mother brings her two youngsters for passport photographs.

Brown has delivered his recitation in tones of unflagging good cheer. When the studio finally quiets once again, Brown is asked how he maintains such optimism.

"Polly. Simple as that. I even liked her shrink better. Great guy. Pol and I really enjoy each other. We like to do the same things. It's a pretty nifty setup because she has enough income to keep her end of the family going. The only real demands on me are for my own children. We pool our resources—our talent, money—and have put together a really enviable life."

Another call. His tax lawyer, this time.

"When Polly and I met," he resumes, "she was peddling photographs on street corners. I'd always taken pictures, of course, so we had that in common. The summer after we first got together, we went to Nantucket to see if we could make it as a team. If Nantucket has a ghetto, we found it. The place we got cost fifteen hundred for the season. Really tacky. Negatives drying in the shower, all that. We called our corporation the Naked Eye, which startled the classified-ad lady at the local newspaper. The first month, we had one commission. The second, fifteen jobs. When we got back to New York, I continued doing child photography on weekends. We were getting pretty well known and began to believe we could make it just with that."

Of all the creative crafts, photography is the most likely to provide employment, and it rarely requires formal training. Most successful are those photographers who focus on two or three specialties, building their reputations and client lists. Jim and Polly Brown have some problems with that.

"As a going photographic concern, we've been erratic in our directions," he says. "I hate to be stereotyped as a person who does only tabletop setups, for instance, or food, or shoes, or fashion. We did a promotion for Gruen Watch Company on their LEDs and their factory. And there was a job for Lee Bailey, on his helicopter. He wanted to sell it at the French Air Show. We had a lot of fun and hard work last summer doing yacht photography. I really love sailing. Done it all my life. We had quite a few sales with that, but we got to feeling we were a charitable organization for yacht owners. Photography is an expensive business on any level—the cameras, film, processing materials, lights, all that. When you get into something which requires chartering boats and hiring crew, where weather can kill days of picture time, there isn't much profit left.

Creating

"We still don't value ourselves enough as workers—because of our backgrounds, I suppose. We didn't charge enough for our work, we'd even give away the proofs. Nobody does that, because it kills repeat business. To make money at this, we're going to have to narrow our interests. We dig travel photography, the kiddie stuff, underwater macrophotography, minutiae shots of bugs and leaves. For most of that, there's no market at all. Even the child portraiture is limited. Industrial things, commercial accounts, catalog projects—that's where the money is. I guess we'll have to work in that direction. We've been doing things mainly that we really wanted to do. It's been really nifty but not very practical."

The Browns' future will continue to hold distractions. The court hearings and appeals go on. The Stock Exchange, the IRS, and his former wife will insist upon chunks of his income for years to come. Jim's ankle may require another operation. And, a few months ago, they took over a photo store in Marblehead. It's in the red.

But Jim has Polly, their children, their spacious home in a beguiling New England village, and engrossing work in which they delight and share. On balance, a satisfying existence.

Nifty, one might say.

Gratification in the arts and allied craft professions has a direct relationship, in immediacy and continuity, to the length of time spent in preparation of any given performance or project. After a few days or weeks of rehearsal, the stage actor or musician receives an instant verdict: applause, followed by the critics' judgments. Then the work begins again.

A novelist expends lonely months and years with only the intermittent urgings of his editor to acknowledge his efforts. Once completed, though, his book can bring satisfactions that space themselves over as much time: paperback and book-club interest, periodical serializations, prepublication reviews, press and TV and radio promotional interviews, cocktail-party lapel grabbings and ego massages. All this lasting as far as his next publication and beyond.

Anticipation of ultimate response is the artist's most profound anguish; favorable reception, his most exhilarating joy. The actor or singer or painter who professes no interest in the reactions of peers and public "as long as the money is there" deceives no one. A book unread, an aria unheard, a watercolor unseen, a ceramic untouched—all are meaningless. Expression is only part of the artistic transaction. Communication completes it. Creators who choose not to recognize this, or those who cannot tolerate rejection, can anticipate only frustration and lack of fulfillment, the potential for posthumous appreciation notwithstanding.

Those contemplating one of the arts or crafts are reminded, therefore, that life at the easel, on the stage, or behind a typewriter does not bring freedom from the exigencies of distribution, negotiation, and financial management, or from people who tender those services. Indeed, as performers and craftsmen are largely self-employed, they are more involved with these tedious necessities than are wage earners. Taxes, contracts, loans. Agents, lawyers, editors, producers, impresarios, accountants, publishers.

And theaters, galleries, stores. To communicate emotions or ideas, in whatever form, artists must have outlets and a firm understanding of how they operate.

The Great Barrington Pottery demonstrates an approach to creating and marketing that many craftsmen favor and few execute. In 1965, Richard Bennett bought a farmhouse in the Berkshires of western Massachusetts, equidistant from Boston and New York. He built a three-chambered Japanese wood-burning kiln with the help of an expert he imported from Kyoto. It was the first one ever constructed in the western hemisphere.

Then Bennett sat down and started making pots and plates and pitchers and cups, 150 to 200 a day. When he had enough, he opened retail shops in the Back Bay area and Greenwich Village. He took on apprentices to help meet the demand and because he wanted to pass on what he was learning. After seven years, he closed the stores, locked up his farmhouse, and returned to Japan.

According to his original plan, he was going to stay there until 1979, then move to Europe for another seven years. The design was short-circuited. The woman he had married his first time in Japan did not want to return to her homeland, and Bennett found that his work there was not so gratifying as he had expected. He came back to the Berkshires.

The driveway turns off Route 41, runs past the low, long shed that houses the pottery and kiln, passes a barn, the showroom, and doubles back to the house on the road. A slender man, shorter than most, appears at the screen door and asks the visitor to remove his shoes before entering. Bennett then guides the newcomer through several white rooms, cautioning him to watch out for the pots and dishes placed on the floors.

Pouring two glasses of Chablis, he waves the guest to a reed chair. Bennett's manner is distracted. He is gracious enough, but socially out of sync, as one might be who has spent many years in two distinct cultures without completing the transition to either. From time to time, he halts in his speech to find the right word, mentally translating from Japanese to English as often as the other way around.

Born in Boston to a family that rarely conceded the existence of institutions other than Harvard, Bennett intentionally chose the University of Michigan when his time came. He drifted into Oriental languages and philosophy and a junior year in Japan. His attorney-mother and physician-uncles forgave his skirmish with unseemly iconoclasm when he accepted a fellowship at Harvard for his graduate study. He should have gone to Berkeley, he now reflects. They had a better program. But Harvard seemed the best place in terms of career placement, and he cared about those things then.

He imagined he'd become a professor, not out of compulsion, but because nothing else crossed his mind. After two years on the Ph.D. treadmill, though, he decided that "academe was nice enough, but you could get just as trapped as working for a company, and the rate of advancement was even more limited." So he gave up the idea and joined the army. This was in 1958, and he had to go in sooner or later. After his discharge, he found a job as assistant manager in an import-export firm with offices in Tokyo, Seoul, Hong Kong, Rio, and New York. He chose Tokyo and became, despite misgivings, an utterly conventional business executive. The company owned a fleet of 20,000-ton freighters, petrochemical factories, and vast commercial interests throughout the Far East.

Bennett, in his late twenties, was drawing a salary well over $25,000. A house, a chauffeur, a maid. Tax-free. He married a Japanese artist—secretly, because the firm wouldn't have approved. Increasingly discontented, he sought counsel from his wife's Buddhist priest, a man thought to be clairvoyant by his 200,000 adherents, asking if he should quit his job. (Bennett was the first Westerner the priest had met.) Yes, was the answer. Should he take one of the other business opportunities available to him? No. Should he become a potter? Yes.

Bennett had taken up pottery a few months before as a hobby. He was not set afire by it, but intrigued. After the conference with the priest, he returned to his office and handed in his resignation.

The priest had an "annex" in Fujima, a tiny village outside the small coastal city of Matsue. The area was known for the production of slipware pottery, made by covering red clay with a film of white clay before firing.

"Matsue was a feudal fief right into this century," Bennett says. "Other than that, there was no particular reason to go there. It is very isolated, even though it's on the main island of Japan. To me, though, it sounded very romantic. I went up there and walked into a pottery with fifteen workers. The man in charge asked if I'd like to study there. I said yes right away. There was a one-room house overlooking a lake the man had built next door for his son, who was subsequently ostracized because he was a Socialist. That wasn't an acceptable thing to be, back then. I leased the house for about two hundred and forty dollars for the entire year.

"I moved all my things from Tokyo and started working in the pottery immediately. A foreigner, I found, never actually becomes an apprentice, because apprentices are trained only to work right in that place for the rest of their lives. A foreigner is always an outsider—a *gaikokujin*. The rules don't really apply to you because someday you're going to leave and you can never really be part of them. As it worked out, then, they just thought it was very nice of this foreigner to try to learn what they were doing.

"This meant I was not in any program, because they wouldn't think of imposing one on me. Everything I wanted to learn, I had to ask. I had to proceed through centuries of evolution by demanding to be shown each stage. Since I spoke Japanese and several dialects, I was very much a center of attention. They'd bring people in to show off the rich foreigner.

"After three and a half months, my lung collapsed. I was in the hospital for three months, came out, worked for twenty days, and my lung collapsed again. One of my cousins, another doctor, heard about it and insisted I come home. I'd only had barely five months of training, so I was very unhappy about leaving, but my priest said I should go home. He said he'd send my teacher to work with me for two years in the States."

Bennett bought the farm. Then his teacher decided not to come, and the Buddhist priest flew over to Great Barrington himself, distressed that he couldn't make good on his promise. The priest, though a millionaire, had never traveled outside Japan but felt that he was obligated to look after the future of this new member of his flock. He offered Bennett three jobs in Japan through his congregational connections, but Bennett insisted he must stay. Resigned, the priest spent a day blessing his adherent's new property, then left. Bennett's teacher arrived two months later.

They built the kiln together and made pottery for six weeks. After the teacher went home, Bennett was left with $2,000 a month in undeferrable bills, no income, a cumulative total of seven months' training, and a great many clay pots.

"I don't know what I did, really. I worked hard every day, eight to five. People stopped by and bought things. I went to Japan every year to speak to my teacher and the priest. I opened the two stores. And five thousand people a year asked to be my apprentice."

In the tactile crafts, whether it be pottery or weaving or glassblowing or blacksmithing, there are essentially four categories of artisans. At one extreme is the craftsman who is nearly indistinguishable from the creative artist, except in choice of material. He or she designs and fabricates works either as one of a kind or in limited editions. At the other is the production artisan, who turns out large quantities of tapestries or bottles or place settings of similar dimension and color. (The Russells of Rockport exemplify this type, and Bennett comes close.) Within these extremes are designers who have others execute their creations, and folk artisans such as the ones with whom Bennett studied in Fujima.

And the craftworkers, who are employed or apprenticed to do whatever must be done. Bennett has mixed feelings about apprentices, and as a result has taken on as many as eight at a time and gone without for equally long periods. "It's been very disappointing. The idea was to train people to go out and train others. Trouble is, very few of them are making beautiful things, so the end result is that I've put a lot of ugly things on the market.

"I stopped taking anybody for a while because the whole thing was

Second Chance

too aggravating. They never knew what they wanted. I'm not against someone trying to 'find' himself, but not at my expense. I'm just not interested in getting emotionally involved. All I want is to teach technique, but they want more, and I can't give that.

"The only way to do pottery is to work at it regularly, constantly. It isn't easy to drag yourself over to the wheel every morning, but that's the only way it can be learned. They don't understand that. They think I'm just treating them as machines."

When he is so inclined, Bennett accepts apprentices for $5,000 a year for room, board, and instruction. He bought a nearby building and converted it into apartments for this purpose. An apprentice who lives elsewhere pays $3,500. Bennett thinks they should stay with him for two years, but few do. And he acknowledges his own limited training before he began work.

There are other ways to learn a craft. Recognizing the growing enthusiasm for crafts, more than a thousand colleges now have fully developed programs. Boston University even blends "artisanry" with liberal arts in a curriculum leading to a bachelor's degree. More relevant here, however, are the hundreds of small schools, studios, and colonies in every section of the country which concentrate exclusively on training in the desired craft. Bennett sees no reason why a talented beginner cannot be producing and selling in a year.

"All you need is a small room, clay, a wheel, and access to a kiln. Less than a thousand dollars, plus rent.

"Beyond that, you must sit and work and produce," he says. "I don't really know why I'm making pottery. *It* chose *me*. It takes at least ten years to get this 'oneness' with the clay. Some say thirty. I'm starting to feel close on certain things, very far away on others. What happens is—you don't *know* what's happening. I look at this bowl and almost wonder who made it. I've made hundreds of these but never felt I was repeating. I think—always—how it will feel to the lip, to the hand. Each time, I'm trying to make the ultimate piece.

"I wouldn't do it if I didn't think I made beautiful things. My work is a product of everything I do and everything I have been."

7
Farming

*Nature may be rather accounted a stepmother, than a mother,
unto us, all things considered . . . we must not therefore hope
to have all things answer our expectation.*
*Wine, measurably drunk, and in time, brings gladness
and chearfulness of mind.*
— Robert Burton, *The Anatomy of Melancholy*

The narrow back road out of Hesston, Indiana, pitches and
yaws between peach orchards and pastures. Another rise, another dip,
and the converted dairy barn housing the Banholzer Winecellars suddenly appears. Triangular pennants flutter above the ridgepole. On the
golden folds of ground surrounding the building, black fingers of vine-
root reach up, their tips recently clipped. Later on, new leaves will fold
over, quivering in the tiny puffs of air spilling over the far ridge.

Inside, the barn is cool and dim after the glare of the parking lot.
Steps lead up to the tasting room, which runs the width of the building
and stretches to the roof beam. There is a twelve-foot bar against the
end wall, its buffed wooden top covered with glasses and rows of bottles.

The people bellied up to the edge are both crew-cut and long-
haired, denimed and polyestered. A portly man in a powder-blue leisure
suit, aviator shades, and peaked pompadour lifts his glass by the thumb
and forefinger. He swirls the wine, thrusts his nose over the rim,
inhales. Swirls again, thoughtfully. Sips. Sucks air through his mouth
while the claret pools on his tongue. Finally, he swallows, tapping his
lips together.

"Hot damn!" he proclaims in evaluation. "How 'bout 'nother
daba that, honey?"

The expressions on the other faces at the tasting bar range from
joviality to uncertainty. No one wants to seem a klutz, but then no one
is sure of the procedures in such a place. Like meeting the queen. On
the one hand, this isn't a saloon, and the samples are free. There is a

faintly ecclesiastical tone to this vaulted space, despite its commercial purpose. Yet alcohol is being served, and that implies a different kind of behavior. Some meet this head-on, with an "I-don't-know-wine-but-I-know-what-I-like" heartiness. Others toe the floor and try not to gape. Most, though, simply utilize an open-minded, down-home sociability, intrigued but not awed.

Sylvia Obert makes it easy. She is pouring today. There is not a whiff of pretension about her, not the smallest crease between her eyebrows at even the most uninformed of questions. Sommeliers, as a class, cultivate a manner that causes even sophisticated diners to feel as if they had called for ketchup for the pâté maison. Not Ms. Obert. Or Carl Banholzer, the round, bespectacled majordomo who takes over when Sylvia conducts a tour of the winery. (The vats and presses are down where the cow stalls were, and she painted the scenes of historical wine making which illustrate her talk.) Or soft-spoken Janet Banholzer, who presides sometimes when Carl must attend to other business. All of them seem able to recall just which wine a patron drank three glasses ago. All are unabashed at requests for "something sweeter" than the almost sugary rosé just served. (They simply switch to the Sweet Harvest May Wine.)

Up another flight of stairs is one more level, overlooking the bar. Customers may bring their picnic baskets and glasses here or to the thirty tables arranged in a pavilion outside. A lunch of assorted cheeses and bread for two people is available for $1.50. Although the Banholzers may shudder, they don't object if patrons bring their own beverages as well.

Carl's office is down a narrow hall off this floor, next to the room in which he stores his bottled wines. He takes today's inquisitive visitor there, pausing for a moment to select a bottle. He sits behind the desk and pours some of his Neumonthal into two tulip glasses.

The interviewer is a not-very-secret wine snob from the East, given to oenological pronouncements based upon a scanty book knowledge of the Gironde Valley and Napa County, snippets of axioms on the joys of the grape, and a vastly incomplete understanding of where and how vines are grown and wines created. He dismisses New York wines as "foxy," and California Burgundies as "cloying." Because he can name a few châteaus and list the constituent varietals of a *grand cru* Bordeaux, his friends deem him expert. He endeavors to conceal his skepticism that a Cabernet Sauvignon or even a Baco Noir grown in *Indiana* can be acceptable to a civilized palate.

Wrong again. The Banholzer Neumonthal is crisp, flinty, unusually full-bodied for a white. A revelation. Carl pours some more.

Banholzer is the son of German immigrants. Until 1971, he helped his father in their small tool-and-die factory in Chicago. That year, Indiana made it legal to make and sell wine. The Banholzers sold their house in the city, their acreage in Michigan, and bought this former dairy farm. He already knew which grapes would prosper in this region, and he planted them, along with some experimental vines of European thoroughbreds. The first vintage was bottled in 1974. By the end of 1976, he was breaking even.

"Wine making was an avocation for me for ten years," he says, turning the corkscrew in his hands. "My father always made wine at home, and his father owned a vineyard in Germany. We lived on Dayton Street in Chicago, a German ghetto. I was born here but couldn't speak English when I entered kindergarten because no one else did in my neighborhood. I'd go down to the Thirty-fifth Street freight yards with my father when the railroad cars full of grapes came in from California. You could almost identify the types of grapes in each car by the ethnic groups gathered around them. Poles, Czechs, Germans, Hungarians. When there were red grapes, my father would say, 'We don't take that shit. That's for the Italians.'

"We couldn't always afford the good varietals from the West Coast or couldn't get them, so we'd have to use Concords and Niagaras, the ones you associate with the 'foxy' taste. But if Dad had a few dollars, he'd buy a good Moselle at the deli, and after that, the Lambruscas were almost undrinkable. Finish this up?"

Carl drains the Neumonthal into the visitor's glass.

"My father learned tool-and-die manufacturing in Germany because there were too many people making wine. Then, in 1929, there wasn't work anywhere, so he came to the States. When I was grown, I went to the University of Arizona for health reasons. I majored in government but grew flowers and vegetables in a little plot behind the hotel I was living in. I graduated in 1959, married Janet, and went to work with my father at the factory. Eventually I was general manager. We had thirty employees and were making good money, but I didn't like it, and I don't think my father did."

He excuses himself to answer the telephone, then leaves the office for a moment. He returns with another bottle, the Vidalesque this time. It soon reveals itself as softer, more delicate than the Neumonthal, with a certain taste of the fruit. The visitor remembers to ask how Banholzer came to make the break from the family business.

"We were making Allen-type fasteners. They're a totally standardized product and provide no opportunity for creativity. The money was pretty good, though, so as soon as we could, I bought the property in Michigan. Agriculture as a livelihood still had not occurred to me as a real possibility. Farming was so remote from our lives. I just wanted to grow grapes for my own pleasure. The more we worked at it, though, the more the idea grew.

"Looking down the road, I knew I wasn't going to stay in my father's business. Sooner or later, I'd leave. The summer of 1970, my wife and I confronted it. Weekend farming was just too hairy. I couldn't go both ways anymore. But I'm an emotional person, and I didn't want to let that destroy my judgment or jeopardize my family. Janet didn't really care one way or the other. She isn't motivated by financial considerations. She just wanted to see me happy.

"Have some more," he says, tipping the rest of the Vidalesque into the glasses. "Then we started looking carefully for a bigger place. The farm in Michigan was too small, and I'd planted too many varieties. We started taking exploratory drives every weekend, taking aerial maps of each area with us. There hadn't really been any careful study isolating prime growing areas for the less hardy European vines in the Midwest as there had been in New York. One development in Illinois failed because the soils were too heavy and there was no buffering of climatic conditions. It was right out in the open. It could go from very warm weather to below freezing in a matter of hours.

"We don't have that here." (Banholzer's vineyard is on an inland ridge paralleling the southeastern shore of Lake Superior and running through adjacent corners of Indiana and Michigan. It has been a minor grape-growing region since the last century.) "The cold winds come out of the north and west, across the lake. So in the spring we get cooler weather right here than five miles south. Just the opposite is true in the fall, because the west winds blow across the lake, which is then much warmer. The first frost is delayed until December, two months later than just a little way downstate.

"So we focused on this region. The peach orchards were tip-offs, and all these forests. Fruit trees only flourish in highly buffered zones and in soil that isn't much good for grain or any of the more usual crops. Gravelly soil or sandy loam with high internal drainage is desirable. You don't want too much water sitting in the primary root systems, because it gets pumped into the vines and swells the berries with moisture.

"We wanted slopes like this for air drainage. The cold air flows down into pockets, and the vines at the top stay warmer. You don't want an overly rich soil, either, because then the plants put too much energy into growing leaves, not grapes. This is very poor ground for corn or wheat, for example. It's not worth a damn for anything but fruit crops. When we saw this place—rocky, sandy, rolling—we knew it was the right place. We knocked on the door and asked the farmer to sell it to us."

A look at farming as a new-life occupation is necessary to this consideration, because wine making is really only another version of the chicken-farm syndrome. The civil servant retiree of the past who thought to take his pension and raise Plymouth Rocks has been joined by back-to-basics suburban dropouts understandably offended by apples which taste like potatoes and packaged dinners with more chemicals in them than food. Unfortunately, realization of the wish to be a full-time farmer is so unlikely as to be irrational. Assuming, that is, that one is neither wealthy nor an heir.

However, it is surprising how many people are unintimidated. Robert S. Blumberg, coauthor of *The Fine Wines of California*, lists a dozen men drawn to wine making from other fields. Without too much thought, he lists a former corporate airline pilot, a Stanford University scientist, a Los Angeles realtor, a contractor, a musical comedy actor, a retired police inspector—all with their own wineries. Back East, there is a Hudson Valley wine maker who was once a magazine illustrator, and a Westinghouse executive with the only vineyard on Martha's Vineyard, an island off the Massachusetts coast.

The figures are chilling, nonetheless. The per-capita personal income of the American farm population was $4,759 in 1974—but only $2,496 of that came from working their spreads. According to a study by the Agriculture Department, nearly 60 percent of U.S. farm families rely on outside jobs to make ends meet. And many are just scraping by: *72.4 percent* live *below* the poverty line of $5,000 per year when only farm income is taken into account. A Vermont dairyman with forty cows and property valued at $100,000 regards a $10,000 profit as a very good year—as would a Georgia peanut farmer, with certain notable exceptions.

It takes a lot of money to enjoy this threadbare estate. The Department of Agriculture also estimates that to earn an annual profit of at least $8,000, an *experienced* farmer must make an *initial* investment of *at least* $40,000. Even this would be in high-yield, low-expense crops in the least costly regions of the country. Most of that profit, of course, must be plowed right back into seed, fuel, fertilizer, and equipment payments. And try to find an experienced farmer who believes that $40,000 is anywhere near enough.

Jim Martin, the CB man in Indiana, has made it his business to know the financial demands on his farmer clients. Martin claims that the lowest base figure he's heard is $200,000—just to get started—with a total investment of $500,000.

Banholzer thinks that is about right. "For an operation such as this," he says, "figure on at least that amount to start up *and* continuing in your present occupation for another five years after you make your first move. Anything else is just too reckless. And it will be *ten* years before you can put away the red ink. For a vineyard and winery sufficient to support a family, you need a minimum of forty usable acres. Around here, the necessary acreage, with open ground and a modest home, costs around a hundred and fifty thousand dollars. Then labor, machinery, supplies—another hundred and fifty thousand. Finally, two hundred thousand for housing and equipping the winery.

"You need much more labor starting out than you do later. Winegrowing requires constant cultivation, and you must erect hundreds of trellises, stakes, and fences. The workers have to be paid, and this is before you have a cent coming in. At first, we had to buy grapes elsewhere, to put the equipment to work. A press costs nine thousand dollars; and a crusher, five thousand. Plus stainless-steel tanks and pumps. I have two tractors—thirteen thousand dollars. When the man delivered those, I waited until he left before I tried them out. I didn't want to admit I had no idea how they worked."

There are ways to reduce these intimidating sums, certainly. Lease acreage instead of buying it. Buy as little equipment as possible, and preferably secondhand. Better still, rent it. Check all sources of financing. The Farmers Home Administration lent Banholzer a quarter of a million dollars, for example. Make friends of neighbors, to get advice and to swap labor. Work for another wine maker (or orchardman, or soybean grower, or whatever) before buying property. If he is established in a grape-growing area, an aspiring vintner can simply buy his raw material down the road, planting his own grapes later. Conversely, the farmer can put off building his winery until his vines are established. Also, labor and property costs vary geographically, by as much as 50 percent. Wine grapes are profitably grown in Maryland, Georgia, Oregon, Ohio, Arkansas, and Michigan, among other places, in districts known for both severe winters and searing heat. Most people assume that no market exists for American wines produced without the cachet of California or, secondarily, New York's Finger Lakes. The relative prosperity of the Banholzer vineyard and winery proves the opposite. A small winery may even be at a greater disadvantage if it is in direct competition with such multimillion-gallon producers as Gallo and Inglenook than if it is isolated in rye-and-bourbon backwaters. Banholzer is creating his own market. In the process, he sees no reason to engage in the niceties of wine appreciation that a more worldly, but distant, clientele expects.

"The public in this area is not knowledgeable about wine, as a rule," he understates. "They are ignorant of the meaning of vintage, so there's not much point in vintage labels, and the difference between a bottle of a single varietal and a blend of several would be lost on them. I'm getting over my own fussiness, too. So we have this Vidalesque, which is a blend of Vidal Blanc, Seyval Blanc, Aligote, and Baco Noir grapes, and this Seyval-Ravat-Chardonnay we call Neumonthal. And this Kaiserthal is Foch and Pinot Noir in blend. Here, try some."

Another bottle, another cork, another glass. These are wines for quaffing, not nibbling, and Carl pours such generous dollops of each that a surpassing will is required to restrain from snapping them back like red-eye. The Banholzers produce ten labels altogether, plus occasional special bottlings. There are six whites, two reds, and two rosés, ranging in price from $3.03 to $5.00 the fifth. He expects a yield of 24,000 gallons this year, or 220,000 bottles. Half of that will be retailed on the premises, the other half wholesaled. His goal is to move 90 percent at the tasting room, and he does not restrain himself from the necessary promotion of his wares.

"The Saturday after Labor Day, we hold a 'wine stomp,' " he says. "Forty young ladies are invited to stamp as much juice as they can from a hundred pounds of grapes, in hallowed tradition." The race goes more often to the sturdy than the swift. "The night before, there is food, dancing, and singing to a couple of country and western bands. We only charge a dollar for entrance.

"Anyone who purchases six bottles of wine automatically becomes a member of our wine society, the principal benefits of which are a regular newsletter and the 'bacchanals' on the first Fridays of May and November. There is live entertainment, and members can eat and drink all they want, for free." The last time, the 150 members in attendance bought up $4,400 worth of recent pressings. "They really love it, have a fine time, and keep coming back."

And the cut-rate lunches, the vineyard tours, the discounts for quantity purchases—all contribute to the balance sheet. Carl is an active cheerleader for his corner of Hoosierland, too. As president of the local chamber of commerce, he notes that within fifteen minutes' drive there are beach resorts, three ski areas, a three-mile railroad track traversed by antique steam engines, many campgrounds, and Indiana Dunes National Park, on the lake. Brochures are handed out in the tasting room. Carl observes that anyone starting a winery is wise to consider what other attractions in the region may draw customers, and to help in publicizing them.

Every bottle leaving the Banholzer tasting room sells at twice the gross dollar of one sold at the distributor level. Carl uses those outside sales merely to get rid of his production, which in turn must be maintained at current levels to keep costs down.

The obvious question in the interviewer's mind (only the most obvious ones are occurring to him at this point) is: Why not double production and grower losts—er—lower costs further?

"We have our hands full with what we have," Carl says. "My greatest fear is that if we got any bigger, I'd be relegated to doing what I didn't want to do when I came here—paperwork. As it is, with only five to ten people working for me, I can still involve myself with the operation in all its phases. I'm doing the cuttings, the plant propagation and training, right through to the harvest and wine making and promoting and serving the product.

"That's really elating. To cut the vine, nurture it, grow the grapes, and eventually pour a glass and see someone enjoy what you know to be a fine product—there's a continuity and gratification you can't find in anything else. I have no ambitions beyond that. Finish this up?"

8
Trucking

But the most pleasant of all outward pastimes is . . . to make
a pretty progress, a merry journey now and then with some
good companions, to visit friend, see cities, towns. . . .
—Robert Burton, *The Anatomy of Melancholy*

Bathed in green light, the crown of the Empire State Building
hangs in the sky above the rows of tenements sloping to the Hudson.
The night is piercingly cold. Out back of the restaurant and filling
station of the Vince Lombardi Service Plaza on the Jersey Turnpike,
a score of Peterbilts and Whites and Kenworths rumble in place. Most
of the cabs are dark.

Michael Kritch is holding court in a booth inside. Everyone knows
him. Last week, he was featured in an article in *Money* magazine about
white-collar people in blue-collar jobs. Not that it mattered. Kritch cuts
a wide path.

"Alice," he says to one of the squad of waitresses who make
excuses to pass his table, "pick a number from one to ten."

She is a woman no longer in first youth. "Five," she giggles.

"You lose," says Kritch. "Take off all your clothes."

"Go to hell," she ripostes, delighted.

"Nobody ever finishes playing that game," he sighs. "And Alice
is so horny tonight, too. Alice, bring those other two girls over here."

"You mean you're a cradle robber and a pervert besides?"

"Alice, just ask them if they want to meet a guy with an eighteen-
inch bionic chicken."

"You wish," she says, adjusting the salt-and-pepper shakers, reluctant to leave.

Another waitress, younger, brings a cup of coffee for the stranger
sitting with Michael.

"Hi, doll," says Kritch. "This is Tracy. She is very horny, too. We've made it six times in my truck."

"That's a lie," she says, grinning and reddening at once.

"Sorry," he says. "*Eight* times. And I would like to go on record —she's good! Take a deep breath, Tracy. Hmm. Very nice."

The waitress rushes away, trying not to wriggle.

"I've retained one thing from my career as a salesman," Kritch says to the stranger. "I'm still shy and introverted."

He was something more than a salesman. Until last spring, he was national sales manager for a food manufacturer.

"I was *very* successful," he says. "Made forty-two thousand as a base salary, plus commissions. I carried ten company credit cards, had a hundred and sixty-eight men working for me, and I was in demand. I could have had a dozen jobs."

But after thirteen years, he quit his job, divorced his wife, and brought his truck.

"I wanted to be a trucker all along, but my first wife didn't want any part of it. She was caught up in that phony world of country clubs and playin' the role. I just got fed up with that. Sold the house I built with my own hands. Threw my golf clubs in the garbage can. I'll never play that game again. Now I'm the happiest, most comfortable sonuvabitch in the world. I couldn't care less if I have a pot to pee in the rest of my life. As long as I have a truck and can make a livin'.

"Alice, why do you keep fillin' this guy's cup? Don't I mean anything to you anymore?"

"Don't bother me," she says, meaning the opposite.

"Alice, you wanna go out to the truck and fool around?"

"No."

"Wanna do it here?"

"Shut up," she says, pouring him another cup.

There are two other men with Kritch. They are lean, laconic good ol' boys who look older than they are, with webs of creases around the eyes from years of squinting into sun and headlights. They seem both entranced with and embarrassed by Kritch's banter with the waitresses. Their handles are "Shortarm" and "Crooked Stick." Kritch calls himself "Blue Moon," and he is as different from them as a captain in the Haganah from a pair of Montana sheepherders. Kritch has the outsized features of a Nez Percé shaman and a body proportioned like a pillar of granite. When the *Money* reporter—a pale and jumpy Holyoke type, according to Kritch—asked him to describe himself, he said he was "a six-foot-two-inch, 200-pound, stomping, dynamic, good-looking Jew." He repeats that appraisal now, with the reasonable assumption that no one will contest it.

"I'm a trucker," he continues, "because it's the roughest, dirtiest, all-man business there is. And truckin' down the highway, bullshittin' your buddies on the CB, is like jumpin' into a bar on Friday night and raisin' hell. Right?"

Shortarm and Stick nod in agreement.

"You'd have to get into a truck and do it, to see what I mean. You're fightin' every element there is. You fight for the best load, then you fight against time, sleep, cars, the Smokies, the weather. You hope your truck holds together, and when you get there, you fight to get it delivered and unloaded and to pick up another load. Then you do the whole thing over again.

"And every time I end, I feel like, 'I did it! I beat it again!' It makes me feel really great, every time. Isn't that it, you guys?"

Nods. These men—and thousands of others—have bought the legend. They are technology's cowboys, the last of the loners, with their own code, their own language. They grumble about the trucker's lot, but, deep down, they retain the romantic vision fashioned for them and by them. They mock the TV truckers ("You'd starve to death stoppin' to help widows and orphans every trip") and watch the shows as eagerly as policemen watch *their* video counterparts, scoffing all the while, but, at the same time, believing.

The CB rage serves to propagate the myth of trucking, especially in its outlaw connotations. Despite Kritch's contentions that "real pros" don't use the radios to evade the law, the two-way units began to proliferate with the lowering of the national speed limit to fifty-five. Since independents like Kritch and Shortarm are contracted—paid by the mile or the load or a combination of both—they make their money by driving as far and as fast as traffic and their kidneys permit. One or two tickets can wipe out their profits on a small load and maybe suspend their means of livelihood.

Being stopped by a state trooper means more than a ticket. Interstate Commerce Commission regulations do not permit truckers to drive any more than ten hours at a stretch, with eight-hour intervals of rest. The owner-operators routinely break that rule. Twelve straight hours or more behind the wheel is the norm. A policeman can demand to see the driver's log, known to both as a "comic book." Loads often exceed state limits, too. Indeed, a cross-country trucker may leave Topeka with a legal load but violate ten different laws before he reaches New York. And there are regional stipulations on tire size, brake types, trailer connections. . . .

So, the CB. Where are the highway-patrol cruisers up ahead? Is the weigh station open? Are there radar setups? Accidents? Road construction? Bad weather? While it's at it, the CB provides entertainment, helps fight sleep, brings another human presence into the lonely cab.

"We lie to each other, make jokes, have friends we've never met," says Kritch. "We talk to girls and hookers in four-wheelers and zap each other. Like 'Red Wine'—that's his handle, never saw him—he's the proverbial screwer of a snake. He turns down nothing. Or the Roadway drivers. They're the ethnic jokes of the interstates.

"Ever seen their trucks—orange and blue, long nose, all look the same? In order to get hired by Roadway, you cannot be able to write your name. Roadway trucks only have one seat in them—behind the wheel. That's so the guy knows where to sit. When you call a Roadway driver on the CB, he *always* tells you he has forty-two thousand bushel on. That's forty-two thousand pounds. On a good day, they carry five thousand. Roadway trucks are extremely fast, but only downhill.

"I went into a truck stop with my wife once. She's a model and doesn't look like your average trucker's woman. There's about twenty drivers inside. One of them hears my wife ask, 'What's Swiss steak?' This asshole yells that it's 'dead beaver meat.' Without even looking up, she says, 'Must be a Roadway driver.' It was. That's the kind of guys they are."

For every underclass, an elite. The patricians of the industry are the men (and occasional women) who own and drive their own rigs, especially those fortunate enough to possess a Kenworth or Peterbilt tractor-trailer. These gleaming, thundering eighteen-wheel monsters are fifty-five feet long and at least 50,000 pounds, empty. They have thirteen speeds, sometimes more, and may have two gearboxes and shift levers. They can do 120 miles per hour. Their transmissions are custom built, according to the type of driving the owners expect to do.

Above the cockpit is a sleeping alcove adequate for two people. These are often equipped with stereo and sometimes TV; at least one independent installed a water bed. The whole thing can cost as much as $65,000. A good credit rating helps.

"Let's say the tractor costs forty thousand bucks," Kritch says. "If you have no experience, as I didn't, the minimum down payment they'll take is around ten grand. 'Course, you can only finance it over five years. It's not like a house, even though it costs about as much. You're looking at nine hundred a month in payments. That's a helluva nut. Now you gotta get a trailer. A good reefer [refrigerated trailer] is gonna be over twenty thou. With a quarter down, the trailer is four hundred a month. That's thirteen hundred right off the top. You don't necessarily have to buy a trailer, but if you rent one, it'll cost almost that much. And if you just haul one of your contractor's, instead of paying you seventy-five percent of the tab on the load, he'll give you maybe sixty percent. So, you gotta have a trailer. Then you got maintenance, equipment. Just one tire is a hundred and twenty-five bucks. If you're careful, it'll last eighty thousand miles. I put that on it in less than a year.

"An average, legal independent can expect to gross fifty thou a year. He'd have to, to net twenty. But that's not hustlin', and it's assumin' he's got all brand-new equipment to pay off. I won't tell you what I make."

Even a hint?

"Well . . . Last week, I made eighteen hundred comin' out—Chicago to here—and four-fifty goin' back. I was ridiculously illegal last week, of course. Most owner-operators are very well off, contrary to impressions, if they've been in it awhile. A forty-thou net isn't unusual if he moves. I know a black dude, talks with a voice box where his larynx used to be. Don't owe nothing on his rig, pulls twenty-three hundred a week minimum. And if you have a good accountant, even when you're makin' big bucks you can work it to where you don't have to pay income tax. My accountant is takin' my records for the last four years back. Figures he'll get me refunds even for then, because of my large capital investment.

"Tracy, come out in the cab. I left the ropes and chains home, I promise. No? Next week?"

Most truckers must run heavy—over the limit—to make that

much money. Apart from the one indiscretion nagged from him, Kritch denies he ever does. Most truckers use pills to stay awake. Kritch and Shortarm and Stick deny that they do. Most truckers carry weapons because they carry hundreds of dollars on each trip. Kritch and his friends never do, of course.

"You can't follow the letter of the law," he says. "Truckers get shit on by everyone. You gotta be everything—mechanic, businessman, driver, cop. And you hafta be mean. You can't be a nice guy. Like, you pull into a station, you gotta stand there and watch the guy fill it up. What he could do, if you walk inside, is take the hose outta your tank and put it in his buddy's truck, right next to yours. Then you get charged for a hundred and fifty gallons of fuel when you only have fifty. You gotta figure everyone's out to take you, because they are."

What about that "cop" role?

"You're driving down the street. In back, you have boxed steaks. While you're sittin' fifty-five feet away, guys come up and start breakin' open your doors with crowbars. Nice? I've had that happen. I had to get out and beat on guys. You gotta convince them that they can't do that. You get nasty because you have to. Never any real cops around at a time like that. They're all out on the highway givin' tickets."

This leads the three truckers into another discourse on the harsh demands of the work, from there to comparisons of equipment, and on to tales of the Alcan—the road to Alaska traveled only by the biggest, toughest, nastiest, most suicidal truck jockeys in North America. Even Kritch and Shortarm speak of them in tones of awe.

"Only idiots go up there," says Shortarm. "I'd like to, though, just once. Wintertime's great up there, they tell me, 'cause the road's smooth. Solid ice. You put chains on everything, even the steering wheel, 'cause when you look in your mirror and see the trailer comin' up on ya and you're at a ninety-degree angle and there ain't nothin' you can do about it, your only hope is to put the hammer down and drive out of it. And you can't do that without chains. In the summer, you dodge potholes so bad they give you eighteen hours' pay for a hundred-fifty-mile run."

On good loads: "For a flatbed, electronics and used machinery pay the best. For reefers, perishable produce brings the bucks. The next best is swingin' beef. For vans, plastic. Liquid pays good because it moves, like beef, always to the wrong side when you're makin' a turn.

It's lousy money, though. You can go over even on an easy turn. Explosives pay tremendously high, and wide loads, like earth-moving machinery."

On budgeting: "You can make a damn good living as long as you keep working and watch your money. You can't be a lunatic and pee it away. You gotta live in your truck. You don't check into motels and go partying and play cards and go out with women. That's all bullshit. There's an incredibly high mortality rate among independents. They see these fat accounts receivable comin' in, and forget they got an accounts payable due three weeks later. That's how they die."

On arriving home: "I fall into the house after three days on the road and take a shower. I can tell you, that's better than makin' love. You don't know how good that water can feel. First, you peel your socks off, takin' a layer of skin with them. Then dinner. Then I just fall out. Next morning, I spend the whole day doing preventive maintenance on the truck. Thursday, maybe I take the day off. Friday, I go down to Chicago, get a load. Saturday, I clean up, pack up, go truckin'. Three hard days till I get back."

On training: "When I wanted to learn, I contacted a truck-driving school. I went over there, paid fifty bucks, got the books. It was supposed to be a twelve-week home-study course. The books were written on a sixth-grade level. I finished them in four hours. The next day, I called them and told them what they could do with the balance of their course. That was to be eighteen hundred bucks. Never paid them. Not goin' to. A real rip-off racket. They sucker people with the 'glamour' of truck drivin'. And if there is anything this is, it ain't glamorous. Anyway, all I did was buy a truck and start drivin'. I fucked up a lot at first, but I didn't have to buy anyone to tell me how to do it."

On truckers these days: "They're more highly educated. I've run into engineers, attorneys, executives. . . . Amazing, the guys who have quit good professions. And why not? They're their own people now. No shit. They're doin' for themselves. They owe nobody. They're free."

Kritch is tired, and he's bored by speaking with an outsider. "I like the myth. It's kicky. Kids in station wagons wave to me. Their fathers give me a break. They have a better idea what you're tryin' to do. You don't want to admit it's an ego builder, but it's fun. It ain't bad, bein' a hero.

"Like Alice, here. First time I walked in, she said she wanted my body."

"Like hell," Alice demurs. "First time he came in, I asked why they didn't lock the doors. Thought we had a high-class clientele."

"Ten-four, Alice," says Kritch. Then, aside, "It ain't easy bein' a hero."

It is inaccurate to infer that all efforts to transform lives prevail despite the odds. There are those who are deceived, who lack vision or tenacity, who are underfinanced, undermined, uninspired, or unlucky. Their failures should serve as cautionary examples, however, not as excuses never to dare.

One such is Clarence Horton. His Savage Trucking Company is just down the road from the Pattersons' inn in Chester, Vermont.

Horton is angry this afternoon. He has just returned from the bank, where he was refused a $6,000 loan. Since he has a $25,000 savings account there, he believes his application was rejected because he is black. Perhaps. But Clarence Horton and the Savage Trucking Company are in deep trouble.

When he talks, it is of his past, a long, meandering recitation of his ten years as a labor organizer and civil rights activist. He is reluctant to tell of his decision to buy this visibly decrepit firm. He seems to have reached the point where he can no longer confront the disintegration of his business and his life.

"I am," he says proudly, portentously, "a black male American, age forty-three, educated in Nashville, a veteran of the Korean War. My mother was a domestic, and I went to an all-black school. Many of my friends were white boys, though, and I could never understand why I couldn't go to Florida with them on vacation or why my guidance counselor told me I couldn't attend the same colleges. This was 1950, remember.

"After high school, I got on a bus and joined the army. When I went to the PX that first week, two white MPs told me I couldn't go in. That was my first real taste of what it was going to be like to be black in this country.

"I was discharged in '52, as a sergeant. I'd saved two thousand dollars and decided to go up North to get a job driving earth-moving equipment. They were letting blacks do that down in Oklahoma, so I figured I could do even better up there. After a month, I found work as a tractor-trailer driver for forty-five a week. I was the first black to drive into Newark. Then I had an accident. The newspapers reported me dead. I sued the company because it was their faulty equipment that did it to me. I won twenty-five hundred, but I couldn't get another job with trucks because I was blackballed. Never had anything to do with trucks from then until now."

Having touched that subject, Horton veers away. He was hired as a machine operator with an all-black cement company. It was a bad place, he says. "After breathing in that stuff all day, you'd go home at night and shit little rocks." His fellow workers started drinking by noon Friday and didn't stop until they ran out of money on Monday. Gibralter Jones, one of Horton's best friends, died of TB. Horton has always believed it was due to the cement dust Jones inhaled every working day of his adult life. Horton left before it happened to him.

He found a position on the assembly line at the General Motors plant in New Jersey. Sixty-two cars an hour. Two white men on the other side did the same operation he was expected to accomplish single-handedly. Horton complained. The union delegate took him off the line and made him a plant committeeman. He made waves, was laid off, filed a protest, was rehired. As the years passed, he became a representative to the union for the interests of minority members. Then he was moved outside, as a community relations specialist. He joined the NAACP, the Urban League, and, after he heard Malcolm X speak, the Nation of Islam. He drifted away from the union and the Black Muslims when he met some of Martin Luther King's lieutenants.

By 1970, he had organized an association of black truck drivers, later adding white members. There were 187 owner-operators. To be free of the contractors for whom they hauled freight, Horton began to search for a company holding ICC rights. These are, in effect, federal licenses to transport goods across state lines, and are very difficult to obtain. (Mike Kritch and other independents work for companies which already hold the "rights" instead of trying to get their own, a virtually impossible task.)

It was three years before Horton was steered to the Savage Trucking Company. He filled his car with his associates to drive up to Chester to look the company over. "Man, where in hell is we goin'?" said one as the snow by the road deepened and the heater whirred furiously. Savage had eighteen trailers, twelve tractors, six milk tanks, and six van and dump trucks. The owner handed Horton a sheaf of papers, identifying them as the company's ICC rights. Apparently Savage was permitted to work in twenty-one states. The asking price was $1.2 million.

At this point in his story, Horton reaches into his filing cabinet, pulls out a folder, and drops it on the desk before his visitor.

"You ever seen a set of rights?" he demands. "Those things look like they might be? They did to me, too. I saw them, and the trucks outside, and I said to myself, 'By God, we gonna do some *truckin'!*"

Negotiations began. Four of his partners dropped out along the way. They didn't want to sign their lives away. In the end, it was Horton and his wife who wrote their names on the loan agreement. With $350,000 up front, Savage was theirs.

Driving his family to Vermont, Horton saw a man jogging by the roadside. "Look there!" he said excitedly. "It's a black man! 'Least we won't be the only ones up here."

He knocked on doors in Chester and asked if people would mind having him as a neighbor. They said no, and Horton has had no reason to believe the contrary. Maybe because he, his wife, and three daughters were an unthreatening novelty, or maybe because Savage was the largest employer in Chester.

Horton pulled into the garage lot, ready to complete the formal transfer. He couldn't put his finger on it, but there was "something funny." The former owner wasn't there. Half the trucks and trailers couldn't be accounted for, the dispatcher told him. "And, Mr. Horton," the man continued, clearly embarrassed, "the men say they won't work for you. It's not what you think. It's because of the rumors about the company."

The missing vehicles never showed up. Loads and drivers were difficult to find. The loan was in arrears. An organization of consultants to minority businessmen tried to sort out the accounts, the chaotic piles of bills of lading, the maintenance records. They didn't have much success. The bank was calling for immediate payment of the debt.

Horton is glowering across the desk, defiance and defeat warring in the lines around his eyes and jaw.

"What we got here," he says after a very long moment, "what we have in those papers, this building, those trucks outside, is nothing. Absolutely nothing. In a month—in a week, maybe—there won't be no Savage Trucking Company. Nothing."

He turns, looks through the window at the snow beginning to fall, but doesn't see it. There were forms to sign and people to see, so it took two months before the Savage Trucking Company was acknowledged to be officially bankrupt.

Clarence Horton's experience summons up the hoariest of admonitions. If it can go wrong, it will. Don't throw good money after bad. Let the buyer beware. Look before you leap. Carl Banholzer has a more colorful summation. "Making good wine from bad grapes is like making meatballs from manure."

9
Teaching

Learning is not so quickly got . . . few can compass it. After many expenses, he is fit for preferment. Where shall he have it? The most parable and easie, and about which many are imployed, is to teach a school, turn lecturer or curat; and for that, he shall have faulkners wages.
—Robert Burton, *The Anatomy of Melancholy*

Until now, this consideration has centered on those who have fled Establishment, organizational professions for some variety of frequently offbeat self-employment. There are other routes, other needs, other drives. Dissatisfaction may lie in the mastery of a vocation as readily as in an exhausting expansion of its demands. There may be a wish to serve others which is not satisfied by voting dividends to stockholders. Careers devoted to the profit of a few may make one yearn to help satisfy the intellectual or emotional requirements of many. And there are those hardy few who run *to* challenge, not away from it.

Malcolm Boyd fits in there. In 1951, he was a prosperous advertising and television executive. He became an Episcopal priest, later writing such controversial books of prayer as *Are You Running with Me, Jesus?* and actively participating in the peace movement.

Dr. Benjamin Spock fits in there. And so does Charles Lord, albeit in a less celebrated role. Lord left the presidency of a pharmaceuticals firm without rancor, but with purpose. He warmly recalls hearing his superior announce that he would hold Lord's job open for three years in the event the incipient educator "came to his senses." Then Lord went off to become the assistant headmaster of the Maumee Valley Country Day School, on the southern rim of Toledo, Ohio. He said he wanted to influence lives.

Lord is an open, articulate man who seems a bit uncomfortable acknowledging that lofty motivation. He has the bearing and manner of the well-born and -bred, but without the arrogance. In conversation, he persistently credits his listener with perspicacity and rare sensitivity. It is as if he held diplomas from Yale *and* Esalen. (Also, he is wearing a dreadful tie. J. Press would whirl in his sarcophagus.) The visitor, as a rule irrationally intimidated by the sons of Eli, adjusts his creases and relaxes. Why, he wonders, did Lord pick such a time to enter education? Support for schools is harder to come by than ever, and with neither teaching experience nor advanced degrees, Lord doesn't have the credentials normally required for even an entry-level position.

"This will be a long answer," he says, almost apologetically. "Altruism is in my genes, I guess. My family has always been oriented toward people, to service to others. My mother was a delegate to the UN and the Human Rights Commission and did a lot of things in Democratic politics and social work for years before that. My brother was one of Kissinger's top aides, and my father was always very supportive of those kinds of activities. That kind of rather idealistic outlook —that something *can* be done about people's problems—influenced me, too.

"I like working with people. When I was in business in Panama and Guatemala, I was running my own little company, a Squibb subsidiary. A lot of the satisfaction was dealing with the people who worked there—to see the Indian gardener move into a technical job, to see others in a position to feed their families with a measure of confidence they'd never had before. When I was called back in a promotion to the home office, I got involved in the traditional big-company situation and found myself more and more removed from the real concerns of human beings.

"To offset that, I started working in my spare time with an organization devoted to finding jobs for youthful offenders. That led to a trusteeship of a private school in New York. I believed then, as I do now, that private education still has an important role. Not as an elitist institution, but as a leader. That became part of the equation of my move.

"My perspectives were changing. I decided I had to get into a smaller company to recover the satisfactions I'd had when I was abroad. I found a vice-presidency in a medical products firm. Under an alcoholic president, as it turned out. When they got rid of him, I was given his post. It was good in a number of ways, but it still seemed an unreal world."

There it is again. The conviction—or rationalization—that what one *is* doing is somehow insulated from life, while the projected alternative is awash in relevance. Was Lord aware of the contradiction?

"If I wasn't," he smiles, "it was brought home to me. The first time I came here, one of the parents asked me if I was a failure in business. Was that why I was here? he asked. Was I migrating out of the 'real' world? Reality, I suppose, means involving yourself in the things that are truly meaningful to you. Accomplishment by itself is not enough. It must have an impact on the concerns which are central to you.

"To get back to your original question, though. It was somewhat quixotic of me, I guess, to think that schools would beat a path to my door when I made my availability known, when I had no real experience in education. But I felt that my business background was an asset. Educators are not trained to be managers. But the old days when a school found itself with a deficit and just called up a few benefactors to cover it—those no longer exist. You can't ask people for money anymore unless they know you're running your school in a businesslike way. The educators I met understood this, that if private schools and colleges are going to continue to exist, they have to get their houses in order. They also warned me I might get pegged as a business manager and never do anything else. That's why I came to this particular place, where I'm able to do many things. I teach, I'm the assistant football coach, I'm adviser to a number of students, and I administer. About seventy percent of my time is still in management, but I'm working toward the point when it will be fifty-fifty. That's the kind of balance I'm looking for."

A professional manager instinctively weighs all facets of any issue before *and* after the decision. He never acts impulsively, and once he makes a decision, he continues to appraise the situation. In everything he thinks or does, Lord exemplifies this quality.

He is a Republican—but of the moderate Ripon Society stripe. Discontented as a business executive, he nonetheless admires much that is done in that arena, and the men who do it. He is pleased with his new work but can readily list its deficiencies. He is a churchgoer but not devout, neither a teetotaler nor a persistent drinker, a cityphile but at a distance.

"I have never felt I possessed final answers," he says. "I always analyze and evaluate. Everything is a compromise; there is never a sudden conversion. Our situation here in Toledo is a good example. I don't make even half the money in salary I did before, but the rent on our house is less than the maintenance charges on the co-op apartment in New York we had already paid for, and my children receive free tuition here. We miss the cultural atmosphere of New York—the zip, the involvements with fascinating people. It's different here—there's not as much available. But we take better advantage of the things that *are* available. And it's marvelous in terms of the family. We rely on each other more here—there's less outside stimulus. I'm home more of the time because I'm no longer a commuter. There are fewer social events—fortunately, there seem to be almost no cocktail parties here —but now we have two or three couples for dinner fairly often. We get to know people better. We tried to do that in New York, but people were always scurrying in so many directions, it was difficult.

"So we miss things, and we compensate. But we also gain."

And, some parents "are a pain in the neck," but "the kids are a joy." Life was luxurious in Guatemala, but "guerrillas were blowing up the warehouse." He's not "actively looking for another position" and expects to stay "another two to five years," but "ultimately we'll go back East" unless "there's a school in San Francisco. . . ."

All of which may give the impression that Lord is indecisive, but "thoughtful" is more nearly accurate. Life changers who are unyieldingly convinced of their rectitude are suspect. Having activated one option, they slam all others shut by their insistence that they have seized the one and only course available to them. Rather, the first move should be regarded merely as the liberation necessary to exploit *all* of one's aptitudes and to explore all the nuances of personal relationships. Not compulsively or urgently, to be sure, but with a full comprehension of possibilities. The intent should be, in Richard Gill's phrase, to "test all muscles," not simply to become a true believer in another cause. Charles Lord is not wishy-washy. He is guarding the freedom he has wrested for himself.

Stillman Drake has something of the same quality. He became disenchanted with San Francisco and admires Toronto, his new home, but he recognizes the continued attractions of the former and notes the latter's warts. He is horrified by what he views as the decline of the United States, while conceding distress with the recent petulance and self-righteousness of official Canada. And he, like Lord, sees much virtue in the world of commerce he departed, while retaining his right to proclaim the deficiencies, as well as the satisfactions, of academic life.

"I find I have nostalgic feelings about the financial community I left behind," he says. "So much so, it's difficult for me to say which I really prefer—that [municipal bonds] or this [professor of the history of science]. After I got the hang of things here, I'd often sit back and compare. General attitudes are quite different, of course. The fact is, I'm still more comfortable in the business world. In the financial business, a very high premium is placed on production, on making money. As a result, you have a clear, sharp focus on your objectives. You don't have that in a university. Also, the quality of people in finance is, at least in my experience, very, very high. They were of great intelligence, with strict standards and unwavering principles of ethical conduct. You got used to people giving their word and keeping it, and to their thinking before they talked. If they don't, they are ostracized. In almost any other department of society, this is not true. People don't think first, they don't keep their word, they don't admit their mistakes or make good for them. So, generally speaking, I'm more at home among individuals who trust each other than in institutions that have massive sets of rules and regulations where everything is spelled out but no one really pays much attention."

By inference, then, universities are muddled in purpose, and their inhabitants are untrustworthy?

Drake won't say that, exactly. "There is a lot of jargon and hocus-pocus about what constitutes something academically meritorious. There's quite a bit of pretense, I feel, which makes this environment somewhat less congenial to me."

Why make the move, then?

"I put in thirty-three years in business, in pretty much the same field. I was curious to try other things. Besides, in your old age, you don't think as fast and you're not as receptive to changes. You get in the way. I always had in mind to spend my last few years in academic work, so when the offer was made to come to the University of Toronto, I took it. I haven't been sorry."

It wasn't the first time a university faculty had sought him out, but he had turned those earlier inquiries aside. The interest in him was generated by what he called his "hobby"—translating the works of Galileo and writing about the scientific revolution. He started in 1938, four years after graduating from Berkeley. After a number of scholarly articles, Drake's first book was published, a translation of Galileo's *Dialogue* on the two chief world systems. That was in 1953. Subsequent efforts committed to English all of Galileo's scientific works and some of his pieces on other issues. Drake was not offered teaching posts in the United States because he lacked advanced degrees. The credential fetish is less pronounced in Canada, and Drake had long respected the head of the history department at the University of Toronto. When this position was tendered, he accepted. He was afraid it might be his last chance.

His move to Toronto coincided with that city's emergence as one of the most livable in North America. Once notable only for its Calvinist propriety, the dowager had turned sassy and provocative. Developers renovated old buildings instead of tearing them down. A tide of immigrants brought not crime and poverty but sprightliness and color. Thruways were rejected, parks prevailed, imaginative shopping and residential districts bloomed. It was called the "city that works."

Drake anticipated none of this. It was a bonus, and though he views the evolution with benign detachment, he intends to stay after his retirement.

"Mainly, I suppose, it's that Toronto is thirty years behind cities in the U.S.—meaning they have fewer problems. That's an advantage when you start to get old," he says dryly. "You rather *like* the way things were, thirty years before.

"I had no real feelings about Toronto one way or the other. I simply talked to a few professor friends, and they immediately encouraged me to take a good look. Mainly on the basis of the university, though. At first, the city struck me as being very flat, since I had always lived in hills before. But then I turned onto University Avenue. It is the widest boulevard this side of London, with all those plantings in the middle and the trees and impressive buildings. I took that as a sample of the rest of the city, which wasn't accurate. But it is such a fine city to walk in. There are parks every few blocks, and there's no sense of foreboding at all. I often walk my dog in the park at eleven P.M., and there are young people walking and holding hands—it's really incredible. In San Francisco, no one in his right mind ever goes to

Golden Gate Park after dark. And there's really no campus in the States that's quite as attractive as ours.

"This recycling of older buildings and restraint on new construction is part of the reason that Toronto is so livable. But to do that, Canadians have taken for granted restrictions that would bring out the vigilante in a Californian. Americans wouldn't take it for a minute. Some of it is quite maddening. They don't put the same premium on individual liberty as we do. Their emphasis is on the public good. Canadians always make anything mandatory if they possibly can.

"We're landed immigrants, not citizens. But if you're born here, you're a colonial, the 'subject' of a sovereign, in effect. Those are words that don't mean much to an American—nor to a Canadian anymore —but the psychology of the tradition lingers on. The result is that an American here is frequently surprised that everyone doesn't go up in smoke and indignation when some new bit of bureaucratic foolishness is foisted on them.

"I haven't suffered much from the hostility that Canadians feel toward Americans who live here but don't take up citizenship. At least, it didn't affect me until recently." Surging Canadian nationalism has lately pushed American-owned publishing firms out of business, withheld funds from museums purchasing foreign (read "American") art, endeavored to jam television and radio broadcasts from south of the border, and escalated costs of gas and oil piped to the States. The debate over "foreign influence" (read "Yankee imperialism") has spread into the universities as well. Almost 15 percent of the Canadian professoriate are Americans. There have been efforts to reduce that group, and Drake was a target of them.

"I will stay in Canada, and it seemed the right thing to do to take out citizenship. But just at the time I became eligible, pressure was building to fire any American professors who wouldn't take out citizenship. Because of that, I haven't any intention of applying. I rebel. Even though they were trying to make me do something I was going to do anyway, I won't be forced. It wasn't that I have any affection for Washington—hell, that's one of the reasons I came here—but I will *not* be told what to do."

Drake admits he isn't much of a teacher, but he was hired primarily for his scholarship, so the deficiency doesn't trouble him. He is given ample time to pursue his research. In business, his study and writing was done evenings and weekends and during three weeks' vacation a year.

"Here," he says, "the school year is effectively over by mid-April or the first of May and doesn't begin again until September. That gives me four months of unbroken time for research. It's much better than the situation for professors at American universities."

Time is the major benefit of educational work, especially for faculty on the collegiate level. Given normal teaching loads, the typical professor's classroom responsibilities, including time for preparation, boil down to an eight-month year of twenty-hour workweeks. Even a school or college administrator enjoys more discretionary time than his or her opposite number in the private sector, although rarely as much as teachers and taxpayers believe.

"I'm not going to sit here in my suntan in the middle of April and pretend I don't have more free time than I did before," says Charles Lord. "Perhaps fifty percent more. During the summer, I take perhaps four weeks; and while I'm here, I might take off at four o'clock some afternoons to play some tennis. Then there's a week at Christmas, another week in spring.

"Otherwise, it is illusory. People don't realize the amount of external relations required in a school like this—promoting the idea of an independent school, raising money. And there are night meetings with the parents, alumni, the steering committee, the finance committee, and so on, as well as social activities of one kind or another. It means three or four evenings a week. Faculty, on the other hand—with some exceptions—can get out of here at three thirty or four, most days."

It may be thought that educators exchange time for money. The stereotype of genteel poverty dies hard. Neither Drake nor Lord will reveal his salary, but it is fair to guess that each draws in excess of $20,000. In Drake's case, perhaps much more. The mean salary of college professors in the United States is over $15,000, and of secondary and elementary teachers, over $12,000. Not very grand, to be sure, but adequate, especially when combined with generous allowances of free time. And, depending upon location and type of institution, it is no longer unusual for professors to receive over $30,000 or elementary-school teachers over $20,000.

Financial considerations were unimportant to Drake and Lord. Both were highly paid before their moves, both have substantial investments, both accepted heavy cuts in salary. Their motives are evident, and their attitudes toward the future are predictable.

"I don't want to know what I'll be doing in ten years," says Lord, "but right now I'm happier than I've ever been in my life."

"I don't see the point in planning more than six months ahead," says Drake. "Who knows what the world will be like? Do you?"

10
Trading

And, if we scape Scylla, we fall foul on Charybdis . . . in perpetual fear, labour, anguish, we run from one plague, one mischief, one burden, to another.
—Robert Burton, *The Anatomy of Melancholy*

For all those who want to teach what they've learned, there are others who rush in the opposite direction. Richard Gill, for one. Don Kawash, for another. Kawash was a history instructor at Temple University when the administration dropped his course in Western Civilization. Instead of looking for another professorial post, he decided to play ragtime piano at a fashionable club in Philadelphia. One of his singers was another ex-professor.

And Charles Perry: teacher, administrator, and, eventually, president of Florida International University. Perry left to start a second career as publisher of a Sunday newspaper supplement. His decision is evidence that change need not be synonymous with escape. Swapping one set of responsibilities for another may appear a futile exercise, solving nothing. But while Perry's move may not have the drama of a banker turning beachnik, it was for him as energizing and required a similar sacrifice of the known for the unknown.

There is no more thankless job than that of university president. The position's several contentious constituencies—students, faculty, alumni, trustees, community, staff, politicians, contributors—ensure that no action, however evenhanded, is ever accepted by more than a grudging plurality. There is no social or organizational disorder the president is spared—and often, as with drug use and political unrest, he has to confront them long before anyone else. For many, the job means heart trouble, ulcers, nervous conditions, alcoholism. For the survivors, it is a gray, juiceless existence in which every view, no matter how outrageous, must be heard, for to do otherwise is to invite conflict.

In that sense, Charles Perry may be said to have jumped from the fire into the frying pan. The number of views he must accommodate is diminished, and objectives are fewer and more broadly shared.

"Woodrow Wilson said that the politics of higher education made the politics of politics seem like nothing," Perry observes. He is sucking a pipe to life in his spacious corner office in midtown Manhattan. "In the university, you're surrounded by very bright people, and that's why it can be so vicious. All that intellectual power. And the days of the folksy old college 'prexy' are over. I was the manager of an academic enterprise with a thirty-five-million-dollar annual operating budget and a one-hundred-million-dollar capital budget, with fifteen hundred employees, thirteen thousand students, two campuses. I had to deal with labor unions, architects, construction, land-use planning, public relations. I had to be an academician, super with students, a tough administrator, an orator, a fund raiser, and have skin as thick as an alligator's. I wasn't equally successful at all those things, perhaps, but that's what was expected.

"As president and publisher of *Family Weekly*, my authority is restricted. It is the fourth-largest magazine in the country in terms of circulation, appears in three hundred and twelve newspapers, and goes to nearly twelve million readers. But I have limited direct power over editorial content and production and none at all over budget, once it's finalized. My authority is in the areas of advertising and newspaper relations. We're in the process of—ah—altering those relationships within the conglomerate of which *Family Weekly* is a part.

"In any event," he says, slipping away from what is apparently a delicate in-house issue, "I've found that fewer of the skills I developed at Florida International are called into play here. But one is central to any kind of management: the ability to work with people on all levels. I have that, and I use it."

There can be no doubt that he does. He is adroitly loquacious—telling much, revealing little. It is easy, certainly, for others to suspect his intent, but nonetheless difficult to resist his persuasion. His is a confidence that is one part self-esteem, another part assurance. Perry is not a man who permits himself disappointment. Or stagnation. Along the way, he has mastered the executive art of "euphemoptimism," a special language which masks immodesty while asserting strength, casting even fiasco in a positive light.

He accepted his present position to "develop a new pattern for his economic life-style." That is, he wanted to make more money. "I never want to become complacent." Which is to say, he'd gone as far as he could go. "I felt a new challenge would be good for the soul, that it would be stimulating." He'd become proficient in the techniques of higher-education administration and craved new excitements. "I wanted to exercise my skills in a new arena." He wanted to see if power, deftly manipulated, brought the same satisfactions in other fields.

And: "If I ever relaxed, I'd be a total wreck." Meaning, if he ever relaxed, he'd be a total wreck.

None of this is presented with judgmental intent. The addiction to achievement is no less noble than the flight from pretense. They even overlap. The thrust should be to test *all* personal capabilities—psychic, aesthetic, social, intellectual. In that sense, Charles Perry differs little from Richard Gill or Michael Kritch or Richard Bennett or Carl Banholzer, surface dissimilarities aside. None of them submits to confinement or concedes he has reached an ending. Or admits he has exhausted his potential.

Certainly not Charles Perry. "It has been a long-term, methodically planned process," he says. "Originally, I intended to stay in higher education until I was forty, and then switch. But I started quite young and became the founding president of the university at thirty-one, ahead of schedule. After six years, it was time to move. You should leave when you're on top. So many of my colleagues stayed too long. Nothing I shall ever do will top that experience. It was exciting, stimulating, demanding—and I'd wrung it just about dry. When I announced I was leaving, there wasn't a dry eye in the house. Except mine.

"I'm young enough to have a twenty-year career in the private sector and still have a third career beyond that, perhaps in foundation work or in government."

There is no "perhaps" about it. It isn't difficult to connect Perry's admitted interest in building his financial resources—something he could not do as a university president—with one of his earlier comments.

"I might have gone into politics," he said then, "but I didn't have any money. When you don't have money in politics, somebody owns you. I'm too damned independent for that. This is a way to reach that point. Publishing just happens to be where I landed. It could as easily have been banking or finance or manufacturing. I programmed the change but not the direction. And this is just transition, not finality."

Given Perry's stamina, ambition, and predilection for twenty-hour workdays, there is no reason to believe that even a gubernatorial or senatorial chair will satisfy him.

No two people could be less alike than Charles Perry and Charles Hepner. Perry is short; Hepner is tall. At fifty, Hepner looks younger than Perry, who is thirteen years his junior. Hepner matches Perry's sleek competence with diffidence. In his dealings with others, Hepner practices a form of self-effacement that he has polished into an art. While both have the same first name, Perry surely is called a brisk, precise "Chuck," while Hepner could be nothing but "Charlie."

But they have one thing in common: both traded one demanding profession for another. After fifteen years as an electrical engineer, with a wife and two children established on a small farm at the farthest end of the Penn Central railroad, Charlie Hepner resigned. Yale Law School accepted him despite his advanced age, and he matriculated for the three-year, full-time program. His family and friends thought it an irrational act, of course. Charlie allows that they may have been right.

"Gee," he says, "I'm not sure why I did it. I know I wanted to change, but that's a common occurrence around that age. Most people don't really plan their lives up to that point. They find they're doing whatever it was they fell into. Halfway through, I just thought I should have another life. Simple as that, I guess.

"I was just an engineer. I'm not the kind of guy who likes to supervise other people. But that's the only way you can move up in engineering—become an administrator. I found I wasn't that great technically, but I was fairly good at taking other engineers' ideas and writing them up. Did a lot of proposal writing. That's how I got interested in patent law. I was helping the chief engineer at Electric Boat get a patent for an invention a couple of guys came up with. It looked like an area where I could work by myself—which is what I prefer—yet still be a little more successful than as just an engineer."

Charlie's projection of himself as an amiable nebbish doesn't bear examination. He is a graduate of two very competitive engineering schools, Berkeley and MIT. Neither institution suffers the halt or infirm. When he took the Law School Admission Test, he drew a score of 725 (out of 800). Many of his classmates, half his age and a notoriously aggressive, hard-driving lot, would have sold their sisters for a rating that high. And Yale Law took him, although it is acknowledged to be one of the two finest schools of its type in the country and can take its pick.

But Charlie persists. "Law school is mostly just psyching out what each course is all about. Once you have, you don't have to crank out too much work. Of course"—he smiles at his ineptitude—"I never really figured the courses out. Probably I wasn't flexible enough. Law is so different from engineering. Every question has an answer, I'd always thought. Something was, or it wasn't. With law, there are too many variables. Two plus two can equal five or six as well as four. Law is a matter of nuances, and it was tough changing the thinking habits of a lifetime, which is why I didn't get any higher than the middle of the class."

Asked why he picked Yale, where it was necessary to attend full-time, rather than a night school where he could retain his job and income, Charlie says he needed "as much going for him as he could get." A Yale degree carries clout, certainly, but tuition came to nearly $10,000. (It's much more now.) All that money going out, and none coming in. Charlie's wife, Anne, had to care for their three-year-old son, so she couldn't work.

"And he was a terror," she says now, erupting in a squeal of laughter, as she does often. "He locked me in the closet twice! Before he could even walk! You can imagine what it was like when he gained full mobility. I've always thought Charlie went to law school just to get away from his son."

Charlie denies the accusation. Anne isn't so sure.

"Money wasn't *too* big a problem," he continues. "My father left me a little, and Anne had some. I had to use up about half my savings, though, and a long period of no income is probably something from which you never fully recover. It was years before I had recovered the income level I had when I left Electric Boat. Even now, although I'm making about thirty-one thousand, which is more than I would have if I'd stayed there, inflation has eaten up the difference."

Presumably there are other satisfactions, then?

"Oh, yes. I've done more rewarding work in the last five years than in the whole rest of my career."

Anne is skeptical but silent as she spoons out a cottage cheese salad garnished with walnuts, blueberries, and tangerine slices. The sunroom, added to the main house three years ago, is awash with light. Across the carefully tended lawn, Bob, now thirteen, is running across the roof of the barn. Anne runs to the door to hail him down. He sits but doesn't leave. Anne settles for that.

"It's true," Charlie continues, trying to persuade himself as well as his wife and visitor. "There are things you don't like in any work. But I've been able to carve a niche that suits me. I don't get involved in litigations. I'm not the sort of person who could deal with the adversary situation in the courtroom. My preference is with a kind of 'preventive' law, anticipating patent problems so they can be solved before things get messy. I like that—it suits my sense of order.

"Even when I'm at my lowest, I'm glad I did it. I look back and think: Gee, if I hadn't done it, I'd be back doing something I really loathed."

How about the commuting? Charlie gets up at five in the morning and often isn't home before eight in the evening.

"It's like the Navy," he says, with a sidelong glance at Anne. "If you love your wife, you get to be with her half the year. If you hate her, you can stay away half the year. It takes me four hours a day, door-to-door. I don't really mind it, though. If it weren't for the subway from Grand Central Station to downtown, it would be quite pleasant, actually. The Penn Central is a lot better than it used to be, and I do a fair amount of reading and writing both ways. It's a sort of decompression chamber between work and family."

Then there is a good deal of pressure?

"Quite a bit. It's something I didn't realize about law. There's an awful lot of work. A sixty-hour week, at the least."

"He never goes anywhere without his briefcase," Anne says, edgily eyeing Bob, who is now practicing standing schusses on the barn roof. "He even takes it to our ski lodge in Vermont."

"When it gets to be six thirty at the office," Charlie says, "it's a question as to whether to bother going home. Two or three nights a week, I wind up sleeping on Mr. Kenyon's couch. I keep a toilet kit and pajamas in my desk.

"And you have to remember that the hardest thing about a new professional career is that you start at the same level as everyone else, guys twenty years younger. There's no advantage in being older. I don't have the strength and resilience they do, at thirty. And New York is still the Big Apple, so my firm can hire the top people, and they are *really* good. It can be salutary to find you're not as brilliant as you thought you were, but it hurts, too. I don't have their drive, either."

"Charlie never has been a high-energy person. Bob! Get down!"

"That's not true," Charlie retorts, wounded. "If you can just get me to wake up, I have a *lot* of energy."

Is he suggesting that in the face of that competition he has gone as far as he is likely to go?

"Gee, I hope not. I'm certainly not going to change again. Getting to be a partner is where the income gets better. I'm still just an associate. Every partner has six or seven of us working on his cases, and he gets about two-thirds of everything we bring in. Our top partner is probably in the two-hundred-thousand-dollar range, but even the junior ones make sixty thousand or more. As an associate, you're not always doing income-producing work. There's a lot of housekeeping and spadework and keeping your records in order. Then if the partner has given a client an advance fee estimate below the amount of work actually done, he may turn around and cut your share.

"I was just passed over for the first partnership for which I was eligible, but maybe next year. . . ."

"Bob, dear," Anne trills, trying another tack, "here's your favorite! Apple pie! Bob?"

Regrets, Charlie?

"Sure, some. I don't see as much of my family as I'd like, I don't have time to keep this place up as well as I'd like, we don't get to see people very often. . . . But I wouldn't go back for anything. I've never done anything so stimulating, and in the law, no one hands you a watch when you reach sixty-five. You can do this forever. One of our partners just retired at eighty-six. Mm. It *is* good pie."

"Good Lord," says Anne. "Now he's sliding down the drainpipe."

11
Women

Others are much tortured to see themselves rejected, con-
demned, scorned, disabled, diffamed, detracted, undervalued.
—Robert Burton, *The Anatomy of Melancholy*

She married young, just a sophomore in college. Two years ago, at thirty-nine, she had her fifth child.

"Every three and a half years, I dropped a foal—like a brood mare," is the way she puts it.

Now, Betty Praeger is a senior at the New School for Social Research in New York City and plans to continue for a master's degree in social work.

"Making a baby was my answer for everything. When my marriage seemed shaky, I'd have a baby. When I questioned my direction, I'd have a baby. When I was at loose ends, I'd have a baby. I've always been hyper, and while child raising is never easy, especially when they turn teenager on you, it is most demanding in the first two years. You don't have a chance to take a good look at yourself. As soon as one of mine was toilet-trained, I'd start feeling unnecessary and underused. So I'd get myself pregnant again. That would keep me occupied for another three years.

"Jack was tolerant. If that was what I wanted, he'd say, we could afford them. He's quite successful. Started making good money right out of college. And when you're young, it's hard to take middle age seriously. I knew the time would come when I couldn't have babies anymore, but it had no meaning for me. It was so far away!

"Then the time came, and I was panic-stricken. *Now* what? I felt cheated, which I recognize is an attitude of every in-between generation. Too old to do all those things the kids were doing at college in the sixties, too young to accept the values of my parents. I was more dependent on my children than they were on me, and on my husband, who reinforced the reliance, in a well-meaning, passive way. When the feminists started up, I became defensive. So maybe it wasn't such a marvelous thing to have the seven neatest sets of hospital corners on the block, but who were they to say that my entire life was a waste?

"I still have my doubts about the women's movement, but when that final shock came, I was at least able to recognize that they had created an environment in which women like me had the opportunity to take ourselves seriously. And here I am."

Betty Praeger is one of half a million older women enrolled in colleges across the country. In this case, "older" means "beyond normal college age," primarily between thirty and forty-five. Hundreds—perhaps thousands—of programs have been designed especially for these women in the last ten years. The Center for Continuing Education at Sarah Lawrence College is one.

"They come here wearing masks," says Martha Green, associate director of the center, "doing all the things you do when you're scared or insecure. One of the things they're looking for is to save their lives, but they won't say that. They want a chance to take a look at themselves as much as to find careers. Programs like this are one way to do both."

But the ultimate goal is a job?

"A *career*, not a job," says Green forcefully. "Women don't make the distinction, and they should. Fifty percent of the nation's women work—with banks, in hospitals, real-estate agencies. Nine out of ten will work outside the home at some time in their lives. But these are just jobs, and they move from one to another without purpose. Partly it's because they move around as their husbands' careers require. Mostly it's because it's not in their heads to have long-range plans. They've been conditioned to avoid responsibilities which might interfere with their family obligations."

Most life changers require, in Jay Guben's phrase, an emotional "support system." When lovers, homes, friends, hobbies, parents, children, and spouses aren't enough, college often fills out the formula. But each outreach requires new skills or the resurrection of old ones.

"I hadn't written a term paper in twenty years," Betty Praeger says. "The only times I went to the library were to pick up best-sellers to pass the time in the labor room. I was terrified of the first time I'd have to speak up in class, of all those bright young things who were hardened veterans of the learning process."

That's why she picked the New School, which has always specialized in the adult student, and why the Sarah Lawrence Center for Continuing Education segregates its matriculants from the college's regular undergraduates for at least the first four courses.

"A woman will say she wants to go back to school," Green says, "and she'll get flak from all around the dinner table. 'Why would you do that? You must be crazy!' Or she says she thinks she'd like to go back to work, and they say, 'What could you do?' Now, she already *believes* she can't do anything. She's *sure* of it. When she does it anyway, her husband doesn't understand why she has to study all weekend, or why she can't keep the house as neat as before, or why meals are a lot less interesting. The attitudes of husbands and children tend toward subtle negativism. 'Let her go off and do it if she must, as long as everything else stays as it was.' It takes a lot of working out. After a while, it smooths out in most families. They learn to accept the adjustments."

"It took me a semester to get past my own insecurities," says Praeger. "Then I started *loving* it. When I looked around for someone to blame for denying me this gratification for so many years, the scapegoats were right there. It was *him. Them.* All six of them. I saw Jack's tolerance as being patronizing—which it was, but just a little. I couldn't see why *I* had to wash out diapers all the time, why my role was cooking six variations on every meal because of the schedules or taste preferences of *these people!* My family became opponents. I've gotten past that. Now I'm dreading the day I go out to look for work. It'll start all over again."

"Almost everyone who goes through here," says Martha Green, "is a candidate for divorce."

Inevitable. The tiniest taste of liberation brings jarring recognition of what has been missed. For a woman who has defined herself exclusively as a housewife and mother, the shock is magnified. There is the sudden sense of time irretrievably lost, of creativity lain fallow. When combined with the termination of the childbearing capability, the distress is intensified. With half of her identity cut away, the woman *must* change or she will wither. Whatever her husband's misgivings about the course he has set for himself, he at least can continue on that path. His role is undiminished, even enhanced, by his wife's greater dependence.

"When I saw myself sliding into those endless rounds of alcoholic confessionals of barren women," Betty Praeger says, "I knew it was time to shake myself out of it. It was hard, terribly hard, and still is. But I *had* to start living for myself, not for and through others. To be selfish to the point where I can accept the possibility that my marriage won't survive."

Sometimes the interests and restlessness of husband and wife coincide. They are the fortunate few, and their relationships grow richer, stronger. Wine makers Janet and Carl Banholzer, innkeepers Jim and Audrey Patterson, rug dealers Anna and Steve Foster are among them. And they are exceptions. For others, the choices are harsh. Betty Praeger is prepared to make them. So must any woman unwilling to consign the second half of her life to torpor and aimlessness.

"Reading *The Doll's House* helps," says Karen Olsen, only half in jest.

Olsen, an insurance saleswoman, is also one of four people who brought to life the *Compleat Women's Classified.* The directory, revised annually, lists woman-owned businesses and women professionals in the New York metropolitan area. Included are doctors, dentists, locksmiths, attorneys, designers, photographers, retailers, carpenters, caterers, psychiatrists, mechanics, movers.

With her question-mark posture and hyphen of a mouth, Olsen appears physically destined to be a listener. As it happens, she is not glib, but she has intense convictions about women and their need to help each other.

"We didn't get involved with the directory just to make money," she says. "It's a lot easier to sell life insurance, believe me. No contest. But the directory is intended to stimulate economic activity for us and the people listed, and it has a wider purpose. There is still the social psychology that women's labor should be voluntary. I have very strong feelings about that. It's outdated. It's castrating. Essentially, it says that men are worth money and women are not. Women have an obligation to place a fair value on themselves and their work. Labor should be compensated, whoever does it.

"Some women have political reasons for searching out the services of women. Others feel more secure with unknown women working in their homes or private offices than with unknown men. I hadn't sought out women myself until one day when I was waiting to see a client. There was a bulletin board in her outer office covered with the business notices of woman-owned enterprises. I took down several of the names because I needed their services. It occurred to me that a great many women would prefer to deal with women—for any number of reasons —but that the effort to find them was too time-consuming. So, the directory."

Olsen and her three colleagues all had demanding jobs. It took two years of evening and weekend research to discover that there were at least 50,000 concerns and independent professionals who fit their criteria. Most of these were circularized, and 240 bought ads. With the publicity that followed publication, and their own renewed efforts, the four women expect to double or triple the listings in the next edition.

Not that they haven't encountered resistance. There were eligible advertisers who protested that they wanted business because they were good, not because they were women, as well as those who felt they had achieved their positions without regard to their sex. One order blank was returned to Olsen with "feminist pig" scrawled across it.

"There are women who are very successful and feel they did it themselves and that the only reason other women don't make it is because they behave in an unprofessional fashion and they don't like to associate with women because men are more fun," Olsen says in a rush, as if to acknowledge and dismiss in one sentence the fact that certain sisters are intransigent. "I even heard one distinguished businesswoman tell a dinner meeting of one hundred women there was no such thing as sex discrimination. She got torn apart, of course.

"At the age of twenty-one," Olsen admits, "I felt the same way. I was very proud of having mostly male friends and masculine interests. I was not interested in typing or nursing or being a stewardess or a schoolteacher. I looked upon 'women's interests' as childish and repugnant. I was almost ashamed of being a good cook.

"Eventually, though, I realized that by looking down on women, I was looking down on myself. Despite my interests, I was never going to be a man and didn't want to behave like a man. So I stopped. But I still see women who never grow out of this attitude. Some of them strive to become successful by following male models and really believe they did it themselves.

"Yet if it weren't for a bunch of radical women getting the vote in 1919 and the actions of successive feminist movements since then, no woman would be able to do more than type for a man to this day."

She marks her own reassessment from the time she entered the insurance business. Divorced, with a daughter, she wanted to make a place for herself in a profession less subject to unpredictable fluctuations in the economy than the real-estate business she had left. Further, she hoped to be able to tailor her services to the needs of a clientele she found for herself, instead of fitting customers to products.

"And I select whom I want as clients. I spend my time with people I choose—mostly women, because they're bypassed by other insurance people. Some men, too. My schedule is flexible, and I spend very little time in people's living rooms after dinner. The insurance industry hasn't actively sought women workers, but I haven't encountered too much resistance, either.

"I like this business, and I'm good at it."

It is a straightforward and accurate declaration. By the end of the conversation, Olsen has sold a policy to her interviewer.

Agents of change are invariably veterans of the process themselves. Martha Green of Sarah Lawrence worked in politics for several years before taking herself out of the job market to devote a decade to her children. When she was widowed, she found her way into educational administration and counseling. She agrees with Olsen about "volunteerism."

"Women must stop giving away their time," she says, "until men recognize the value of volunteer work and get involved themselves on a similar scale."

As an ideological point, that stance has merit. From the standpoint of a long-term housewife and volunteer who wants work, however, it is neither very useful nor entirely true.

Harriet Anderson's case is illustrative. In 1958, her marriage of twenty-four years disintegrated. To obtain the divorce, she agreed to waive alimony and to accept monthly support payments of only $175 for her six-year-old son. She surrendered their house without compensation. There were no savings, annuities, or investments. She possessed only a high-school diploma and had held no paying position at any time during the marriage, which she entered before her twentieth birthday. There was the Depression. The war. By the time her husband had regained a comfortable income following his military service, their two older children were ready for college. She never had the chance for a degree for herself. Now she was forty-three, with her mother and son as dependents, with no husband, no income, no job.

Over those years, however, Harriet Anderson was a compulsive volunteer. Den mother, League of Women Voters, library trustee, OPA, PTA, hospital worker, school board trustee . . . At one point, her husband tallied Harriet's simultaneous membership in fifty-three organizations, committees, boards, and subcommittees. Those activities even became a prime issue of dispute during litigation in family court.

Over all those hours of service, Harriet made friends, established contacts, and did favors. Now she started telephoning and interviewing and pushing. Before the divorce decree was final, she had found a position as director of volunteers for a nearby hospital. Two years ago, she was promoted to a fund-raising post. She never did go to college, as she had wanted, but she does lecture to graduate students majoring in public administration.

It is no surprise that Harriet Anderson disputes the arguments of Green and Olsen on "volunteerism," but primarily to assert that women who find themselves needing work must use whatever resources and backgrounds they have. Formal retraining is not always possible. Sometimes it isn't even necessary, as when converting a long-standing avocation to a livelihood—the antiques collector into dealer, the church-dinner cook into caterer, the amateur painter to greeting-card designer.

Nor is a full-length college program always required. Many of the older women at Sarah Lawrence and in similar curricula elsewhere want to develop personal priorities without regard to vocation, or intend further study in law, medicine, psychology, or social work. But others have not the time, funds, or inclination. Rosslyn Barnes, for one. She's listed in Karen Olsen's directory as a "cabinetmaker." While employed by a publishing firm in New York, she chanced to take an evening crafts course at the YWCA. That led to a government-sponsored crafts cooperative in New Jersey and, later, employment at two custom-furniture shops back in the city. Eventually, she opened her own business.

Or Stephanie Wallach. After Wells College, she found work as a film editor. When she had gathered enough experience, she went free-lance.

"That was fun," she says now, "but half my energy was devoted to getting new assignments, and it was pretty much a hand-to-mouth existence."

After four years of that, she signed up for flying lessons. Just for a lark.

"It was the most exciting thing I'd ever done. The day I soloed, my face was sore from grinning. I flew *all* the time. *Any* excuse to get up there. I took friends anywhere they wanted, as long as they'd help pay for gas, just so I could fly and build up hours for my license."

Stephanie started thinking about an airline career. But at twenty-six, she was afraid she was already over the hill. The airlines preferred to hire pilots who were under twenty-five—rarely did they want anyone over thirty—and she still had to accumulate 160 hours of flying time for her commercial rating. Not to mention the problems of being a woman. Even by 1976, the Airline Pilots Association was reporting that of their 37,000 members, only 11 were women. By then, Stephanie Wallach was one of them.

She was an unlikely candidate to spearhead the entry of women into what may be the most exclusively male profession of all. Typecasting would produce a stern-jawed, thick-shouldered creature, grimly resolute and given to sensible shoes and tailored suits. Wallach doesn't fit. Here, in the apartment she shares with her mother in a high-rise on Manhattan's Upper East Side, she perches cross-legged on the sofa. Striped skinny top. Trim boutique jeans. Shoulder-length auburn hair. A trace of lipstick. Slender to the edge of fragility. The finely traced features of a Saint Laurent mannequin. Friendly, ingenuous. Unwary, uncontrived. Determined, surely, but not pugnacious.

"It's no longer *that* big a deal," she says. "I'm not the first woman airline pilot, or even the second or third. And Braniff has been very good about it. They've never exploited me in a public-relations way. Emily Howell, who *was* the first, probably had more of that sort of thing to deal with. But not me."

Wallach is not a crusading feminist, but she does acknowledge a personal obligation to others of her sex. "It wouldn't be good if one of us quit, after being given this chance. *I* certainly won't. It would hurt other women. *Guys* don't leave airline jobs, and I'm not going to make

Second Chance

it tough on women who might follow me by doing so. Not that that's a problem. There is no better job in the world as far as I'm concerned. I never, *ever* thought there could be *anything* I could like this much."

It was expensive getting there. It takes most people only about fifty-five hours to qualify for the private pilot license. Although fees vary depending upon locale and equipment, they average $25 per hour for rental of the plane and $10 for the instructor. That's $1,000 or more, just for the first small step. Instrument, commercial, flight-instructor and multiengine ratings must then be won, in sequence. Finally, there is flight-engineer training. At one time, airlines hired people without it, then provided the necessary schooling. Now, there are too many pilots available. Stephanie had to pay for it herself—$5,000. Altogether, $10,000. The total is even higher now, and it's tacked onto the frequent airline requirement that pilots possess college degrees.

There are ways to reduce the bite. "I had a boyfriend who was moving to California from New York. By that time, I was really hating my editing job. It was just sitting at the Movieola or the rewinds, day in, day out. So I left and drove across country. When we got there, he introduced me to this super TWA pilot who showed me around and introduced me to people. I hung around the airport as much as I could, and started working as a dispatcher two or three days a week. That gave me an employee discount for use of the airplanes. The instructors were my friends, so, as often as not, they wouldn't charge me. When I'd picked up all the ratings except multiengine, I found a job at Van Nuys as an instructor. That meant I could earn money while I was accumulating flying time. In six months, I had the multiengine.

"I kept teaching, but you had to work awfully hard, and the money wasn't too good. I kept hearing rumors that this or the other airline was going to hire pilots—followed by announcements that Pan Am had just laid off six hundred pilots. I figured my only chance was to get the flight-engineer training, so I went to the United Airlines school in Denver. Had to pay for it myself. When I finished in late summer of '75, I started applying to all the airlines. Braniff hired me. It was fluky, I guess, but I hit them at a time they happened to need a few pilots. Other lines were still laying people off."

Flight engineers don't fly planes. They sit at a small desk just inside the door to the flight deck, or cockpit, before a panel of gauges positioned at a right angle to the nose. If all goes as she hopes, Stephanie will move up to the copilot's seat in four years, to the captain's in another eight. Captains draw $60,000 or more in salary, but a flight engineer doesn't break $20,000 for three years and is on probation for nearly half that time.

Stephanie doesn't care. The eventual financial rewards are not unimportant to her, but she is so pleased with her good fortune, she can think of little else.

"I'm so worried about missing a trip, about getting caught in traffic, that I'm always at the airport two or three hours ahead of time. Actually, you have to do something really awful to be dropped from employment, but I want to be perfect." She knocks wood. "All they really expect is that you show up on time, that you're sober, that you don't bounce checks. They're not concerned with the way you conduct your personal life, as long as you don't get a reputation as an inflight floozy."

Wallach bridles at the visitor's suggestion she is a "company person," uncritical of airline policy, despite employment practices which have long excluded women from the flight deck.

"That's not true. I just haven't found anything to be unhappy about."

Very well. How have the flight attendants—mostly women— treated her?

"They've been fabulous."

No resentments, envy?

"No, none. They've been really nice. Not a trace of hostility."

The pilots?

"The same. Really nice guys. We have good times. They let me do my job. They don't say, 'Let me do that, honey.' "

The passengers?

"Oh, once in a while one will ask me to hang up a coat or hold a baby's bottle, but that doesn't bother me. I've got the job, so I don't care."

Finally, she does allow mildly that "most pilots are a little Rotarian" and she doesn't care too much for her uniform cap and she wishes she could be assigned to a domicile city with more sunshine. That is the length and breadth of her dissatisfaction. "It's too bad everyone can't be as happy in their work as I am."

An increasing number of women concur. The Federal Aviation Agency reckons there are 34,780 female pilots in the country, clustered mostly in Southern and Western states where weather permits year-round flying time. One of them is Peggy Nauman, once a physical-education teacher, now the owner of a flying school in New Jersey. Another is helicopter pilot Sue Matheis, who stayed home to care for her four children before she became a traffic reporter for a Saint Louis radio station. A third is former stockbroker and concert pianist Lauretta Foy, currently demonstration pilot for the Bell Helicopter Company. Others are corporate and charter pilots, instructors and aircraft sales-people.

They are an exuberant and disparate breed, united only in their love for flying, as one can readily see by attending a meeting of a regional chapter of the Ninety-Nines, a women's pilot group founded by Amelia Earhart. There is one in or near most large population centers. The dominant personality at the Ninety-Nine local in West-chester County is Penny Amabile. She carries a business card which announces her expertise and availability as "aviatrix, barnstormer, balloonist, adventurer." Today she is wearing a T-shirt bearing Earhart's likeness.

"Amelia has mumps, Penny," says one of the twelve women at the table.

They roar with laughter. The male visitor timorously asks why they are all so enamored of flying.

"The exercise of power over a machine."

"Mastering the challenge."

"It's the second biggest kick there is."

"No, the first."

"Great way to keep from waxing the floor."

"Great way to meet men."

How can the cost of learning be reduced?

"Join a flying club. Every airport has one. You can usually rent a two-seater plane for fifteen dollars an hour, about ten dollars less than a flying school."

"Go to Florida. At schools there, you can fly eight or nine hours a day, sometimes at a discount from once-a-week individual lessons."

"Check nearby colleges. Some have programs which are much cheaper because they own the planes."

"Fly your friends to their vacation spots and have them pick up the rental, gas, and landing fees."

"Get a job with a flying school. Employee discounts."

"Find a man who owns a plane and thinks you're sexy."

How young can you start?

"As soon as you can reach the pedals. Solo at sixteen."

How old can you start?

"As long as you can *push* the pedals. Sixty, seventy."

Penny winds the meeting up. She and a friend are departing tonight on a fifty-hour round trip to Bangkok, and she wants to go up in her own plane before she leaves. Everyone at the table understands.

The point is, women eager to break free of confining life roles cannot permit themselves to be intimidated by expense, training, or preconceived ideas about what roles are suitable for them. Every woman who wants to rise above the typing pool and the nurses' counter faces the likelihood of being the "first ever" of something. It is one more roadblock women face.

A psychiatrist whose practice is composed largely of women has evolved a set of convictions about successful women. They are, she believes, people determined to develop whatever potential they possess. They are impatient and assertive and have trained themselves not to care if those qualities are interpreted as pushy or aggressive. They do not wait for others to pioneer. In fact, they rarely consider whether what they are doing is innovatory for their sex. They are markedly iconoclastic, often self-absorbed. They are not joiners, at least not until they have surpassed their initial goals. They pare their personal and social relationships to a manageable and meaningful few. They shepherd their energies, channeling them toward specific objectives. They do nothing out of boredom. They are always players, never cheerleaders.

The psychiatrist (who prefers anonymity) concedes that she has oversimplified. Everyone broods about mistakes and lost opportunities and wasted years. It is a question of degree—between brief interludes of regret and stultifying immobility. That is the difference between women who achieve and those who do not—or never begin. The former permit themselves little time for recrimination and doubt. And they are—or become—loners, at least in the sense that they are not inclined to reveal themselves to others. However unconsciously, friends reinforce weakness and uncertainty more often than they build esteem. ("Do you think that's wise? Do you know what you're getting into? Do you want to give up everything? Wait. Wait and see.") The woman who cuts loose keeps her own counsel.

Then why does the psychiatrist see *any* women she can define as successful?

"I *said* there were no absolutes," she snaps. "A woman who breaks the mold inevitably realizes stress. But therapy for an achiever is nearly always less difficult and of shorter duration than for a nonachiever."

As regards life change in general, she observes that "dramatic change in a man's life is usually associated with jumping from one career to another, normally after many years, and frequently in middle age. It is commonly judged a commendable act, even though men have *always* retained the greater flexibility for themselves. In an important way, women are making an adjustment of the same magnitude *whenever* they reject their traditionally subordinate role, whether that be at twenty-five or forty-five. They are *born* into that role, while men are given until adulthood to find one with which they are compatible."

Oversimplifying again?

"Perhaps. We are in the beginnings of an evening-out process. But I am speaking of internalized perceptions as much as of objective reality. We must confront ourselves, overcome the ideas of inferiority and worthlessness we took in with mother's milk. No one will do it for us."

It is not surprising, given those opinions, that the psychiatrist is skeptical of the value of encounter groups and consciousness-raising sessions. "Those things may be of limited help for some people, under the proper conditions and leadership," she says, "but I'm afraid they are more often masturbatory exercises composed of counterproductive faultfinding and blame assigning.

"Sensitivity groups and courses in personal interaction are a crutch. They can help to modify behavior patterns somewhat, or to codify them, which can be fun, but in the end they are essentially time wasters. A woman who feels the need for them will be wise to put them off until *after* she has taken the plunge into a new career. *Then,* they might help, when she has daily situations to confront. Taken before an effort has been made to secure a foothold in the real world, they are simply an excuse for procrastination, a luxury most women can't afford. They've lost too much time to the laundry and the kitchen."

Jorene Holaday is noteworthy in this context. She had neither the leisure nor the funds to dawdle over formal education or protracted self-examination. With six children, there were more pressing needs. She went from housewife to vice-president of a Wall Street brokerage house in less than five years—and insists she did nothing remarkable.

"It just happened," she says, a trifle bewildered that anyone might think her progress unusual. "We needed the money."

The wartime bride of a musician-turned-pilot, Holaday was pregnant with the first of four sons before she graduated from Douglas College in 1946. She didn't stop producing until the birth of her second daughter in 1960. By then, she had found a part-time job as an assistant to the minister of the Unitarian church in Plainfield, New Jersey. It was enjoyable, but it didn't pay well. While she was trying to decide whether to find full-time work—there was the prospect of four children in college at the same time—a friend asked if she would like to be a contestant on a quiz show called "Camouflage."

"I said, 'Why not?' and was very lucky, as it turned out. I won eight thousand dollars, an Oldsmobile station wagon, a motorcycle, a television, a freezer—all kinds of stuff. I'm good at games. Kind of a ridiculous thing to be good at, but there it is. Anyway, I had to keep going back to the studio to play the game, and I got to know the producers. One of the girls had to go back to California, and they asked if I'd like a job for the summer. The church was closed then, so I said I would. While I was there, they sold another show, 'Fractured Phrases.' They needed to build a staff for it and asked me if I'd like to stay on.

"That was it. I had to decide whether to take the plunge or go back to the church and probably stay on for another ten years. I took it. A big step, going into a full-time thing. Up until then, my identity was pretty much as a housewife and mother. This was something else entirely.

"Anyway, it went the way of most game shows. Lasted just a little over one season, and I was out of work. I couldn't very well go back to my old situation. I started looking for something else in television. One day while I was going to interviews in New York, I bumped into

Sam Strasbourger. We'd met at a party in Plainfield. After some conversation, he said I should come work for him at his brokerage house. I told him he had to be kidding, that I almost didn't get into college because I was so bad in math. He said that was all right, that he had machines that took care of that.

"I thanked him but said I wanted to stay in television. So I kept looking—everywhere—but couldn't find anything. When I went back to Sam a month later, he said he thought I'd show up."

It was 1966, and everyone on the Street was making money. Strasbourger paid for Jo's preparation for the exam to become a registered broker. She decided she'd do it by correspondence, using the three hours of daily commuting time to study. It took her only six months, the minimum time permitted.

"There was a lot to learn, and my college major in history and political science wasn't much help. But I pulled an A and a B."

Why did she do it?

"To keep the job, of course."

No—why did she decide to go for a career of *any* kind?

"For the money."

No other reasons?

"I love New York. Sam is a great guy to work for. And it's working with people, not figures. He travels a lot, and I take care of his accounts, as well as my own, when he's away. That's one of the reasons he hired me. Thinks I'm good on the telephone. Besides, I can't really imagine myself sitting around the house. No woman should settle for that."

In Jo's office, the phones are beginning to ring with greater insistency. The market has opened, and the Dow Jones is down from yesterday. She picks up the receiver. It is an anxious client from Detroit. Jo punches a query into the console in front of her. The viewing screen displays the action on the caller's stock. It's up. She reassures him. Not to worry. Give it another day or so.

Across the room, another woman is attending to a customer. She, too, is a vice-president. There are three women at Strasbourger, Pearson, Tulcin, Wolff, not counting secretaries. Jo's visitor wonders if that is unusual. There have been only two female floor brokers in the history of the New York Stock Exchange.

"I suppose it is," she answers. "I haven't thought about it, really."

Isn't she conscious of her sex in relation to her profession?

"Oh, some. Women aren't treated without prejudice anywhere. We have to be a lot more energetic to make it than men do. I just happened to be in the right place."

How does her husband deal with the fact that she brings in the larger share of their income?

"He's just glad," she says, laughing. "When you have a house and six children, you don't worry about where the money's coming from as long as it's there. Anyway, he's not the kind of person who would regard it as a threat to his masculinity."

Has her career altered their lives in any way?

"*Living* has altered our lives, not the job. Most of the couples we've hung around with have split up. We don't do as much entertaining as we used to because of that. *We* haven't changed, *they* did. If anything, we spend more time together than ever."

The increasing number of female workers in the labor force and of older women reentering it are two trends which are profoundly influenced by singlehood. One in every three adults is now unmarried, widowed, or divorced. Of all working women, 56.7 percent are single. Unmarried men and women soon will comprise two-fifths of all workers.

Popular surveys of the implications of this trend have focused on the titillating aspects of the single life-style, as might be expected. Print and broadcast accounts imply that the waking hours of singles are a bitter brew of intemperate sexuality, crushing loneliness, and mindless motion. They also give the impression, to marrieds, that the single person has an unfettered freedom of choice. However, these stereotypes hardly apply to single parents whose children are not yet fully grown.

For one subcategory of the singles group, however—those never-married and without dependents—it might seem that opportunities for change are unlimited. With no responsibilities beyond oneself, one can conceivably live anywhere, work anywhere, shuffle relationships. At will. In superficial comparison with a married couple with aging parents and children approaching college age, the picture is not inaccurate. A single person with a $20,000 salary can withstand a 50 percent cut in behalf of a more intriguing job, but a breadwinner for a family of four cannot. An unmarried man or woman need consult no one to move from Buffalo to Taos, to accept a different position, to buy a car or a condominium, to pick a wallpaper pattern, to decide what to have for dinner. No money is spent for day camp or orthodontia, no sleep is lost waiting for teenagers to get home, no hours sacrificed to PTA meetings or chauffeuring to pep rallies and birthday parties.

But an unmarried life changer living alone does not have a partner to bring in money during the thin spots of high expenditures and little income at the beginning of a new venture. A single's tax deductions and exemptions are fewer, and the IRS bite is 15 to 20 percent higher, on average. There is no one else to clean the apartment or shop or wash clothes or walk the dog or wait for repairmen. Illness is suffered alone, as are the breakdowns in heating systems and plumbing and appliances.

More critical, no one shares the single person's stake in the future. Friends cannot provide the same intensity of emotional support as a spouse and children. Without the pressure of a continuing responsibility to others of the household, drift and indecision and simple sloth loom as special enemies of the unpartnered single. Coupling as the primary form of social organization serves not only to protect the weak and to share work but to stimulate effort.

"After my divorce," says one childless architect, "I found I had enormous difficulty getting myself to take on the simplest tasks. To rake the leaves or fix a stuck window—or even get out of bed, for that matter. There was no presence around the place to give me pause as I reached for the gin for the fourth time in an evening. My ex-wife never told me I was drinking too much or getting too fat, but I could always feel those negative vibrations emanating from her, and that was enough to pull me up short. At the time, I always thought of it as a kind of subliminal nagging. Sometimes I even yelled at her for it when she hadn't said a thing. Now I find I have to look around to find horrible examples of lazy, unmotivated people to remind myself of what I could so easily become. When you answer to no one but yourself, you have to work three times as hard to overcome your own inertia. Mine enemy is me."

It comes to that. Woman, man, married, single. Anyone who would form a new life must conquer the cowardly sluggard within. There are scores of ways, and as many reasons to choose one.

12
On the Path

That we must pray to God, no man doubts: but, whether we should pray to saints in such cases, or whether they can do us any good, it may be lawfully controverted. . . . And as he that is invited to a feast eats what is set before him and looks for no other, enjoy that thou hast, and aske no more of God than what he thinks fit to bestow upon thee.
—Robert Burton, *The Anatomy of Melancholy*

"I was a profound atheist," says wine maker Carl Banholzer, "up until the time I became involved with farming. I'm still not a Christian, nor do I believe in a Higher Being, but I'm now very skeptical about atheism and agnosticism.

"When you work with the soil, you become very primitive as far as nature and the elements are concerned. Everything you work with causes an almost unbidden spiritualism.

"Think of the grapevine, for instance. It has any number of ways of reproducing itself. Seeds, of course. Birds pluck them from the ground, digest them, then expel them as feces, which then fertilize and sprout. Or, the vine regenerates itself by layering. A cane falls. The buds underneath throw rootlets, and a daughter plant grows. Then another. And if you cut a plant, it simply stops that angle of growth and branches off in another direction.

"It does these things to accomplish tasks. John Dewey referred to man as a 'problem-solving animal,' yet plants do the same thing. There is also a form of innate quality control. The quality of fruit relates directly to the quantity of fruit any given plant can produce. If you have a huge crop in a plant which can tolerate it, such as a Thompson Seedless, the quality of fruit is inevitably lower. Even the birds are then less interested in it than in the sweeter grapes of the shyest producer.

"Now I still do not propose that there is a grand design, nor that a plant has a soul. But that vine certainly has determination. At times, it almost seems to be thinking. It's as if that Thompson 'decides' that since its fruit isn't too good, it will produce a lot of it to compensate.

"All this has brought me to a kind of religious revelation. Not conclusions, but a recognition that something is there."

Of all the forces and events which bring people to these seemingly abrupt turnings—divorce, discontent, departure—none is more pervasive than that of spiritual discovery. Often, one merely accepts the existence of supernatural forces passively, without acknowledging that they have authority over one's behavior. For Carl Banholzer, it is a matter of tantalizing speculation, nothing more. Others surrender themselves. Potter Richard Bennett has a Buddhist shrine in his house. Innkeeper Tom Wells makes no important decisions without consulting his astrological charts. And Jim Russell simply defers to destiny.

In doing so, Russell conducts himself according to the teachings of an Indian guru, Kirpal Singh. To an outsider, the most visible manifestations of Singh's dictates are chastity and vegetarianism. And serenity.

"I have *no* influence over what will happen," says Jim, "although emotionally I might think I do from time to time. We are taught that we don't have control, to just let it flow. And it does. Who can say what will happen? People spend so much time planning their futures, making one life plan after another, each of which has to be amended and twisted around to meet unanticipated circumstances. Why bother? There's no sense to it.

"You see, we run this not as a real business but a pretend business. It is not real. It is a game. It is just what we are doing in this life. If it goes well, that's okay. If it doesn't, it doesn't."

Kirpal Singh isn't one of the major-league gurus. He has no more than 4,000 followers in the United States. They believe not that he is the Messiah but that he "reflects the presence of God," in the way of Christ and Buddha. God is Absolute Truth, and unknowable. He manifests Himself as spiritual light and sound, to which man is blind and deaf from birth. A master—Singh—can open man's inner ear and eye to see and hear this celestial light and sound. So say his disciples.

In order to do this, and to take the disciple "out of the body into higher spiritual universes" and into "perfect union with God," Singh insists that those desiring initiation "cultivate and practice (1) noninjury to others, (2) truthfulness, (3) chastity, (4) love for all, (5) selfless service." In addition, they are to follow "right conduct," a vegetarian diet, an honest livelihood, and to shun drugs and alcohol.

When it is suggested by a visitor that this code of conduct does not leave much in the way of diversion on the earthly plane, Jim turns earnest and voluble.

"Sex leads to violence, emotional instability, heavy interpersonal problems. In the outside society we are taught that people should have sex. That's absolute nonsense! Absurd! Psychologists will go to the lower forms of animals to buttress all of their conclusions—except for sex! They use mice, apes, chickens to prove everything else, but not that. And this is because only human beings engage in indiscriminate sex.

"Violence is so popular on television because it has a direct correlation to unchaste thought. The deodorant business would die if all human beings eschewed carnal desire, because the body stops smelling when one is chaste. All of this is pure, scientific fact! It is! Look around!"

What about procreation?

"We do not reject that. On the contrary. When sex is to have children, it is a mutual coupling to promote the race, and it's a beautiful thing, at that level. Otherwise, sex is an egotistical, self-gratifying act.

"As for the vegetarian aspect, there are reasons for that. Most people can't conceive of going through the day without having their slab of flesh. We don't need it. We don't make graveyards out of our bodies. It interferes with meditation.

"Meditation is to help us rise above body consciousness. Look, we are in a kind of department store. This physical plane is the subbasement where all the junk is stored, the garbage, the glitter. That's where we are now. We learn through meditation to take the escalator up to the first floor and then to take the elevator, rising through all five planes, all the way up. It works! We experience leaving the body. We're not our bodies, you know. I'm not a six-foot-five pile of decaying matter. Not that. It's not our intelligence, either. *Beyond* that. It's what the Christians call a soul. There are other words for it, but it's that force that makes the body alive. That's what leaves the body and becomes free—and permits us to know what others will only experience at death."

Kirpal Singh's soul is no longer in his body. In other words, he is dead. Russell says that Singh is still his teacher, but he is seeking that physical being in which the "power of God" now resides.

"Once you have made that bond with a guru, it's indestructible.

It follows you the rest of your life. It's there because the guru's astral form is here"—Russell points to his forehead—"at the third eye. He is constantly aware of what I am doing, and he advises me. Some gurus offer only peace of mind. I want more than that. I want a continual state of God-intoxication."

He has not yet reached that goal. "We work at it," he says. "We try. One step leads to another. But there are no saints here."

Asked if he would object to his business's being taken over by someone not "on the path," Russell professes to be unconcerned. Karma. Then he does not consider that followers of Singh are in any way superior people?

"Not at all. Everyone has a soul with a link to God. It's just that some people are in the position to be working to 'get back,' and others haven't yet reached that stage. It has to do with what happened in past lives. The fact that I follow Kirpal Singh does not make me different from you or anyone else. It's just that I have chosen to recognize that this earthly plane is beginning to lose its appeal. Now I can go on to the other things. It's like living in a slum and deciding to move to the country and breathe the fresh air. Many people are content to live in slums. You know that. The realization that they want to move comes through the grace of God. It just happens. No effort is required. Karma."

The signals to salvation came unbidden to these people. Whether they make themselves known as an unexpected awakening which instigates a fresh direction or as a recognition that grows with the insights born of the new life, these spiritual discoveries reinforce a characteristic universal in life changers—an acute sense of preordination. *Que será, será.*

Russell gives witness to this, as does Richard Bennett, who maintains a duly sanctified Buddhist shrine next to his dining room. "Maybe that's what keeps us going," says the phlegmatic potter, "but I don't try to figure anything out. I just work. I produce. I am loved, or I am hated. That's the way it is."

And Steve and Anna Foster. "You must be willing to surrender yourself," says Anna, "to put your faith and trust in God. When you let Jesus be the Lord of your life, you no longer have to carry the bondage of fear and sin. The Lord provides."

Terminology differs, but the essence is the same. Jim Russell and the Fosters use similar techniques to communicate with their respective versions of God. Prayer, meditation. Striving to understand His message and, once comprehending it, accepting. If there is a variation in method, it is that Russell uses an intermediary, while the Fosters speak directly to their deity.

"I take things to the Lord," says Steve, "and He gives me the answers. Whenever I try to direct my life myself, it's always . . ."

". . . a fiasco," says Anna.

"True. I am so *un*mechanically inclined," Steve continues. "I can't change a flat without problems."

"He gets mad."

"I have tantrums. I kick the tire like a little kid. When we moved in here, I *had* to do something about the plumbing. It was sixty years old. I had to change a faucet assembly in the kitchen. I sure dreaded that."

"And, you know, *I* was afraid. Steve has such a temper."

"So I went off, and I said, 'Lord, listen to me. I'm not going to change that faucet, you're going to. You get into my hands and zap those bolts and things off there.' I didn't have the proper tools, either, you see. And I said to Him, 'I expect you to do that, Lord. There's going to be no cursing, no nothing, because you're going to do it. You invented plumbing, Lord, you know all about it.'"

Anna is giggling.

"This is simple faith. I got my one wrench. It all came right off. I didn't even know what I was looking at. Everything fit. Put it all back together. Prayed it wouldn't leak. It didn't. Never seen anything like it. If it'd been me, I'd still be doing it. But it wasn't me. It was Him, and He's very good at plumbing."

This is related with good humor, dramatic gestures, much laughter, and total conviction. It reveals, as well, another commonality. The new-life people have shed anxiety over the unknown. God, Christ, nature, fate—whatever—will provide.

"Every time I come up with a big debt and I haven't a cent," says Richard Bennett, "bigger than shit, the money shows up. Always! I own this other house down the road. It needed refurbishing, a new plumbing system, other things, before I could charge enough rent to bring in any profit. But I just didn't have the money. Then one New Year's Eve, I went away. The oil man didn't make his delivery, and the pipes burst. The insurance came to fifteen thousand dollars, which took care of both the plumbing and the refurbishing. Never fails."

Foster tells comparable stories. "One day the IRS audited us," Steve is saying. "Told us we owed forty-five hundred dollars and to pay up by the next Monday, otherwise they'd close us up. Monday morning came, and I still didn't have any money. So I prayed. 'This is it, God. It's in your hands.' Then this guy walks into the shop. He looks at these three Kirmans I'd had a real long time and couldn't sell. I tell him I'll give them to him for fifty-three hundred, which is a twenty percent discount. He says if I agree to still another discount, he'll give me cash, and peels off forty-five one-hundred-dollar bills. I took it. Went right over to the IRS and slapped all those bucks on the guy's desk."

"We hang over these cliffs all the time," says Anna. "We live by that kind of miracle because we've given ourselves to God."

"The Scripture says, 'All things work for the good of those who love God.' He always turns them around. A tornado came through, leveled the town, hit our shop, put us out of business. 'Woe is me!' we said, because we still didn't have enough faith. But we rebuilt, with a better place than ever."

"God saw we needed a new building, but our partner at the time wouldn't agree to putting in the money. So God sent the tornado."

"Then, a month ago, the exterior needed to be painted again, but we didn't have the money. We needed a new sign, too. It is so funny, what always happens when Satan tries to get us. About three in the morning, Satan sends this nut. He's out of his tree, really drunk. Possessed, obviously. He throws firecrackers in the trees out in front of the store, sets them on fire. That catches on the awnings and the sign. I go down and see that and cry, 'Praise the Lord!' because I know what He's done. Two weeks, the insurance company pays up, and I get everything done over. Made that old buzzard Satan so *mad!* He's always trying stuff like that! God always comes through."

On a tour of the house, with its Tiffany windows and magnificent carpets, the visitor is compelled to observe that "God has terrific taste." Steve nods. "He ain't tacky," he says. Isn't there a certain smugness in the Fosters' protestations of divine guidance, a note of superiority in having discovered "truth" when so many others have not? Foster insists not, as did Russell.

"During those long drives in the other life," he says, "I got to know God on a one-to-one basis. I built up a relationship with Him, but I feel no evangelical responsibility. God doesn't need anybody, but He does anoint certain people for a ministry. He hasn't done that to me, except temporarily. Like now. The Lord said to me, 'Ye must witness to this man.' That's why I agreed to speak to you. I am confident the Holy Spirit will come upon you and give you the urge to hear. You have heard our testimony. You are witness to what God has done. If you refuse to listen, you're as blind as poor Joe." He nods in the direction of his friend, the Iranian Jew. "I do what God tells me. He uses different people for different things. If he says I must, I will be a street sweeper."

"We want everyone to know about the sweetness and faithfulness of God," Anna says. "I'm not a particularly nice person, and we're not very smart. We know where the credit for our success belongs. It doesn't matter, because our joy is in Him. Jesus cares in you. He loves."

It is not enough for these life changers that they have done what so many others long to do. They insist that others act. Whatever their religious persuasions—or lack of them—these people feel compelled to share the joys of their rejuvenations.

13
Prelude

All his youth was full of perplexity, danger, and misery, till
forty yeares were past; and then upon a sudden the sun of his
honour brake out, as through a cloud.
      —Robert Burton, *The Anatomy of Melancholy*

The preconditions of life change are manifold, their permutations unpredictable. There is no single age at which they are most likely to coalesce and rouse one to action. As these profiles attest, that can happen at any time, any stage. The impulse is forever there, underneath our protestations of satisfaction, our frustrations and our doubts.

We develop at uneven rates—the teenager who first menstruates years after her contemporaries, the man still spry at eighty, the woman discovering a flair for management in middle age, the young executive discontent with early success, the fat person suddenly svelte, the energetic person lethargic. In recent years, much has been made of "the seven stages" and "predictable crises" of life, with a special emphasis on the travails and trauma of midlife. "Midolescence," Fred McMorrow has called it, a variation on Russell Baker's earlier "middlescent." It is a "dangerous" period, according to McMorrow, a "time when a man recognizes and/or rejects the truth about himself, that for better or worse, he has reached the point at which he has achieved, if not all he thought he *would* achieve in life, just about all he ever *will.*" Or, as someone else described it: "The time when you are doing fewer and fewer things for the first time and more and more things for the last time." Then, too, traversing this slough of despond and scaling the crest of euphoria, one may find these to be "wonderful" years of discovery and rejuvenation—"prime time," in the words of Bernice and Morton Hunt.

None of this is inaccurate, but all of it is incomplete. Chartings of human behavior necessarily generalize, and their conclusions can be entertaining, illuminating, or devastating. They are rarely all three and are, therefore, imprecise.

This is not to infer that a realignment of sorts does not occur during the middle years. The "midlife crisis" does exist. It is as real as senility or adolescence, with its own broad commonalities. And just as old age resembles infancy in some ways, so middle age bears similarities to the postpubescent years. How each individual responds to these influences is another matter. For some, the crises of the various identifiable stages are mere hiccups. Their life commencements are negotiated without hesitation. Only the accidents of their lives are noticeable. For others, interruptions in life cycles are cataclysmic, resulting in the sociopathic teenager, the menopausal divorcée, the runaway husband.

Consider these sketches of a typical midlife man and woman. He experiences severe swings in mood, from brooding to beatific, introspective to gregarious. He dawdles, daydreams, imagines himself the victim of disease. He is frequently withdrawn, peevish, belligerent, consumed with doubt. He grieves over his loss of libido, his diminishing authority over his children, his falling hair, his failing strength. He is dismayed by the sexual initiatives of his wife, his reduced capacity for intimacy, his lack of interest in other people. When he is not slumped in his chair, chin on chest, sighing deeply and often, he is quarrelsome and self-pitying. Because of a hormonal imbalance attributable to the early climacteric, his skin erupts in blemishes, blotches, even pimples. He indulges in erotic fantasies, certain he couldn't appreciate them were they to materialize. He thinks his wife doesn't understand him, and he's right.

She, on the other hand, experiences a reawakening of sexual desire and a surge in aggressiveness. There seem to be attractive men all around her, and she does something about it, certainly flirting, often consummating. She is alarmed by a renewed growth of hair on her forearms, chin, and upper lip, the result of an instability in her androgen-estrogen balance. The imminent termination of her procreative powers depresses her—when she is not elated by the liberation that it implies. She is inclined to quote beer commercials ("You only go around once, so grab all the gusto you can") and grows desperate over actual or imagined restrictions on her enjoyment of her last good years. She persuades herself that she has more to offer than flesh, but frets about sagging buttocks and crinkly thighs. She thinks her husband doesn't care for her as much as he once did, and she's right.

Matching oneself or friends or relatives against such vignettes as these can be diverting for those so disposed. It's not unlike comparing events to the daily horoscope or completing Sunday supplement quizzes on "your compatibility quotient." There are bound to be parallels. A variation of the game, popular with social scientists, is to draw self-fulfilling comparisons within the tabulations they have made. In the eyes of psychologists, then, midlife becomes a "second adolescence." As evidence, they note that teenager and middle-ager share the characteristics of violent mood swings and skin eruptions, but they scrupulously ignore *un*shared traits, as in physical strength or sex drive. When the connective threads are spun too long, they break. The reader begins to concoct symptoms to fit the box assigned or remains merely confused. Why am I disturbed when I'm supposed to be placid? Why is he content when he's supposed to be distraught? What's wrong with him? With me?

We defy the classifiers. If marriage is most threatened at forty, what is to be made of the equally insidious "seven-year itch"? If a woman's midlife crisis ends with menopause, what is the effect of sterility imposed by illness or surgery at twenty-eight? If the onset of the climacteric promotes divorce, alcoholism, ennui, depression, weight gain, and sexual incompatibility, what reason is there to believe those occurrences are more virulent than at any other age? Any of thousands of unforeseeable events invalidate the social scientists' pronouncements.

There is comfort, perhaps, in the knowledge that our dysfunctions of the moment are not unique to us. But not much. That everyone else in the sophomore class has whiteheads doesn't make the affliction more endearing. Old people on park benches listen to descriptions of each others' ailments primarily so they will have an audience for a list of their own. The middle-ager is bracketed by two sets of dependents—children and parents—both of which are inclined to couch their demands in unyielding terms. Psychologists believe that Oedipal feelings reappear now and complicate relationships with aging parents. And the two sets of dependents insist upon both freedom of choice *and* unwavering loyalty.

Yes, middle age is a time of ambivalence, and at that growth-inhibiting juncture, one must take stock of his situation. The preliminary conclusions of an ongoing study by researchers at the University of Connecticut should be heartening. Even though middle-aged life changers risk their financial security and are apt to be branded "dropouts," those studied were found to have happier marriages than before and closer ties with their children. They felt they had gained direct control of their lives and their work. According to an article in the *Hartford Courant,* the seventy-five subjects included a systems analyst who became a kindergarten teacher, an engineer turned bookstore owner, a merchant now a college professor, and a data-processing manager who became a clergyman. Most retained "mainstream values" but "sought ways in which they could better control their destinies, see the results of their work, and help other people at the same time." The "highly ambitious men retained a drive to achieve success, but it was no longer just directed at making money."

There is time enough, and more. At forty, far more than half of one's adult life still lies ahead. And if ours is a youth-oriented society, it is controlled, nevertheless, by the middle-aged. They have the power and the money. Because they married younger than their parents and possessed the first effective means of birth control, their responsibilities in child rearing are over sooner. Their health is better. They have the financial resources and experience to cushion the first years after a life change, and two decades or more of business associates and contacts to whom to turn.

The moment for transformation does not pass with the forties, although many think it does. Look at Professor Stillman Drake, a financial expert until fifty-six. Or at Senator S. I. Hayakawa, a semanticist and academician until his first political campaign—at seventy. Or Kentucky Colonel Sanders, who didn't begin franchising his chicken until he was well past his sixty-fifth birthday.

There *is* no "last chance," no final termination of options. Just as forty can be—should be—regenerative, so, too, should the years beyond. Children are grown and gone. Expenses are down, but income is the same or higher. Large homes no longer need be maintained. The station wagon can be swapped for a long-deferred sports car. The only psyches to be contemplated and catered to are each others'. Blunders are permissible and tolerable, for personal responsibilities are fewer.

Nor is there one "best" time. Nearly half the people described in these pages made their changes in their twenties and early thirties. They didn't wait to build equity or seniority, and most will not settle permanently where they are. The opportunity is always with us, waiting. "Salute thyself," said the English poet George Herbert, "see what thy soul doth wear." The right moment is anytime.

There are signals, clues. Check these, at any age. Frequent sleepiness, even shortly after waking. A lack of concern about appearance and grooming. Extended daydreaming. Unusual irritability. Accumulations of uncompleted tasks, alibied by "no time." Ten extra pounds that won't go away. Listlessness. Two visits a week to the liquor store, when one used to be enough. Nothing to say to old friends except what was said last weekend. Love affairs more intense, less casual than intended. Inability to sleep through the night. Indigestion. Daily doses of Valium. Obsession with aging. A conviction that politics/golf/art/religion/weather/Super Bowls/air fares/the economy/inflation/gun control/abortion/capital punishment/World Series/flycasting/crime/schools/journalists/zoning/ecology not only cannot be improved or resolved but do not matter.

Do not grade from one to ten. Recognizing oneself in this roster can mean merely that one has reached a temporary plateau, a resting place before the next climb. But if these indicators of malaise fit all too snugly, if there are no other peaks in view, the right moment is now.

This is not to counsel that one immediately abandon one's mate or partner, embrace the occult, shed neckties, or buy a windmill. Gently, gently. Positive life change is precipitous only on the surface. A life built upon mainstream morality and the work ethic will founder on an existence of organic, vegetarian, communal funkiness that has been embarked upon in haste. Rather, test in small bites and construct atop known skills and insights. Quit smoking. Take a course. Sort options. Lose weight. Talk to people who aren't friends. Take a break from people who are. Keep a journal. And consider: is the change desired this year the same as the one two years back?

Ed Morrow worked for CARE in Ecuador, Algeria, and Guatemala. Barbara Morrow went with him. By 1969, their children were nearing school age, and they were starting to show foreign-service-brat symptoms. Ed and Barbara came home. He found employment with a mutual fund, she with a travel agency, among other things. He loathed commuting from Croton, she was dissatisfied with the noncareers available to her, and they were beginning to not like each other very much.

The solution, they thought, might lie in doing something together. Their "wouldn't-it-be-nice-to-[blank]" pillow talks increased. On a ferry trip to Martha's Vineyard, they decided that the first thing to do was detach themselves from the magnetic field of New York. They didn't know whether to pick a place and then choose a livelihood, or the other way around. A small-town newspaper, perhaps. A country store. A restaurant. Something like that.

Every weekend, they traveled the coast of New England, from Stamford to Seal Harbor. Then they struck inland—Vermont, New Hampshire. For nearly two years, they used every spare day to drive, to talk, to watch. The newspaper idea was discarded. Ed's parents were journalists, but Barbara carried a bad taste for the breed after prolonged exposure to foreign correspondents. The restaurant, too, was eliminated. Ed had never recovered from a summer as a pantryboy on a freighter. They narrowed to retailing. But what kind? Poring over juicily worded ads in the classifieds, they eliminated general stores and ice-cream parlors, ski shops and clothing emporia. A bookstore! That was it! Both were voracious readers, Barbara had been a librarian, and Ed had solid business experience.

They signed up for four days of dawn-to-dinner workshops offered by the American Booksellers Association. The faculty—booksellers all —was impressive. "There was nothing they wouldn't share with me," says Ed, "even though I was a potential competitor. And every one of them was positive and without reservation about the business. I was terribly impressed with their openness." Ed and Barbara were convinced. They started looking for New England towns that were without bookstores. There weren't many, at least in good market areas. So they walked into existing stores and asked the owners if they were prepared to sell. Barbara wanted an established place, but Ed hoped to start from scratch. They visited over 200 locations, and in the end bought a building in Manchester Center, Vermont.

It seemed a precarious choice, especially after all their research. The population of the town is 3,500, and there were already three bookstores, more than in many small cities. "It was pretty brazen of us," Ed supposes. "But our guess was that Manchester wasn't being properly served." One of the other places featured mass-market paperbacks exclusively; another, mostly old and used books. All kept abbreviated hours. Barbara and Ed put together a Fifth Avenue–style shop, with tapes of classical music in the background, imaginative displays of both hardcover and softbound releases, and a restful atmosphere that encourages browsing. They stay open seven days a week—until nine, some evenings—and they have made it known that they eagerly accept special orders, no matter how exotic.

The planning, talking, researching, driving, training, and evaluating paid off. By the end of their sixth week of operation, the weekly gross of the Northshire Bookstore exceeded what they had projected for two years away.

Theirs is the pattern to follow. Change should not be a complete break. Continuity should be preserved. Old skills are transferable, old talents renewable. There is only folly in taking on a life unrelated in any particular to the one departed. Bailey Alexander was a published writer for ten years before he left educational administration. Carl Banholzer had a weekend test farm long before he opened his vineyard. Tom Wells used his background as an interior designer in renovating his inn. Charlie Hepner needed three years of law school, but his eventual specialty—patents—was an extension of his previous career in engineering.

Nor should we become transfixed by the romantic conventionalities of life change—escape from the city, a potter's shed by a waterfall, black soil between the fingers. None will assure untrammeled contentment. It may be more appropriate to run in the direction opposite to the stampede. Ceramist Kitty Bright sold her farm in Pennsylvania and moved to a SoHo loft to produce terra-cotta planters. And for all the stockbrokers who fled to camera and easel and kitchen, there is Jo Holaday, delightedly ensconced on the thirty-sixth floor of 60 Broad Street, overlooking the Stock Exchange. She can't wait until her youngest is grown and she can move to a Manhattan co-op. A minority alternative, perhaps, but not one to be rejected out of hand, especially if the dissatisfaction lies less in career and location than in friendships. It is lonely on a mountaintop.

Much of the substance of this book has been devoted to livelihood. This is only reasonable, since most of us define ourselves, favorably or not, by our work. All the modish therapies and salves—est, TM, TA, orgone, rolfing, bioenergetics, Arica, Scientology, primal scream—will not alter that fact. Apart from true believers or the socially aggrieved, we respond to questions about ourselves by saying, "I sell collapsible tubes," or, "I'm a homemaker." Work is, in Desmond Morris's phrase, "stylized hunting," an activity in which we "make a killing" out in that "jungle" and "bring home the bacon." It is that basic—and so necessary that we are compelled to invest it with heroism or, failing that, with tortured dignity. An executive has "scratched and clawed his way to the top of his trade," and a garbage dump is a "sanitary landfill" serviced by "sanitation specialists."

Still, we must give ourselves permission to flee, and that goes beyond occupation. Whether it is that Faustian rite of passage at midlife or the early rejection of a path briefly followed, it is painful to reject our own past assumptions and those of people about whom we care. Those embarking on a life change are considered neurotic by psychologists, irresponsible and starry-eyed by friends and relatives. It is not fair, they are advised, to desert colleagues or to jeopardize the well-being of partners and dependents in pursuit of ephemeral gratification. The reactions may range from astonishment and threat to martyrdom and sympathy:

"Give it a little longer. Things are improving."

"How can you give up everything we've worked for?"

"You won't be able to come back."

"It's a phase. It happens. Ride it out."

"Pull yourself together."

"Don't expect me to be here waiting."

"Why not wait till the kids are through school?"

"What will you live on?"

"Come see me when you come to your senses. I'll keep it open as long as I can."

"It's your life, but. . . ."

"Gamble *everything*? On—on—*this*?"

"Boy, I wish I had your guts. I couldn't swing it. The house, the wife . . ."

"What have I done wrong? I've tried!"

"It's me, isn't it? Oh, don't bother. I know it is."

"You've thought this through, I suppose?"

"If it's really what you want."

In the end, the decision is made alone. There is no other way. It isn't fair to ask someone else to do it. There will always be excuses not to move: inflation, unemployment, recession, cash flow, debt, failure curves, interest rates, age, competition.

"Ginnie and I had a trouble-free marriage," says a onetime magazine editor. "About the only things we ever argued about were her housekeeping and my—ah—casual regard for money matters. I was forever overdrawn, in debt, couldn't get myself to balance the checkbook. This made her wild. I've never figured out why. She came from a well-to-do family, and I always made a pretty good salary. We never got in *real* difficulty. Once we agreed that I'd help around the house and she'd take over the family accounting, things improved even more.

"Then I hit her with this [a print shop in Colorado], and she thought I'd gone mad. After the first outburst, though, she managed to submerge her anxiety. I didn't realize until later just how hard it was for her. No regular check, the bills. She must have been frantic. But I had to get out of Chicago and the magazine business or I'd have fallen apart. She understood that and went along with my unilateral decision, not out of any sense of wifely duty but because she cared.

"Funny thing. Now *I* handle the budget—happily—and she hasn't had the tiniest quiver about where the money is coming from. The change not only did *not* destroy our marriage, it removed one of the major sources of irritation. The people we were before wouldn't have believed it. And when it came right down to the crunch, the admittedly selfish decision I made worked out well for *both* of us."

Overcoming the guilt of an action taken in self-interest is the key. But if we want change, we have a right to it. In the view of Yale psychologist Daniel J. Levinson, quoted in *Vogue*, this former magazine editor was "listening to recurrent themes in his life structure, to parts of himself that have been muted and neglected."

No one else can know that agenda. No one else can decide to make it happen.

14
Balance Sheet

Wisdom hath labour annexed to it, glory, envy; riches and cares, children and incumbrances, pleasure and diseases, rest and beggery, go together. In prosperity we are insolent and intolerable, in all fortunes foolish and miserable. In adversity, I wish for prosperity, and in prosperity, I am afraid of adversity. Where is no temptation?
—Robert Burton, *The Anatomy of Melancholy*

The decision to get out—of the city, the suburbs, the country, the corporation, the union, the rat race, commuting, housework, taxes —is the biggest step, but only the first. A great deal of winnowing, preparation, and soul plumbing remains. It must be determined *exactly* what will be lost, what will be gained, and how to get there.

First person: I want to leave. I have to!

Second person: Okay with me. Where are we going?

First person: I don't know! I just have to!

Second person: Take it easy. Let's talk it over.

Break it down. Make a list, if that helps. Perhaps the life to be left is a job with a large business organization. Is the problem that particular position with that specific firm, or the entire field? Is it having to work for other people, or having to supervise them? Is it the profession itself, or simply its site? Is it working for a salary, slow promotions, lack of a financial stake in the firm's success?

If enough of these problems apply to one's situation, the best solution may be to work out of the home, with a minimum of public contact.

Gained: Independence of movement. Personally controlled working hours. Full reward for individual wit and effort. Freedom to act on one's own ideas, without referring them to superiors or committees. Location of choice. Wardrobe of preference. An end to commuting.

Sacrificed: Communality of shared success and objectives. Assistance with tedious tasks. Use of computers, office machines, mailing service. Paid vacations. Group health plan. Regular paycheck.

One manager turned cabinetmaker came up with this tally of job-related expenses:

Item	This Year	Next Year
Commutation, train	$492	$000
Commutation, subway	$245	$000
Clothing	$450	$ 75
Laundry and dry cleaning	$250	$ 50
Lunches	$720	$260
Daily newspaper	$ 96	$ 48
Coffee breaks	$240	$ 50
Taxi	$100	$000
Totals	$2,593	$483

"It was incredible," the man says now. "Until I sat down and really looked at it, I had no idea how much it was costing me to hold that job. And in nondeductible expenses! At that time, the railroad was charging forty-one bucks for a ticket good for a month, and they had it rigged so you couldn't buy a cheaper ticket if you were going to be away for a week or two. That meant twelve tickets a year, despite vacation times or out-of-town business trips. God knows what they're charging now. I've been in the city exactly once since then, and I drove. The subway charges more now, too.

"Then there were clothes. I had to buy two new suits a year, since we were expected not to wear the same suit twice in any one week. That meant five suits for the summer, five for the winter, each of them lasting about four years apiece, the way they make them now. Then dress shoes, ties, shirts, topcoats. My wife worked, so everything went out to the cleaners. Two-fifty to clean and press a suit! Every time! I'm not all that fastidious, but that was still at least five bucks a week. Now I just throw my jeans into the washer. Haven't worn a suit in over a year.

"And lunches. I wasn't one for those three-course, three-martini spreads. But a hamburger, fries, and a Coke in a greasy spoon can't be had for less than two-fifty, plus tax and tip. I can have the same thing in my own kitchen for a buck, tops. When I got coffee from the cart at the office, it was thirty-five cents a pop and two bits for a jelly roll. Look, it adds up! Even the newspaper. We had it delivered at home, but my wife took it with her, so I had to pick up another copy at the station. Or taxis. Once or twice a week, I'd be so beat I couldn't walk home, or it rained or snowed. Figure it out. I was blowing over two thousand bucks a year for the privilege of busting my chops so someone else could clip coupons."

There are other financial considerations. The obligatory payroll deduction for life insurance that an unmarried person never wanted in the first place, or forced contributions to a pension plan that an individual might prefer to invest in other ways. Even office gift giving is an income reducer. For birthdays, anniversaries, departures, births, funerals, engagements, showers, marriages, and Christmas parties, staff members of even moderate-size organizations can be assessed "voluntary" contributions of $2 a week or more.

More important than the financial considerations is the emotional equation. Some questions to ask:

> In what ways will associations with partners and dependents be altered?
>
> How important is the exercise of authority over others, and in what ways will it be diminished or magnified by the change contemplated?
>
> Do work-related separations place strains on relationships, or do they, in fact, provide necessary distance?
>
> Can spouse or friends take up the slack in the verbal support and sense of common purpose formerly provided by subordinates and colleagues?
>
> Do spouse, partner, or dependents derive substantial satisfaction from status and security provided by the perquisites of the present occupation, and how will they deal with that loss?
>
> Is daily interaction with large numbers of people essential to sense of purpose or well-being?

And vice versa. And so forth. Hazard is normal in life change, and that which is unanticipated or unmeasurable is ample. All else must be weighed, balanced. Barbara Lord agreed, with reservations, when husband Charles said he wanted to become a schoolmaster in Toledo. But with a graduate degree in art history and a compulsion to participate in cultural and social causes, she was leery of leaving America's only world city. Once in Ohio, her fears seemed confirmed. She was "desperately unhappy," according to one friend. There was nothing for her there. She thought herself marooned in a mid-American desert of polyester pantsuits, PTA meetings, and faculty teas.

"She is a woman who's used to being active," Charles says. "The Metropolitan Museum, consumer groups . . . And here she was in a house she never would have picked for herself, servantless. She couldn't imagine what she was going to do from nine to five, at least in terms of something meaningful to her. She'd hoped to work for the local museum, but they were having the same money problems as everyone else. So here she was, stuck in Toledo for two to five years while I went blissfully about my new career.

"What she did was put together some things on a volunteer basis, for which she is now getting paid. She's teaching history of art in our upper-division classes and is working to integrate the study of art in courses throughout the school. She spends hours with the kids involved in medieval history or in French, among other subjects, weaving art with literature and culture and politics. It's a unique concept, and it's all hers. She created it and followed through. But if she hadn't had those qualifications or that energy or determination, she'd have been lost. And so, in the end, would I."

Obviously, change cannot be undertaken in a vacuum. One must anticipate its ramifications for those drawn along in its wake. But the possibility that one's marriage may dissolve should not of itself squelch the impulse. Our first obligation is to ourselves, and we best serve others when we make known our nonnegotiable needs. If those requirements are formulated and expressed with maturity, yet still do not mesh with those of the partner, a temporary compromise merely postpones the inevitable conflict. When the original contract cannot bear the modifications mandated by growth, better to be done with it.

Initial misgivings prove groundless, as often as not. The Pattersons wondered if they could tolerate the pervasive togetherness of a twenty-four-hour enterprise. They soon found the reverse, that their division of duties—Jim out front, Audrey in the kitchen—kept them apart more often than they liked. Some worry that age has sapped their strength and enthusiasm but discover that a new career, location, or realignment of responsibilities refreshes them. And the Morrows of Manchester Center discovered that the constant companionship of running a bookstore rejuvenated their marriage instead of exacerbating its tensions, as they feared it might.

Setbacks do occur—Jim Brown's shattered leg, Richard Bennett's collapsed lung, Jim Martin's kidney, Steve Foster's tornado—but that should not be an excuse to defer the venture. An experience that falls short of prior expectation, when due to misfortune or accident, is not a failure. It brings a richness that could not have happened without the attempt.

When contemplating a life change, one is often bewildered by the countless options. For many, the choice reveals itself through chance encounters or through a pastime that burgeons into a vocation. Others, however, must search for a direction, beginning with little more than the desire for "a business of my own."

The quest sometimes leads to dead ends. Chilling examples are the business expositions which make regular appearances in convention halls of every city in the country. They are, almost without exception, celebrations of the banal.

The recent series of Be Your Own Boss exhibitions, for instance. Drawn by that beguiling theme and undeterred by a stiff admission fee, thousands push through the doors. They find booths manned by fast talkers promoting franchises for: Mr. Whippy Soft Ice Cream, computer portraits, plastic laminate engraving, Pachinko, Goom-Bah Joe's Italian Ice, Subway Famous Giant Foot-Long Sandwiches (thirty-nine units in operation), swimming-pool alarm systems (which aren't working), cologne-spray dispensing machines, Mary Belle Restaurants ("Home of the Original Belgian Waffle"), mobile disotech *(sic)* and light shows, baby-shoe bronzing, Fotomats, Holiday Rent-a-Car, Lee Myles transmission-repair stations, dance studios, upholstery and carpet steam cleaners, Jerry Lewis movie houses, travel agencies, Pied Piper food vendors, and greeting cards with phonograph record inserts featuring the voice of Dennis Day. Visitors are assured "exclusive protected areas," "untouched fields," "working capital," "generous financing terms," and "unexcelled advertising programs"—all for investments of as little as $30,000 and even "nothing at all, ever."

It is, in short, a display certain to curdle the ambition of anyone seeking independence. Beyond that, the solvency of such franchised vendors is no more assured, despite contrary claims, than that of the solitary entrepreneur. The appeal of franchising lies, presumably, in the consumer's instant recognition of a standardized product, aided by regional or national advertising and the hip-pocket supervision of the parent organization. Decisions on site, architectural style, territory, marketing technique, personnel policy, and pricing are taken out of the hands of the unit manager—along with taste, style, initiative, and individual judgment. Under the best of circumstances, the franchisee may be subjected to indoctrination at a "Hamburger University" or "College of Tacos," complete with hymns to alma mater. Under the worst, the innocent find themselves caught up in "pyramiding," where all they do is collect licensing fees.

Those undissuaded can obtain information and counseling from the International Franchise Association in Washington, D.C., among several sources. Prudent individualists will set aside franchising as a concept, at least until they can be the sellers, not the buyers. They can commence by jotting down their hobbies, skills, interests, deleting nothing as too remote or farfetched. The list will be longer than expected, especially if two people are involved. These notations will, in turn, suggest possible enterprises.

Another approach, if that one proves unproductive, is to note all one's dissatisfactions with the products and services of area retailers, with suggestions on how they might be improved. Or, list those commercial ministrations which are absent from the community but might prove desirable. One can often get good ideas by scrutinizing innovative retail operations that have cropped up recently in various parts of the country. San Francisco's Ghiardelli Square, or Toronto's Yorkville Avenue, or the revamped Boston market and waterfront, or Newmarket in Philadelphia, or the more recent recyclings of factories and warehouses in Minneapolis and Denver. Concentrate on offbeat, bohemian sections of the cities, such as Old Town in Chicago and SoHo in New York, for trends are more readily visible there than they are on Michigan and Fifth avenues.

Then, too, a vacation might bring the germ of an idea. An Austrian-style coffee shop, maybe. Glass-topped tables, bowls of fresh flowers, newspapers, and European magazines scattered about. No meals, just plump croissants, crumbly brioches, espresso, hot chocolate. High tea with finger sandwiches and light salads in late afternoon. Poetry readings on Sunday afternoons. A wheezing copper-and-brass coffee machine in the corner.

Or, a wine-and-cheese shop. Box lunches of Gouda and Camembert and Stilton, with chunks of warm bread, grapes, a pear, a carafe of Chablis. A few tables under awnings on the sidewalk. Toothpicked sample slivers of Port Salut and Cheddar on a tray by the cash register. A line of cutting boards and cheese knives. Christmas packages. Party trays for nearby offices. Two or three booths along one wall for informal dinners or after-theater snacks of fondue and soufflé.

The perfect movie theater. Excellent prints of classics and kitsch, and fresh-popped corn (not popcorn lying there from yesterday's feature). No collections at intermission for any charitable cause, ever. Surprise bonus showings of *Red River* and *The Big Country* between the Clint Eastwoods, and mystery midnight features selected from the permanent film library. Never a movie the owner doesn't like himself, and no velvet ropes at the entrance. Twice-weekly program changes, and Louis Trintignant and Oscar-loser festivals.

A bookstore with Saturday coffee hours and reading nooks and Pachabel on the hi-fi.

A cooking school. A crafts store, with lessons. Custom-designed hot-air balloons. A natural-energy power systems factory. A blacksmith shop. A "we-buy-and-do-almost-anything" service. A weaving center, with looms, supplies, and evening classes. Customized, permanent light shows for the home.

Clip the classified sections from the hip/tony magazines—*Saturday Review, New West, New York*—and "business opportunities" from the newspaper. After a month or two, sit down and go over them, one by one. Make more lists.

Reverse possibilities. A country inn in the city, for example. Perhaps it's time to reconsider occupations traditionally held by one sex or race. For instance, women and blacks have stayed away from work in better-quality restaurants not only because of past discrimination but because cooking for a living reinforced distasteful stereotypes.

Intensive research begins once the possibilities have been narrowed down to one or two. In the *Handbook of Associations* at the library, there are organizations and clubs devoted to every interest. Write them for information about membership requirements and benefits. Often they conduct workshops and seminars and keep lists of schools offering training in the field. They may provide leads to consultants and regional affinity groups as well as a variety of financing and lower-cost insurance plans. Don't be reticent. Pester anyone and everyone who might drop useful scraps of advice or know others who can. Most people are pleased to talk about their trades, for they so rarely get the chance.

If formal education seems necessary, don't shy away from it—but keep it to a minimum. Many colleges have reentry or reorientation curricula. Even when they don't, remember that the fastest-growing college student group is the middle-aged. And given the lackadaisical entrance standards of recent years, there is no good reason for older students to be apprehensive that their younger classmates will be too advanced for them to keep up. (There are side benefits. After twenty-three years in the food-service industry, Mal Dixon decided he wanted to be an artist. He enrolled at Fairleigh Dickinson University. While he was at it, he played out another fantasy—he went out for the football team. For four seasons, until he graduated at forty-seven, he was FDU's kicking specialist.)

The guidance counselor at the nearby high school may be willing, even flattered, to help. A comprehensive guidebook to community colleges and technical schools is the *Blue Book of Occupational Education*—among dozens of others.

Much of formal education is repetitious, however, and off the point. It can be agreeable to stroll through the liberal arts, especially at an age when it is not mandatory, but few life changers can afford the expenditure. The traditional credentials for a particular occupation can turn out to be superfluous. Charlie Hepner *had* to go to law school, but Charles Lord and Stillman Drake found employment in education without a teaching course or a master's degree between them. Michael Kritch didn't sign up for a driving school; he just climbed into the cab of his truck and turned the key. There are four- and five-year curricula in nursing and prosthetics and filmmaking and journalism and hundreds of other careers—and thousands working in each who have degrees from two-year colleges or who went no farther than high school. Colleges, schools, and institutes are businesses, and they perpetuate themselves. What was "optional" last year is "required" now. Declarations that *any* form of training is "essential" must be viewed with skepticism, especially when mouthed by representatives of an educational enterprise. A few hours' conversation with a handful of people in a chosen field may be enough. Another way to learn a business is to farm out as a salaried employee or apprentice, or perhaps find a short-term intern program.

When the search has gone this far, other gears must be shifted, too. Excess material and emotional baggage should be pared. Strip to essential possessions and obligations. Draw back from friendships grown routine or humdrum. From an enforced distance, they may prove profitless, as when one becomes just a wailing wall for the rehashing of another's marital or psychic vicissitudes, or when there is simply nothing more to say to one another. Consolidate debt. Eliminate it, if possible. Reexamine life, house, accident, medical, theft, fire insurance. Take to attics, closets, cabinets, and bookshelves with a ruthless hand. Sell whatever can be sold. Give away nothing unless there is no other way to get rid of it. Every cent of profit realized—by selling the sun-porch sofa and the last child's crib to the secondhand store, the forgotten brooches and necklaces to the jeweler—might represent the difference between defeat and triumph when the new life is begun. At this stage, the life changer's best charity is himself.

"When you've lived for years on a regular salary," one warns, "you tend to be cavalier in disposing of the refuse of a housecleaning. You give everything to Goodwill or the Salvation Army, just to be done with it. There are people around here who furnish their houses with the things the rest of us put out on the curb for the garbage men.

"But when you're about to cut loose, and you're underfinanced, as I was, it's plain dumb to throw away your assets. It may sound insignificant or even petty, but I picked up nearly three hundred dollars for a collection of junk I once would have thrown away without a thought. And that, my friend, is a month's groceries. It can get just that close, later on."

Reconsider all possessions: boats, second homes, cameras, cars or recreational vehicles, gun and coin collections, paintings and prints, power tools, appliances, television and radio sets, furs, flatware and extra place settings. Money is the primary issue here, but not the only one. All the items gathered in a lifetime of acquisition erode flexibility. The lighter the load, the better. Examine consuming habits, too. It's as good a time as any to:

Swap the overpriced unisex hairstylist for the corner barber.
Take out a library card.
Decide to keep the car another year.
Determine whether the kids are really enjoying the karate classes,
    horseback lessons, and piano instruction.
Close down the charge accounts.

Say good-bye to a favorite bartender.
Pull the plug on the answering service.
Let the golf membership lapse.
Reduce home entertaining and dining out.
Shift from vintage Bordeaux to jug wines.
Drop the record club and the fruit-of-the-month.
Start the diet.
Brown-bag it.
Use the bus.
Shop the thrift stores.
Quit Friday night poker or Wednesday bridge.
Make do with last summer's bathing suit.

We take on impedimenta of diversion and convenience almost without thinking and permit them to complicate our days. Some of them can be eliminated. The next time the dishwasher breaks down, leave it. See if the initial wrench of its loss doesn't fade after a week or two. And the dryer, the air conditioner, the blender . . .

Alterations in life-style are more difficult to predict, but try. The ex-office manager may have to write, type, and mail his or her own letters, make travel arrangements, and fend off unwanted callers without assistance. Partners may have to adjust daily work patterns, accommodate to the constant presence of the husband or wife. When a geographical move is contemplated, children may find schools not so well equipped but with longer summer vacations and beaches or skiing nearby.

Not that there will be much time to brood. Of the qualities nearly all life changers share, hard work is paramount, although most quibble with the word. " 'Work,' " says one, "is something you do for someone else. We just 'play' a lot longer than we used to. Every day, from the time we get up until we go to bed." Additionally, most emphasize that while they distance themselves from old friends and colleagues, they retain ties. "This may be a bust. We've given ourselves two years. If it doesn't pan out, I may want to go back. I don't put down my old profession, and I didn't stomp out in a rage when I left. I still have dinner with my former boss every now and then. He even throws me some business once in a while." And adaptibility: "We're very pleased. But we don't allege that this is the end. There are other things we might want to try." And limited objectives: "We have been successful beyond reasonable expectation. We could start churning and expanding, I suppose, but then we'd lose touch. We want to keep control. Money is great, but autonomy is better."

15
Financing

Thou hast enough: He that is wet in a bath, can be no more
wet if he be flung into the ocean itself; and if thou hadst all
the world, or a solid masse of gold as big as the world, thou
canst not have more than enough . . . thou art not poor, but
rich.

—Robert Burton, *The Anatomy of Melancholy*

No one who has worked for a salary all his or her life can fully appreciate the impact of leaving corporate or institutional employment until those bonds are finally severed. For all the psychic injury large organizations can inflict, their protection of their employees' material well-being is rarely appreciated. Naturally enough, employees care most about what is in the pay envelope, and have trouble recalling the reason, purpose, and amounts of deductions. This is true even of those managers who negotiate and administer fringe benefits, at least before they tally the outlays they themselves must make to replace previous coverage.

Even the most parsimonious of employers match their workers' Social Security levies and contribute to governmental unemployment funds. They must. Beyond that, most provide membership in group health and medical plans, life insurance, and pension funds. Put aside for the moment what the loss of such extras as a company car, or profit sharing, or club memberships will mean, as those are not so common. Most wage earners have only a vague notion of how much they pay for what coverage. The first step is to examine these items carefully, preferably in consultation with an accountant, and *then* an insurance agent.

Health and Medical Insurance. The former employer probably provided both. Even if the firm did not make any monetary contribution, it made the plan available, at a cost substantially less than to an individual. Most insurance companies abhor the necessity of offering single-person and family medical coverage. With group plans, they can spread their risk; with individual policies, they cannot. To discourage customers, they charge 50 to 80 percent *more* for individuals than for the same coverage under their own group plans. For maternity and dental coverage, their premiums for individuals are tantamount to extortion.

There is a way out. There are a few insurers who have created plans which, in effect, *provide group-plan rates to self-employed individuals.* It comes down to a question of definition, really. These plans offer protection to groups of employ*ers* assembled by the insurers, on the same basis as they would to large organizations. This makes it possible for small businesses to give their employees the same coverage at the same rates as large concerns. Benny's Luncheonette is thus placed on equal footing with General Motors. The insurance company reduces its risk, and the employee at the corner garage pays lower premiums.

Now follow this. Those small businesses are often wholly owned by one person. They are, therefore, "sole proprietorships." Presumably, he or she has employees to be covered, but if the insurer specifies no minimum number, that "sole proprietor" is eligible, anyway. All alone. It isn't stretching things, therefore, to confer that label on *any* self-employed person. *Voilà!* That fledgling novelist, that solitary bookbinder, that single truck driver, that painter, that potter—and their dependents—all are eligible! As "sole proprietors"! The result is the same protection at the same cost as professors in the state university or tool pushers at Exxon.

There are some factors to keep in mind when seeking out these plans. They are not well publicized and are rarely made available by the well-known companies. Typically, they require that the individual be associated with a conventional hospital-surgical plan (such as Blue Cross), and they then cover doctor and hospital bills *beyond* that basic protection. The result is the same. The combined premiums paid each year are roughly equivalent to ordinary group plans, and the protection is as comprehensive. Sometimes, more so. In one, even prescription drugs are covered—beyond a relatively low deductible amount—a feature rarely included in institutional plans.

Alternative paths to explore, if this one proves unprofitable, are professional and special-interest organizations. There is an association to serve every occupation, no matter how esoteric. Many offer group medical programs. Any new-lifer should check this out, for apart from conferences and newsletters, these organizations frequently provide lower-cost life insurance, travel discounts, investment and buying plans, and professional services. Check the *Association Handbook* at the library. It's revised annually and lists addresses, telephone numbers, membership totals, purposes.

Pension Plans. Some may be continued after a person's departure from salaried employment. In most versions, the employer matches the employee's contribution in equal, greater, or lesser sums. In others, the organization makes the total payment. Whichever, it must be determined how much the self-employed participant is expected to pay in his or her new situation. If the pension plan cannot be retained, there are several options. First, of course, is whether it is even needed. For those employed a long time, accumulated payments may already be sufficient to ensure subsistence or even comfort in old age, making a new plan unnecessary or at least deferrable until the new career is on a firmer footing. Second, check those professional organizations. Third, look into the Keogh savings plans and individual retirement accounts (IRAs), which have the same tax-saving features as most company pension plans. (Provisions are subject to frequent modification. At this writing, the Keogh plan permits deductible annual savings of up to $7,500. In both cases, taxes are put off until retirement, when the bite is likely to be smaller, due to reduced income.) Keogh and IRA plans are available through banks. Fourth, examine private annuity programs. Some insurance companies have investment annuity programs which serve a similar goal. After a substantial minimum investment—usually about $10,000—smaller annual additions are made. Taxes are not due on earnings until the investor begins collecting them, which can be thirty years or more in the future, if desired.

Life Insurance. The arguments *against* owning life insurance aren't going to be rehashed here. However, if a person has resigned from an organization in which it was mandatory, whether the employee and/or the company paid the premiums, he should review the issue once more. Policies tend to be tossed in drawers and forgotten. Perhaps former beneficiaries have passed away or are no longer dependent on the policyholder. (A dinner-table game: "Quick! Who is listed as your beneficiary? Your executor?") Perhaps the policyholder is now divorced or widowed. Assuming provision for burial is made, there is no real reason for a single person without dependents to carry life insurance. There are solid reasons to believe that a sound investment program is preferable to life insurance. And again, a prospective life changer may conclude that this expense can be set aside temporarily.

Taxes. This is the big one. As between young and old, married and single, there are both penalties and advantages to self-employment. It is disagreeable for any wage earner to hand over statements of tax liability the fifteenth of every April, but it is much more frustrating and time-consuming for the person working for himself. At least, someone else must deduct the approximate requisite amounts when one works for a company. It isn't necessary to try to save enough through the year or take out a loan every spring. The independent, though, must serve as unpaid tax collector (just as he or she must now justify expense accounts to Uncle Sam directly instead of merely passing swindle sheets over to the accounting department to let it face the steely-eyed representatives of the IRS).

One relatively minor item is that the Social Security assessment increases for the newly self-employed. In early 1975, the difference was 5.8 percent for salaried workers, 7.8 percent for the self-employed. When staff is involved, the proprietor has to match each person's contribution as well.

More annoying, perhaps, is the need to keep easily decipherable, clearly annotated receipts for every potentially deductible expense. Each receipt should include the name of the seller and the purchaser, an exact description of the item or service exchanged, the price, the date of the transaction, *and* the notation that payment was made. Should all that sound stunningly obvious, ask for receipts without these instructions for the next five purchases and see how complete or legible they are. While that isn't too tedious for big buys, it is for boxes of carbon paper or a telephone installation or rubber bands or subscriptions to professional magazines. But even modest expenditures can mount up quickly and are not to be ignored. Bailey Alexander claims to have run up $149.26 of business purchases in his first month as a full-time writer, with no one expenditure greater than for a copy of *Roget's Thesaurus.*

This precision in record keeping has a worthwhile purpose. Apart from budgeting and projections, those scraps of paper are the basis of tax deduction claims. Again, an obvious point. Nevertheless, those who have never worked for themselves have little real understanding of what this can mean. For, properly run, *a personally owned business is the most effective tax shelter of all.*

It is startling how imprecisely this is understood. Even a bright, sophisticated college graduate has been known to ask, "What difference can it really make? All those things had to be bought, anyway."

Take two couples. They both live in the same town. One couple works for the same school system. Between them, they earn $25,000 gross a year. The other pair owns and runs an inn. They take out a joint salary of $25,000. For the sake of illustration, neither couple has dependents, and their tastes and needs are essentially the same. Couple A can take two personal deductions, plus medical expenses, gifts to charity, the interest payments on their house—and that's about it. Couple B can deduct all those things, but also payments of principal on the mortgage, food consumed on the premises, meals and lodging at other inns and restaurants, their car, heating oil, gasoline, automobile maintenance, building repair, even those clothes worn while they perform their duties.

Couple A pays about $3,300 in federal taxes (at current levels), couple B about $1,000 (and only if they're rather conservative in their claims).

Business-related deductions are judgment calls, of course. Is the car used *primarily* for business? Exclusively? Half and half? What portion of the wardrobe is provably worn for business purposes? Are living quarters actually part of the commercial premises, or separate? There can be no certainty, only good guesses and bad guesses. This is why a capable accountant is invaluable. Few owners of small businesses have the necessary experience with tax agencies to know which deductions are normally accepted, which are not, and what are the relative margins of risk. Business people require the services of many professionals—bankers, attorneys, insurance agents—but the accountant is the key adviser.

Admittedly, he or she is the last person from whom to solicit counsel when a change in vocation is being contemplated. Apart from the fact that no one can make that choice but the individual concerned, the accountant almost invariably will regard it as his responsibility to urge cautious forbearance.

Once the decision is made, however, he is the first person to see, especially when the transformation means a shift from wage earner to entrepreneur. Not all change means self-employment, of course, but it is the desired form of liberation for many people, and they should pay scrupulous attention to money issues.

Even the executive turned novelist must adjust his financial affairs, though the study is his office, his only apparent business expenditures are for paper and Ko-Rec-Type, and his staff is composed of members of his family pressed into unpaid service.

Most people in a position to undertake a change in life already have an accountant. That is just as well, for the advice he or she gives is then based upon some knowledge of prior financial habits and circumstances. Apart from preparing tax returns and keeping books in order, the accountant is in a good position to recommend lenders, lawyers, and insurance brokers (remembering that he's likely to spread his referrals around to help *his* business). He can be helpful, too, in designing that critical document, the business plan.

In Chapter 14, it was suggested that every life changer draw up a personal balance sheet. That is simply a device to sort out priorities and is certainly not mandatory. A business plan *is*.

In a booklet published by the Small Business Administration, the editors suggest that the plan answer these questions: What business am I in? What goods or services do I sell? Where is my market? Who will buy? Why will they buy? Who is my competition? What is my sales strategy? What merchandising methods will I use? How much money is needed to operate my company? How will I get the work done? What management controls are needed? How can they be carried out? When should I revise my plan? How will I put the plan into action?

The business plan is not merely a gimmick to clarify objectives and methodology; the individuals or institutions to which a business person must turn will *demand* it.

The questions to be answered fall into six categories.

1. *The Business.* A description of the product or service to be sold. The point in the distribution process in which the business is to be positioned: manufacturing, wholesaling, retailing. The location of sales and delivery.

2. *The Market.* The nature of the competition and its location. The prime selling points in relation to competing products

or services: cheaper, smaller, bigger, better. A customer profile. Description of the market area. Seasonal influences on the product or service. Critical socioeconomic influences.

3. *Sales.* How the product or service is to be sold: by mail, door-to-door, through retail outlets, to wholesalers or manufacturer's agents. Advertising, promotion, graphic design. Plans for market analysis and research.

4. *Production.* Sources and availability of raw materials and/ or finished products. Current costs. Quantities to be stocked. Description of equipment, space, facilities, storage requirements, parking. Whether these are to be purchased or leased.

5. *Personnel.* Numbers and types of managers, salespeople, other workers. Skills and education required. Table of organization. Salary rates. Availability of labor in area. Work résumés of key personnel when they are known, emphasizing evidence of successful prior experience in related business.

6. *Finances.* Projections of sales and expenditures for first twelve months. Estimates on times or periods when payments are expected during first twelve months (known as "cash flow"). Forecasts over three to five years based upon these assumptions.

There is nothing sacrosanct about this outline either in content or sequence, but it follows the general format to which investors or lenders are accustomed.

A narrative description of the proposed business is also customary. Experts are surprised at the number of future owner-managers who don't think this through.

"Many people never really determine what kind of business they're going to have," says Benard Fried, a New York CPA specializing in small enterprises. "They're into wholesaling, retailing, manufacturing, distribution—unrelated products, dissimilar services. You can't *do* that. You have to decide at the outset. Otherwise, you don't do anything well. There's a time for revision later.

"If you want to sell dresses, to whom? The misses market? Juniors? Stouts? Who? Are you selling two-hundred-dollar dresses or ten-dollar dresses, not in terms of price but quality? Are there going to be other lines, such as slacks, blouses, pantsuits, swimwear?"

The prospective entrepreneur must sharpen his focus, whatever the business, not just for operational clarity but for external image. Potential customers, bombarded by messages, must know quickly what is being offered and in what manner. Perhaps cantaloupes and calculators can be sold to both cooks and jobbers in the same store, but there is no need to construct more obstacles than are already inherent in any new enterprise.

Perhaps the product or service is truly unique. If so, it is helpful to give a complete explanation, beyond dimensions and components. Potential investors are understandably skeptical of the alleged promise even of *known* quantities, given the failure rate of most new businesses. They need to know, no matter how innovative the new business, the distinctions of this product or service in relation to existing ones.

Location, location, location. This factor is paramount. The business plan must describe not only the desired facility but where it will be and why. The reasons for this are fairly straightforward. Burger King doesn't award franchises across the street from each other or next door to a McDonald's, not if they can help it. But that isn't an absolute. Many cities have solid blocks of restaurants, all thriving. Antiques rows are common, probably because the sum total of their attractiveness is greater than that of its parts. A painstaking assessment of whether the new business will be helped or hindered by proximity to others of a similar nature is in order. Also, is the facility accessible to shippers, to major thoroughfares, to pedestrians, to motorists? Are other shopping or tourist attractions nearby? Public transportation? Parking? To what degree are these features important to the product or service in question?

After "where?" comes "who?" The customer profile should describe the expected prototypical client in depth. The fast-food shops of Donn Bruce, as he points out, draw under-thirty-five, lower-middle- and working-class males of all races. Country inns attract affluent, white, college-educated professionals in their forties and early fifties, according to the quarterly magazine of the Cornell University hotel school. One is a neighborhood business; the other, regional. Product, service, location, and price must mesh with the available clientele and its ability to pay. The plan should demonstrate convincingly that they will.

Identify and rate the competition. List their names and locations, their estimated shares of the perceived market (in dollar amounts), and what they will lose when the rival business opens. Follow this with a charting of the strengths and weaknesses of each—principal products, facilities, image, marketing techniques—and how they will be met or surpassed. Note whether potential competitors have closed recently or are planning to do so.

If there are *obvious* ways in which the product or service will be at a disadvantage, indicate how these will be overcome—for example, higher cost but greater durability, less flashy styling but dependability, slower delivery but handcrafting.

Describe distribution plans in detail, including costs and any particular aspect which deviates from normal practice. If any customers are already lined up, list their names and their anticipated purchases by dollar amount, type of product, frequency, and percentage of total sales.

Describe market trends over the last several years (how far back depends on the product) and then project them at least five years into the future. Attribute the source of data which led to these conclusions. The Small Business Administration and the U.S. Census Bureau are the first agencies to try, but it may be necessary to engage the services of a market research firm if the planned sales volume warrants that expense. (This latter course, it must be cautioned, is primarily in the interest of promoting the idea, since many such studies simply confirm what empirical observation already determined.) List the names of governmental agencies, trade associations, and private firms or individuals, if any, which assisted in developing the proposal, and those to be contacted later.

If items are to be manufactured, outline the operations involved. Are there unusual storage requirements for, say, special chemicals or highly flammable materials? How will these be met? Equipment, facilities, and operational methods may be subject to federal, state, or local safety regulations, and the prospective entrepreneur should describe how he plans to comply with them.

In the "personnel" segment, the structure of ownership as well as the chain of command must be stated. There are three general types: sole proprietorships, partnerships, and corporations. There are no useful general guidelines as to which is best for a given business, so it is wise to seek professional assistance. The main virtue of incorporation is limited liability for debts incurred. A sole proprietor who signs a ten-year lease, for example, may be liable for payment even if the business fails long before then. A deceased corporation may be stripped by claimants only of that amount invested by the members of the corporation. If a business fails after six months, say, the sole owner, with a monthly rent of $1,000, winds up owing $114,000; the corporation, probably much less. Many people with very small businesses erroneously believe that incorporation saves taxes. Sometimes it will, but not always. In any event, determine the proper course and include it in the plan.

Now the clincher. No part of the business plan will be given closer examination or be more difficult to prepare than the profit-and-loss and cash-flow predictions. They must blend optimism and pragmatism in a balance for which there is no formula. There isn't even agreement on the degree of comprehensiveness. Some advisers stipulate only a one-year projection, others as many as five years. A compromise might be a highly detailed charting of the first year or two, followed by more compact tables for the two or three years thereafter.

The Small Business Administration suggests the following format, in which the columns of figures are entered under each month of the year, ending with the twelve-month totals.

Jan. Feb. Etc.

A. Net Sales
B. Cost of Goods Sold
   1. Raw Materials
   2. Direct Labor
   3. Overhead
      Indirect Labor
      Heat, Light, Power
      Insurance
      Taxes
      Depreciation
C. Gross Margin (Subtract B from A)
D. Selling and Administrative Expenses
   4. Salaries and Commissions
   5. Advertising Expenses
   6. Miscellaneous
E. Net Operating Profit (Subtract B from C)
F. Interest Expenses

G. Net Profit before Taxes (Subtract F
     from E)
H. Estimated Income Tax
I. Net Profit after Income Tax (Subtract H
     from G)

If an accountant has not been involved until this point in preparing the business plan, now is the time. He can evaluate how realistic the figures are as well as suggest modifications and additions relevant to the proposed business. And a copy of his letter can be attached to the plan as evidence that presumably objective professional judgment was involved.

The accountant may recommend including data on expected capitalization, cash forecasts, assets and liabilities, and further details on mortgages and existing loans and financing arrangements. Although most plans are not likely to include them, the particular character of a proposed enterprise may prescribe a detailing of inventory and quality-control procedures. Certainly these are necessary to the business person after start-up, as are methods of keeping track of daily production costs and sales and up-to-date reviews of due dates on bills and major disbursements.

The analytically inclined will also develop a break-even formula, to gauge the point in time, volume, and production at which profits will begin, as in:

$$\text{break-even } \textit{equals} \quad \frac{\text{total fixed costs}}{\text{selling point } \textit{minus} \text{ unit cost}}$$

It would be pleasant to believe that the business plan could be written in frank, everyday language. Certainly, hyperbole should be avoided, but the audience must be kept in mind. In the business and financial community, negative reality is positively slanted. *We are in a temporary downside adjustment phase of a long-term escalatory trend.* While there is no need to be so abstruse, the fledgling entrepreneur is wise to speak in a similar tongue. This is especially true with more visionary concepts. At the same time, the line between felicitously phrased disclosure and outright concealment is to be observed, if only because people in a position to venture investment capital didn't arrive there through credulity.

When the first draft is completed, the plan should be shown to knowledgeable friends and practitioners in the same field as well as the accountant and attorney. (The latter, incidentally, will no doubt insist that a disclaimer be inserted at the front of the formal presentation to the effect that it is a business plan, not a prospectus. This is a legalism, but an important one.) Ideally, at least two months should be allowed for the consultative process. When the corrections are made, a carefully typed copy is prepared and bound, with an introduction page and a table of contents at the front.

The question of financing—of actually raising money—is often immobilizing. It's the rock upon which many dreams shatter. It needn't be so. First, the bad news. Those who know insist that most new businesses are underfinanced. On the other hand, there are many more sources of money and ways to defer its need than most wage earners realize.

To illustrate with a hypothetical case: A woman works as an office manager for a large corporation. Her salary is $15,000, but she has no significant assets or savings because she has only recently paid off loans for her college education. Apart from a few small charge accounts, she has no indebtedness. As she is single, without dependents, she has no responsibilities other than to herself, but no real collateral to offer a lender, either. What is more, she knows that many banks are still chary about lending to women. The odds seem overwhelming.

Nevertheless, she wants to open a small florist's shop and estimates she can do it on $10,000, plus living expenses. She has her eye on a particular store. It needs only a refrigeration case for the flowers and a repainting. First, she persuades the owner to reduce the monthly rent from $500 to $250 in exchange for 5 percent of her gross receipts. Step number one. She has reduced the $10,000 to $7,000, although she will have to adjust her cash-flow projections. If the owner was having difficulty renting the store, she might have argued him out of rent entirely—for the first year, at least. Not likely, but it happens and is worth a try.

She is loath to call on her parents, and she has no rich aunt. Always a gregarious sort, she has many friends. Ten of them are willing to kick in $300 apiece. To keep their relationship friendly as well as business-like, she assigns them a percentage of profits instead of interest and signs a formal agreement with each. She still needs $4,000. The Small Business Administration agrees to lend her $1,500 and suggests she contact the state business development corporation. That agency has aid programs for businesses adjudged to promote tourism. (Not all states do this.) She qualifies, although she is startled by their logic, and they give her $1,000.

With $1,500 to go, she is certain she has exhausted all possible sources. The bank will want collateral, and she has none. If she were requesting a mortgage, the house or store would serve as security, as would a car to be purchased with an automobile loan. The only unsecured debt she has ever incurred was for an island vacation, her bank credit cards, and her overdraft privilege.

She decides to try, anyway. She explains her purpose to a rather stiff, officious man. In answer to his' question, she says that she will be keeping her job for at least six months, having managed to shift her hours to the late afternoon and evening. Friends will watch over the shop from four to six. Her continued steady employment and prompt payment of previous loans is enough. In two days, she is advised that a $1,600 loan has been approved—minus interest, of course.

That does it. She sells most of her furniture, vacates her apartment, and moves into the small room at the back of the store. She needs no new clothes for a year, and her other wants are modest. The salary from her office job will cover them and provide a cushion as well. With luck, she'll break even in four months.

This is not a flighty scenario. Mom and Dad, Chase Manhattan, or their equivalents may come to mind first, but there are many possible sources of funding which haven't even been mentioned.

There are venture capital groups. These aren't the source they used to be for new businesses, because they've retreated nearly as much as banks from uncertain investments in the recent hard times. The chance remains, nevertheless. Venture capital groups take high risks other lenders won't, but they expect a minimum of a threefold return on their money *and* part ownership. Individual venture capitalists may respond to ads under "business opportunities" in big-city newspapers, and a few advertise themselves. More productive and widespread are small business investment companies, (SBICs), licensed by the Small Business Administration (SBA) and found largely—but not exclusively —under the auspices of banks.

Linked to SBICs are minority enterprise small business investment companies (MESBICs), aiding businesses owned primarily by individuals or groups of ethnic or racial minorities. The SBA directly provides economic opportunity loans (EOLs) to economically and/or socially disadvantaged business people. Amounts can go to $50,000, with repayment spread over as many as fifteen years.

In 1975, the SBA distributed over $2 billion. Of this, over 65 percent went to retail and service firms, the rest primarily to small manufacturers. Apart from the EOLs, the two principal varieties of SBA loans are those made directly to applicants and those tendered through banks but guaranteed by the SBA. The former can go to $100,000, the latter to $350,000. Interest is lower on the direct loans.

The drawbacks of SBA loans are admittedly numerous. Only a quarter go to new businesses, processing can take months, and it is usually necessary to prove that requests for assistance have been rejected by two other approved institutions.

Credit unions and insurance policies shouldn't be overlooked. Interest rates are nearly always lower than banks charge. With whole-life policies, the amount of the loan is restricted by the total cash value, so the longer the time since the insurance was initially purchased, the greater the dollar potential. Thus, older people generally realize a higher yield. Credit unions, membership-directed, are less predictable. Some are strictly regional, others depend upon labor union associations, and still others are ideological in intent or sponsorship. Their grants tend to be smaller than from most institutional sources, but easier to obtain, often upon signature alone.

When all else fails, imagination takes over. Proof of a forthcoming inheritance or windfall may be adequate for an otherwise unsecured loan. The Fosters bought rugs and resold them to get started. Presold orders or contracts may supply capital or encourage bank officers.

Finally, quirks in legalese may result in occasional chinks between regulations. In some cases, women find themselves classified as minorities. Men, too. When potter Richard Bennett plunged into the tangles of red tape of the Boston office of the SBA, he emerged with an unsecured loan of $15,000. White, Protestant, and native-born, Bennett qualified under the economic-opportunity category because he was "relocating from a foreign country." A Harvard graduate who grew to his majority in Boston, Bennett had worked in an import-export firm in Japan for four years.

Mysterious are the ways of our bureaucracies.

16
Relocating

Many travel for pleasure to that city to which thou art banished; and what part of the citizens are strangers born in other places? 'Tis no disparagement to be a stranger, or so irksome to be an exile.
—Robert Burton, The Anatomy of Melancholy

Americans confuse location with solution. Always have. Still do. Excluding minors without choice, 6.5 million people move every year. They hope, presumably, to find contentment, to become prosperous, to revitalize their marriages, to pursue new interests, or to find new partners.

It is less surprising that many falter than that so many prevail. Nearly all the people profiled in these pages, for example, moved to different locations as an integral part of the restructuring of their lives.

Fruitful change does not require new surroundings. Sunshine is not all; nor is money. Safety is ephemeral; opportunity has restrictions everywhere. But the question of place is so common a component of the inspiration that it deserves more scrupulous attention than it ordinarily receives. A commercial computer service in Colorado has recognized the possibilities. For a fee, Compare/USA matches a customer's list of desired living conditions with twenty appropriate cities and provides names and addresses of realtors, employment agencies, and chambers of commerce. There is no particular reason to believe the results are any more satisfactory than an IBM 1301 dating service, statistics being subject to the interpretations of the programmer. Nevertheless, there are checkpoints worth consideration.

A number of these compilations and box scores follow. They do not lead to any single, inevitable conclusion, for each place on the map has its minuses as well as its pluses, but these statistics may stimulate close personal analysis.

Some chartings are impossibly ambitious and therefore vulnerable. Witness the 1973 effort of the Midwest Research Institute to do nothing less than rank states and cities by the quality of life they provide their residents. The institute's assessments were based upon evaluations of more than one hundred factors relating, in their estimation, to each of nine major indicators critical to quality of life: individual status (opportunities for self-support and free choice), individual equality, living conditions, agriculture, technology, economic status, education, health and welfare, state and local government.

Still, the results are intriguing and at least provide a point of departure for anyone contemplating relocation. The institute's rating of states by level of living conditions, for example, weighed income, security, costs, weather, motor-vehicle death rates, marriage and divorce rates, and facilities for health care, recreation, libraries, and cultural activities. It came out this way:

1. Massachusetts
2. Connecticut
3. Rhode Island
4. Pennsylvania
5. Colorado
6. Nebraska
7. Wisconsin
8. Utah, New Hampshire
9. New Jersey, New York
10. Iowa, Minnesota
11. Maryland
12. California
13. District of Columbia,
    Kansas, Oregon
14. Wyoming
15. North Dakota
16. Maine, Delaware
17. Washington, South Dakota
18. Montana
19. Hawaii, Oklahoma
20. Michigan
21. Idaho, Illinois
22. Nevada
23. Ohio
24. Indiana, Missouri
25. Vermont
26. Arkansas
27. Texas
28. Virginia, West Virginia
29. Tennessee
30. Florida
31. New Mexico
32. Arizona
33. Georgia, North Carolina
34. South Carolina
35. Kentucky
36. Alabama, Alaska
37. Mississippi
38. Louisiana

When all *nine* of the paramount indicators were collated and weighed, the institute came up with a *top* ten of California, Colorado,

Connecticut, Massachusetts, Montana, Oregon, Rhode Island, Utah, Washington, and Wyoming; and a *bottom* ten of Alabama, Arkansas, Kentucky, Louisiana, Mississippi, North Carolina, South Carolina, Tennessee, Virginia, and West Virginia.

Such a roster is destined to please no one. Coloradans, while acknowledging the perspicacity of the study, can be expected to deplore its implicit encouragement of still greater resource-straining immigration. Virginians will inveigh against the inequity of a judgment which does not consider their state's tradition, culture, and natural beauty. The researchers' benign reply is that people "attribute greater significance to slight variations in state score or rank than is warranted" and that "no two individuals will consider the same set of variables as important in shaping their quality of life."

This last is the key point, certainly. We run to—or away from—different things, and those influences we proclaim openly are not always those we harbor secretly.

Cost seems to be important. Very often it is also illusory, for the accoutrements of the good life vary with location. Air conditioning becomes essential in the South, recreation vehicles desirable in the West. Tom and Rosalind Wells, the New Hampshire innkeepers, talk about differences between their present home and the former one in Chicago.

"You don't spend money in the same ways," Tom says. "Your kid doesn't have to be as stylishly dressed in school as in the city, and you don't, either."

"*But,*" Roz says, "he needs a parka, down-filled gloves, boots. . . ."

"There are other kinds of social competition at work here, too. You need ice skates, kayaks, cross-country skis, downhill skis, canoes. . . ."

"Winter is forever here. It's a test. You have to find things to do in it. The usual New England joke is, 'Summer was on Tuesday last year.' Those boots and gloves are *necessities.* You can freeze in your car—to death! Winter in a city is inconvenient but not paralyzing. Here you don't have control. Snow and sleet take away your options. You can't just hop in the car and go. Plus, your electricity isn't constant, and water and sewage are your own. You don't just turn the tap and expect it to work, or if it doesn't, just call the super. That may be trite, but on a twenty-degree-below morning, you're face-to-face with your inadequacies. What's more, the cost of living may even be higher here than in the city. A house is as expensive. Raw materials often cost more because of transportation. Oil and gasoline rates here are very high. And you have to have two cars. Hard goods are more expensive because there's no competition to induce discounting. You wind up paying list price for that TV or refrigerator."

Still, there are measurable expense factors. Federal taxation of personal income is constant, for instance, but regional levies vary more widely than many think. In fiscal 1974–75, according to the Commerce Clearing House in Chicago, *per capita* state and local tax burdens averaged out as follows:

1. New York, $952
2. Massachusetts, $767
3. Hawaii, $765
4. California, $762
5. Nevada, $738
6. District of Columbia, $725
7. Illinois, $699
8. Wisconsin, $696
9. Minnesota, $695
10. Connecticut, $689
11. New Jersey, $683
12. Michigan, $679
13. Delaware, $679
14. Maryland, $674
15. Vermont, $661
16. Washington, $622
17. Pennsylvania, $615
18. Alaska, $611
19. Rhode Island, $606
20. Maine, $597
21. Wyoming, $590
22. Iowa, $590
23. Colorado, $587
24. Montana, $587
25. Arizona, $582
26. Kansas, $573
27. Oregon, $570
28. Indiana, $547
29. Nebraska, $543
30. Florida, $520
31. South Dakota, $519
32. North Dakota, $517
33. Virginia, $510
34. Missouri, $501
35. Ohio, $497
36. Louisiana, $496
37. New Mexico, $484
38. New Hampshire, $483
39. Idaho, $479
40. Georgia, $477
41. Utah, $472
42. Texas, $467
43. North Carolina, $461
44. West Virginia, $450
45. Oklahoma, $428
46. Mississippi, $425
47. Tennessee, $424
48. South Carolina, $422
49. Kentucky, $411
50. Arkansas, $384
51. Alabama, $383

Put in more dynamic—if simplified—terms, a typical breadwinner living with three dependents in Lowell, Massachusetts, would have paid $3,068 in state and local taxes. If that family had moved just five miles north into New Hampshire, the total would have dropped to $1,932—a differential of $1,136 in discretionary income. Tax structures favor residents of Utah over neighboring Nevada by $1,064 on the same basis, Oregon over California by $768, Pennsylvania over New York by $1,348. When the distance of a bicycle ride can cause such variations in spendable dollars, these statistics are worth considering.

But taxation is still merely *a* factor. Fair return for money spent is far more important. A rich man marooned in the desert is still thirsty. This sort of information can be spun out in a more illuminating way. Three-quarters of us live in cities or their shadows. In the left column below, the Labor Department gives us its 1974 estimates of annual budgets for families of four who wish to maintain an intermediate standard of living (defined as home ownership, occasional dining out, meat regularly on the table, a late-model car). On the right, the same metropolitan areas are ranked according to their positions in another quality-of-life study by the Midwest Research Institute (MRI).

Intermediate Budget, Most to Least	*Quality of Life, Highest to Lowest*
1. Honolulu ($17,019)	1. Seattle
2. Boston ($16,725)	2. Minneapolis–St. Paul
3. New York ($16,648)	3. Hartford
4. Hartford ($15,501)	4. Denver
5. Buffalo ($15,364)	5. San Francisco–Oakland
6. San Francisco–Oakland ($15,127)	6. San Diego
7. District of Columbia ($15,035)	7. Milwaukee
8. Milwaukee ($15,024)	8. Buffalo
9. Minneapolis–St. Paul ($14,917)	9. District of Columbia
10. Chicago ($14,797)	10. Los Angeles
11. Philadelphia ($14,757)	11. Boston
12. Cleveland ($14,617)	12. Cleveland
13. Seattle ($14,487)	13. Houston
14. Baltimore ($14,398)	14. Cincinnati
15. Detroit ($14,390)	15. Honolulu

Intermediate Budget, Most to Least	Quality of Life, Highest to Lowest
16. Indianapolis ($14,120)	16. New York
17. Los Angeles ($14,068)	17. Dallas
18. San Diego ($13,977)	18. Kansas City
19. Kansas City ($13,939)	19. Indianapolis
20. Pittsburgh ($13,876)	20. Chicago
21. St. Louis ($13,859)	21. Detroit
22. Cincinnati ($13,753)	22. Atlanta
23. Denver ($13,606)	23. Nashville
24. Atlanta ($13,098)	24. Pittsburgh
25. Nashville ($12,996)	25. St. Louis
26. Dallas ($12,917)	26. Baltimore
27. Houston ($12,872)	27. Philadelphia

Accepting for a moment the MRI's pronouncements on the right, it is interesting that four of the most expensive urban areas—Honolulu, Boston, New York, Chicago—do not appear among the ten deemed most desirable in terms of quality of life. The six remaining, on the other hand, appear to represent fair value. Even more intriguing are the cities which presumably confer much more than their substantially lower costs of living suggest: Seattle, San Diego, Houston, Denver.

The fragility of such generalizations is apparent. Purely as compilations of statistical data, they really cannot be faulted. The scholars of the Midwest Research Institute permitted little in the way of quantifiable conditions to escape their attention. They fed their computers such information as the number of housing units with television sets, mean annual inversion frequencies, swimming pools per 100,000 population, mean levels of total suspended particulates, ratios of automobile registrations to population, infant mortality rates, crime rates, per capita expenditures on welfare and education, and total acres of parks and nature trails per 1,000 residents—among hundreds of others.

But the institute would be the first to concede that attitudes cannot be measured. They didn't even try. Quite apart from the truism that statistics can be manipulated to prove anything, no one can determine with certitude how others *feel*. Striving and contentment and fear are borderless tracts, shifting in personal and collective impact from day to day, even from moment to moment.

In the Northeast, for instance, what one does for a living is the usual basis of identification. On the West Coast, how *leisure* is spent is more often primary. A lawyer in Boston is known as a skier in California, even though he works as one and plays as the other in both places.

New Yorkers cringe in expectation of violence, many refusing to leave home after dusk. After years of alarums raised by the Manhattan-based press and broadcast media, citizens of other cities are certain that New Yorkers have special cause to be fearful. Even comic strips have picked it up. In one episode, Mary Worth is depicted as departing the home of a relative. Mary invites her to return the visit—in New York. "I'd be afraid," replies the niece. "Why, crime is so common there that comedians make jokes about it!" Wise Mary insists that "New York is as safe as any other large city." She is not convincing. Yet death by homicide is more commonplace in Jacksonville and Cleveland, and forcible rape more routine in Tucson and Ann Arbor.

In 1974, the FBI claimed that all the following cities had higher rates of violent crime (murder, rape, robbery, assault) than New York: Miami, San Francisco, Detroit, Atlanta, Dallas, Los Angeles, Cleveland, Baltimore, Denver, Washington, Chicago, Saint Louis, Houston, San Diego. When *all* forms of crime were included, nearly fifty cities surpassed New York, including Kalamazoo, Eugene, Flint, Fresno, Stockton, Little Rock, Portland (Oregon), and Wichita.

Beyond city limits, relative security from miscreants is most thoroughly enjoyed by residents of these twelve states: North Dakota, Iowa, Maine, Minnesota, Idaho, South Dakota, Wisconsin, Nebraska, New Hampshire, Utah, Vermont, and Connecticut. On the other hand, nonurbanites are in the greatest jeopardy in these twelve: Alabama, South Carolina, Georgia, Florida, North Carolina, Alaska, Kentucky, Wyoming, Arkansas, Louisiana, Tennessee, and Maryland.

Such explorations can be extended endlessly and become more tenuous with each step. In a 1972 *Esquire* article, David Franke collected felony data on the 396 American cities with populations of 50,000 or more. His subsequent computations produced his nominees for the ten "safest" and the ten most "crime-ridden" cities. Those in the first category were inevitably small—for example, Lakewood (Ohio), Florissant (Missouri), Westland (Michigan). In such communities, a handful of burglaries constitutes a crime wave. One of

Franke's ten "safest" was Greenwich, Connecticut. In a recent eight-month period, there were three murders there. They were the first in nearly thirty years, but they render the list invalid. Tragic events which pass unnoticed in Detroit or Baltimore loom large in Greenwich.

There *is*, however, validity in the belief that "smaller is safer." The U.S. Bureau of the Budget defines a standard metropolitan statistical area (SMSA) as one which includes one or more core cities of 50,000 population or more, plus contiguous, economically integrated suburbs. In 1970, there were 270 SMSAs. Their average violent-crime rate was 558 per 100,000 people. The rate was 66 percent lower in smaller cities than large ones, and 73 percent lower in towns, villages, and rural areas. Big-city journalists have pointed with macabre glee to increases in suburban crime, but there is still a very substantial gap, which is unlikely to be narrowed in the near future.

There are other considerations, equally contradictory. The states with the highest personal incomes per capita are: Nevada, Alaska, Connecticut, Illinois, California, and, as many might suspect, the District of Columbia. Those with the highest unemployment: Alaska, Washington, Oregon, California, and Montana. Those with the *lowest* unemployment: Hawaii, Virginia, Georgia, Maryland, North Carolina. Those where the cost of living is *above* the national average: Hawaii, Massachusetts, New York, New Jersey, Connecticut, the District of Columbia, Illinois, Virginia, Washington, California, Maryland, Wisconsin, Minnesota. Those with the *lowest* cost of living: Florida, Mississippi, Georgia, Rhode Island, Texas. Those with the highest divorce rates (because *something* must be wrong): Arkansas, Oklahoma, Florida, Washington, Wyoming, Alaska, Alabama, Colorado, California (and Nevada, of course).

Frequently, city dwellers are convinced that their problems will be solved by moving to the country. While emphasizing that he and his wife sought a "cleaner, safer, saner" life and found it, Tom Wells sounds warning notes.

"There are psychological, mental things. You must learn to cope with yourself, with your partner. You learn to face realities about both of you that you didn't have to confront in the city, where there are so many distractions. If it's two in the morning, you can't run down to an all-night movie theater or pizza parlor. They just aren't there. You read a lot, you think a lot, you discover much about yourself.

"Some people can't stand it. We have city friends who come up for presumably extended stays and leave after two days because 'the days are so *loonnggg!*' They can't take it. They're used to living on big streets with Bonwit's and Bloomingdale's around the corner, with restaurants and theaters and museums. Up here, they're thrown back on themselves. New England has a very high suicide rate, y'know."

Smaller cities may be the answer for those who don't want to surrender completely the advantages of urban life. Manhattanites who speak of art and the theater—but who visit the Guggenheim or the Shubert only once a year—may find that Minneapolis or Sacramento will be able to slake whatever aesthetic thirsts overwhelm them from time to time.

Even Toledo can. Charles Lord weighs the alternatives and does not find his adopted city lacking.

"When you arrive at the airport," Lord reflects, "it could as well be a large Burger King. That was my reaction. Then I drove through this horrendous urban sprawl looking for a hill and not finding one. Everyone told me about the availability of culture in Toledo, and I thought that was just what people could be expected to say.

"But then we looked around. My wife is an art historian. She confirmed what they claim here, that Toledo has one of the top art museums in the country, in both its collection and its research facilities. This is so, we discovered, because Toledans are very supportive of Toledo. The Libby family, the Dana family, and others have contributed heavily. We have been to eight excellent concerts this year, with outstanding soloists and a fine symphony orchestra. We've heard more good music in eight months than in three years in New York, because I have time for it and I can afford it. It's not as varied here, but we take better advantage. Certainly, we miss the involvements and pizzazz of New York. We will always stay as close as we can to our friends there. But it's better in so many ways here."

Some suggest that the era of the metropolis is past, that the big-city brontosaurus no longer serves the needs for which it developed. With instant communication and rapid forms of transportation available to all, it is argued, clustering within a few urban concentrations of arts and commerce is no longer necessary. Perhaps. As relevant, in a time of introspection and popular recognition of the limits of resources, is that the competitive drive has blunted. The compulsion to test one's skills and energies against the very best is dissipating. And there is cause for guarded satisfaction in this reassessment of national and personal priorities.

On the positive side, the individual has many more options. Regional inferiorities have been deemphasized: a film can be made in Atlanta as well as in Hollywood, a sculpture constructed in Omaha as ably as in SoHo, haute cuisine presented as flawlessly in Fort Collins as in New Orleans. Urbanity is no longer a quality confined to a few large cities. Small-town life need not be Sinclair Lewis's "contentment of the quiet dead."

Artistic and financial authority is being redistributed, not forcibly appropriated. Since 1970, only two states have lost population (New York and Rhode Island). While much has been made of a presumed flight to the "sun-belt" states—what one writer has called the "Southern Rim"—few analysts have noted concurrent and equally notable population increases in northern New England and the upper Rocky Mountain States. That would muddle their thesis that power is being seized by reactionary, racist regionalists bent upon bringing the Northern and Eastern Establishment to its knees. This dispersal of ideas and talent is visible in every section of the country. Examples abound.

Exciting restorations and recyclings have spruced up downtown areas and neighborhoods in Galveston (Texas), Corning (New York), Louisville (Kentucky), Allentown (Pennsylvania), New Harmony (Indiana), Taos (New Mexico), Muskegon (Michigan), Salem (Massachusetts), Charleston (South Carolina), Savannah (Georgia), Richmond (Virginia). Desert ghost towns and country hamlets are being renovated. Age has transformed storefronts and industrial blocks from what was deemed ugly not long ago to what is judged charming and graceful now. Renewal has been both spontaneous and planned; the vision, collective and personal. Craftsmen and preservationists have been followed by enlightened industrialists and self-interested merchants. Or vice versa. Or together. It is easy to quibble with results, but the fact it is happening cannot be disputed.

Columbus, Indiana, is a praiseworthy paradigm. Under the low-pitched guidance and material encouragement of J. Irwin Miller, head of a diesel-manufacturing firm, Columbus has become an architectural showplace. Since 1954, Miller's Cummins Engine Foundation has offered to pay the fee for any building designed by a major architect.

This otherwise characteristically Hoosier city of 27,000 now boasts the presence of schools, factories, and churches created by the Saarinens, I. M. Pei, Gunnar Birkerts, and Skidmore, Owens and Merrill. As counterpoint, its Main Street has been primped and preserved, a bridge between treasured past and vigorous present.

Jim Martin chose Columbus. He appreciates what its leaders have done, while retaining the reservations which might be expected of a former city dweller.

"Ah, yes," he says, "it's been called the 'Athens of the Prairie.' So have a few dozen other Midwestern towns. There are other reasons for being here, though. The cost of living is lower, social and racial problems are virtually nonexistent. Indiana has no state debt. The air is clean, the schools are safe. Because of Miller, there's a branch of the Indianapolis Art Museum here, entertainment is brought to the mall he built for the town, there's a lecture program, and the University in Bloomington is just thirty-seven miles away, so we can catch the ballet, concerts, go to the library. . . .

"The truth is, though, I've been too busy getting my business going to take advantage of it all. What's more, I've kinda dropped out of being tuned in. It's rather pleasant, the serenity and repose of ignorance. I know people are criticized for it, but I'm not sure it's so wrong after my years of earnest community endeavor. And let's face it: this is flat, level land, and a flat, level mentality goes with it. The Ku Klux Klan ran the state government not so long ago, and some of those attitudes persist. That fact must be considered by anyone who's relocating."

The type of enterprise to be undertaken can narrow choices. The Fosters needed a moderately large and sophisticated retail market for their Oriental rugs and carpets. Fortunately, divine guidance steered them to Louisville. With 938,000 people within its sphere of influence, it is the largest city in Kentucky. Its unemployment level is below the national average, and its family income is well above. It is a manageable city, with broad greenbelts and stately homes. Their arrival was propitious from a personal standpoint as well.

"We bought the house very reasonably. We paid only fifty-five thousand dollars for it less than two years ago. Judging from recent sales, we could get ninety thousand for it right now." It is a spacious building, nearly a hundred feet across, with four bedrooms, solaria on two floors, and a dormitory for the boys on the third.

"One reason this place didn't sell back then was busing," Steve says.

There were bloody demonstrations in Louisville by antibusing factions. Blacks were attacked; the National Guard was mobilized. But as the school year progressed, hostilities faded. The Louisville school system is the twelfth largest in the country, with 22,600 black and white children in the busing program. It seems to have worked.

"People in the city thought their kids were going to be bused, so they moved outside into the country. Then the court decision came down merging the city and the county school systems. That was one month *after* we bought this place. Now all those people want to be back in the city because it doesn't make any difference anymore."

"And the houses are lovely here in the city," says Anna. "There's texture in the neighborhoods. Now the property values are shooting up again."

"Of course," Steve says, "we increased the value of the house tremendously over what we paid for it by the amount of work we put into it. The place was in terrible shape, a mess. No one else would buy it. But we all pitched in. Anna did a lot of the work—I'm afraid I just did a lot of griping—and even my parents helped."

Their efforts were rewarded. Their home was one stop on a posh house tour.

There is, as well, a reverse reaction to the flight from the major cities. Some people are returning. Philadelphia, for one example, has long been unjustly maligned. W. C. Fields and his Borscht Belt brethren notwithstanding, the Quaker City has become one of the liveliest in the country. It is a place full of sprightly delights, crackling with life. Yet it is consistently denigrated except as a repository of artifacts during a recent national anniversary which will pass without further mention here.

Philadelphia is a city with block after tree-lined block of stately row houses and pocket parks and resting places. It has living historic districts grander in dimension and as lovingly groomed as Beacon Hill and Georgetown. It nurtures a cultural life surpassed in quality by none and second only to New York in scope. Despite the judgments of such observers as the Midwest Research Institute, Philadelphia is safer than most of the largest cities and its cost of living less confiscatory than many. More important, its center-city population has actually *increased* by 6 percent in the last decade, contrary to trends in other cities.

One reason is housing. A three-story locally designated "Father–Son–Holy Ghost" town house goes for as little as $25,000 in less fashionable neighborhoods, a quarter of what it might cost in Brooklyn Heights or Cambridge. Philadelphia is not alone. The cost of housing in the "doughnut" towns surrounding older cities is so high that many people are reexamining the idea of an inner-city home. The national median price of a new house is in excess of $44,000, customarily in the suburbs. A person or family willing to work hard and make the necessary compromises may do better back in town. Possibilities are rife. The Haight-Ashbury district in San Francisco is reviving, as are the Boston waterfront, Brooklyn's Park Slope and Cobble Hill, and portions of Detroit, Chicago, Baltimore, Washington, D.C., and Atlanta. Perversely, the inner-city neighborhoods that millions fled for the suburbs may now represent the best housing bargains available.

All this is presented in the interest of stimulating the incipient life changer to ponder all possibilities. Open-mindedness and imagination are critical.

This may help: many new careers or businesses require locations near, rather than in, cities. Within the orbits of most are regions purely rural in character. In the summer of 1975 (add about 9 percent for each extra year), the Federal Home Loan Bank Board gave estimates of average prices for new and old houses within commuting distance of central cities. In the process, it provided a clue to an often overlooked way to save housing dollars.

Near	New House	Older House
San Francisco	$66,300	$55,600
Los Angeles	$61,000	$55,700
New York	$60,500	$54,700
Dallas	$60,000	$58,500
Washington, D.C.	$57,500	$58,900
Houston	$52,700	$49,600

Notice not only the important cost differentials between new and older houses but how the desirability of each fluctuates by region. Around San Francisco, a buyer might save as much as $11,000 by opting for an older house, but have to pay *more* in the Washington area. As a rule, the gap in price between newer and older houses increases as the buyer moves west, but there are exceptions to that pattern. In the New York area, where the supply of older houses is great, their cost might be expected to be less, as it is. Yet approximately the same range exists in Los Angeles, where most housing is post–World War II. Once again, logic is the victim of fashion and other imponderables.

Location, in real estate as in business, is everything. Two houses of comparable size, condition, age, style, and property a village or two apart can vary in price by as much as 25 percent. If one of those properties is within ready commuting distance of the central city and the other is not, the differential can expand even farther. The same is true of interest rates and required down payments. Even in neighboring communities these can differ by as much as a full percentage point in the first case and ten points in the second. Shopping for credit, as a result, is something to be done *while* looking for a new home, not after.

There are others. Energy costs can jump or dip merely by crossing a county line. In Westchester County, New York, 500 kilowatt hours of electricity costs $44. Upstate, it's $5.35. Miniclimates (as in winemaker Carl Banholzer's example) can warm or cool by as much as ten degrees in as many miles. The nearby Weather Bureau station might help. In suburban areas, houses are most likely to go on the market in June, when the school year is ending and transfers come through; in ski areas, at the end of the snow season; along beaches, at the end of summer.

Since leaving the city is a compelling element of many life changers' plans, selecting a new country residence is a happily anticipated task. There's the village where a cabin was rented one summer, the resort town where several long weekends were spent. The dangers of making a selection on that basis should be obvious but often are not. Crunching through new snow and sipping brandy by the fire are pleasurable pursuits—if someone else is shoveling the walks and lugging the logs. The summer resort bristling with dance festivals, chamber music recitals, and art shows may plunge into somnambulism after Labor Day, not to stir again until Memorial Day.

The best way to confirm one's feelings about a place is to visit often—at the most disagreeable times of year—and stay as long as possible. The charms of a town thought unsurpassed over a weekend may prove illusory when everything has been done three times and people must rely upon their own creativity.

One writer, Rex Roberts, is persuaded that a "two-drugstore

town" is about the right size—large enough for competition, small enough to be unoppressive. It might be more profitable to look closely at those which host colleges or branches of state universities. The students and faculty help keep the movie theater running, attract cultural events, and support bookstores and livelier varieties of shops and boutiques than would a similar-size town without them. Another possibility is a village in which an inn or a fine restaurant is situated, if only because their presence suggests a more sophisticated local clientele than does the usual string of motels and fun-food shacks out on the bypass.

When the search has focused on two or three areas, there are other ways to accelerate the winnowing process—*before* seeing a real-estate agent. Talk to bankers, the police, the tax office, insurance agents, innkeepers, bartenders, merchants. Perhaps there's an appealing property that looks vacant but has no for-sale sign or newspaper listing. What do the locals know about it? The school situation? Teacher unrest and busing disputes may depress asking prices, as they did for the Fosters in Louisville. What are the current controversies? A spreading landfill? A new industrial park or state park or highway? Where? What is the population? The size of the police force? Is the fire department all volunteer? How far is the nearest hospital? Was the school budget voted down recently? By what margin? Are there taxes unique to the area (as on road use or for snow removal)? What is the method of garbage collection?

Usually only expensive properties are advertised in big-city newspapers. For-sale signs may mean that those properties are not even listed with realtors. Jim and Audrey Patterson sold their inn when someone walked up and asked, though they had no thought of leaving until then.

When none of this digging has turned up likely properties, it is time to see a real-estate agent. As the agent is in business to bring together sellers and buyers, but for the profit only of himself and the seller, an ideal arrangement excludes that middleman. Since that may not be possible, a realtor can at least be useful for his or her knowledge of available properties in the region. Any service beyond this, fairly represented and rendered, should be regarded as an unexpected bonus. Other things being equal, it's probably safer to deal with those who are affiliated with the National Association of Real Estate Boards. This organization and its chapters establish codes of ethics—with enforcement powers of fluctuating rigor. Their regional units set commission levels (malcontents might call this "fee fixing") and review complaints against practices of their members. It must be remembered that realtors receive their commissions from sellers. Since a commission may amount to as much as 10 percent of the final sale, and even more in some places, the asking price will allow for this, plus another 10 percent as a bargaining cushion.

The maverick realtor who made these observations also tenders these less controversial (to his colleagues) recommendations.

"With country property, try to confine yourself to listings which have already been surveyed. If they have not, it can take months to have it done. A less desirable option is to draw up a boundary-line agreement signed by all bordering owners, one or more of whom may be absentees. Surveys are expensive, as much as three thousand dollars or more for properties of many acres. Make sure to obtain an estimate of the fee in advance if a survey is required.

"A *local* attorney is a must. Your city lawyer simply won't have the requisite knowledge of ordinances, brokers, engineers, lending institutions, and regional political and legal peculiarities. He might be able to refer you to one, however. If not, ask friends or relatives from the area. Beyond that, you're at the mercy of the Yellow Pages.

"Ask his help in determining whether easements have been given by previous owners to power or telephone companies. Even if there's nothing visible now, it could be constructed later—right across your swimming pond. The longer the property in question has been in the possession of the present owner, the greater the chances of a reassessment for tax purposes. Ask your lawyer or the tax assessor what the probabilities are, especially if there has been recent construction or upgrading.

"Check into the costs and reliability of your water supply. In the country, a drilled (as opposed to 'dug') well is best. Do you have a septic tank or cesspool? Must you be connected to a municipal power or sewage system? At what cost?

"The lawyer makes the title search—to make sure there are no liens or pending actions. He'll be able to help determine the need for a survey. He may assist in finding a mortgage and in filing the application. He's absolutely *essential* at the closing, when the buyer is in a daze from writing out checks and trying to keep track of the proceedings.

Decide what you want from him, at least in rough outline, before you even go to him. He gets paid by the hour. Then nail down his fee *in advance.*

"If you're not too familiar with what problems—past, present, future—may be afflicting the house in which you're genuinely interested, an engineering specialist is a good idea. He'll cost somewhere from a hundred and fifty to three hundred dollars. Determine *his* fee in advance and ask for a *written* report when he's done. Expect him to find negatives, because he will. At least you can make a decision based upon reasonable information, not ignorance. Make sure, by the way, that the engineer has no affiliations with contractors, realtors, aluminum-siding firms, or the like.

"After you've done all this, and let your initial enthusiasm cool, it's time to make a bid. *You* will be expected to open negotiations. It should be at least twenty percent below what they're asking, especially if a broker is involved. On large properties, *thirty* percent isn't out of line. Don't sign a binder agreement or make a 'good-faith' deposit. It may prove to be a legal document, no matter how informal the circumstances. Don't sign *anything* without your lawyer.

"When you agree on price and have made certain that financing will be available, have your attorney get together with the seller's and write up a contract. It should specify what detachable or removable items will stay with the building—drapes, the TV antenna (in fringe reception areas, that can be a big investment), the carpets, the appliances, even the azaleas, if you care. It should also spell out the date the property will be available, its state of cleanliness, that plumbing, electrical, and heating systems will all be in working order at the time of transfer.

"There are things people forget about mortgages and closings, even if they've purchased real estate before. Monthly payments, for example, are for one-twelfth of the annual total for principal, interest, insurance, and *estimated* school and property taxes. If taxes are raised or the bank has underestimated, there can be an unexpectedly large extra payment come January. For the first few years of a long mortgage, the bulk of the payments will be toward interest. Find out if there's a prepayment penalty. Often there will be, up to the time when the principal portion matches or exceeds the interest portion—five years or more on a twenty-five-year mortgage.

"Assuming payments on the present owner's mortgage is often

useful, if he's willing, as it takes advantage of what may have been lower interest rates in effect when it was drawn up. There may be savings in fees and closing costs as well. This only really works, though, if the buyer has the cash to give the seller what's already been paid on the mortgage as well as the seller's profit on the deal. If the buyer must float a loan to obtain the up-front money, the bank may not approve the deal. They want the higher interest which comes with a new mortgage.

"There is no more traumatic experience than the closing. The uninitiated should have some prior knowledge of what to expect, although nothing can quite prepare them. First, bring your checkbook. You'll be writing a lot. The bank's representative, the seller, his lawyer, and yours will all be there. You'll write checks for (1) your down payment on the mortgage, (2) your payment of the 'points' charged by the lender (a one-time charge over and above the interest), (3) advance payment (sometimes) into the bank's escrow fund for its payment of your taxes, (4) title insurance, (5) legal fees to your attorney *and* the bank's, (6) any oil remaining in the tank which the seller purchased beforehand, (7) repayment to the seller for taxes paid beyond the date of sale, and, often, the (8) land-survey fee and (9) mortgage tax.

"Even on a relatively modest forty-thousand-dollar mortgage, all these things and any other little goodies they may dream up can easily total two thousand dollars over and above the down payment and moving costs. And you have to go through that whole dreary mess the next time you get itchy feet."

The mortgage market is volatile. It shifts from region to region, year to year. A down payment of at least 20 percent or possibly as much as 40 percent will be stipulated. Interest rates have hovered around the 8 percent level for several years, but borrowers have to watch out for "points" charged by some lending institutions. For the uninitiated, this is a device created by banks to offset what they believe to be unrealistically low, if legally mandated, interest rates. They require this extra fee for their agreement, usually 1 to 2 percent of the total value of the loan, paid at the time of closing.

As banks are necessarily conservative, they do not always agree with the supplicant's vision of a property. It's difficult to find financing of any duration for unimproved land or for buildings in need of substantial repair. In such cases, a mortgage jointly undertaken by two or more parties may be easier to find. When that doesn't work, the Federal

Housing Administration is a possibility, but they are even more cautious, especially with houses more than twenty years old. When a property is to be used for business or farming purposes, either the Small Business Administration or the Farmers Home Administration might come through.

17
Is It Worth It?

What condition of life is free?
    —Robert Burton, *The Anatomy of Melancholy*

There it is. A new life can be made, and by anyone with the requisite imagination, stamina, and determination. It can bring liberty. Realization. Vigor. Excitement. Renewal. Knowledge. Joy. And despair. Estrangement. Bankruptcy. Emptiness.

It can be done. Should it be? Is it *worth* it?

Ask Charlie Hepner and his wife.

"Yes," he says.

"No," she says. At the same time.

"It hasn't been everything I'd expected. Hoped." Charlie considers where it went wrong and where it didn't. "There are very real frustrations, tensions with the other things I should be doing. Partly it's knowing that you don't have as many years as you'd like to accomplish what you'd like. Partly it's not having the time or energy to give as much as you'd wish to your family or to keeping up your house and other interests."

Anne is nodding vigorously. She wasn't in favor of Charlie's change.

"I'm afraid I might lose my son. We've had so little time together. I've been putting in all kinds of time at the office, and it's beginning to pay off, but I've sacrificed my relationship with my son. He doesn't know me, and I don't know him."

But isn't that the by-product of the new profession he chose?

"I suppose so," he agrees. "Maybe a writer or someone working out of his home shares more with his family. There are other factors, though. Health, for instance. The problem of tiring. I'm not the physical type for heart trouble, but I don't push my luck, either. You have to think about that when you get past your mid-thirties. I have to ease off before I reach the danger point, put the briefcase aside, do something else.

"And you have to face up to yourself. You find out that whatever problems you had inside, you carry with you. However many times you move, you can't escape that. You can't tell yourself it's the conditions of your job. It's all yours.

"That's good, really. You are confronted with yourself, the excuses are wiped away. You must conquer yourself every day.

"Am I glad I did it? Yes. Even when I'm at my lowest. I'm living more, every day."

But with sacrifice. Or trade-offs, at least. For independence from supervisors or subordinates or a career gone stale, pay in depleted savings and retraining. For the charm of distance and pure air and a sense of season, pay in loss of friends and urban vitality. For fresh relationships, the alienation of those long known.

"I said I had no regrets," Peter Russell muses, "and I don't, but this isn't the be-all, end-all, either. We miss some of our friends, and there are still the normal problems of living and relating. You take those things with you."

Potter Richard Bennett accepts. "I didn't choose this. I'm both a pragmatist and a romantic. On one level, how I got into this is still a mystery. I can't even draw a pot. I can't translate three dimensions on paper. I just sit here and try to make beautiful things. Sometimes I succeed. Inside, there must have been something pushing me this way, but without my conscious volition. I knew there was more than being a tool to help my superiors steal, and I wanted to do something that was clean, but that was all. This wasn't a goal. It happened. And it's better, but I didn't really have anything to do with it, and I don't try to make things work out in any particular way."

Charles Lord, a teacher now, says, "I've never felt I had all the final answers. I will always analyze and evaluate. But I'll be willing to put money down that if you come looking for me twenty years from now, you'll find I've spent that time in education.

"That doesn't mean I won't sit down alone and with my wife and look at it periodically along the way. But I've never enjoyed the days as much. Who could believe they'd *like* getting up at six thirty in the morning? I do. I look forward to the day.

"Right at this moment, I have no doubts. Neither am I dogmatic. I think this is right, but I give no pat answers. Maybe it will pall. It hasn't yet.

"Look, I love being home with my family. But if I walk by the baseball field and there's a game going, I also like to stop for a while and belt fungoes. Or just sit in the commons and shoot the breeze with some of the kids or the faculty. That's good, not to have to escape from your job.

"There have been interesting reactions from contemporaries, and they included presidents and vice-presidents of big companies. They said things like 'I wish I'd done that when I could have' and 'I didn't have the courage.' They worried about their families, their homes, their incomes, their *routines*. It's *hard* to throw it all over. I was scared to death myself. I couldn't have done it if my wife hadn't been supportive.

"Yet, looking back, it's a lot easier than you think. The anticipation of problems is always worse than what you actually find. Maybe one of the reasons I wanted to talk about this was the hope that someone out there will be encouraged to try. Certain of my friends have become moribund. They know exactly what they're going to be doing ten years from now—and they hate it. I'd like them to know it doesn't have to be. You have to keep learning. You can't do that if you stay and stay and stay.

"It can be terrible to fail. That's the fear. But I'd hate to be a man who wanted to try something else and didn't. I don't want to be a person who puts down the newspaper one Sunday morning at the age of sixty and says, 'I blew it.'"

We are not a static people. We cannot be, in the face of past history and present technology. That doesn't mean we must permit ourselves to be borne along to new heights of consumption and specialization.

Jim Martin: "More and more people are going to have to do what I have. Living standards are stabilizing because they cost more and more to maintain. The old verities are proving to be the new falsehoods. Education is no longer an automatic meal ticket, turning on a light costs five times what it did a decade ago, ever-increasing industrial production cannot be absorbed by a zero-growth population. There is going to be a radical realignment of individual life choices, a reaction to a society in which only the wealthy can own houses and a college degree is worthless because everyone has one. Sooner or later, that revolution will happen. Why wait to let it happen to you? Why not be part of it? Why not help find the alternatives?"

Tom Wells: "Do it! Why do the safe thing and hate it? Why not fail at something you like? *Do it!*"

Many commentators have issued shrill cries of alarm at the sight of people disengaging themselves from collective action and turning to themselves. "The ME decade," Tom Wolfe called it. "The new alchemical dream," said Wolfe, "is: changing one's personality, remaking, remodeling, elevating, and polishing one's very *self* . . . and observing, studying, and doting on it. (Me!)" This runs counter to the outer-directed, big-view, institutionalized altruism urged—imposed—upon us by intellectuals, theological satraps, and political aristocrats of every well-intentioned ideological persuasion. The fuel is guilt over our selfishness, and the results are foreign conflicts we make worse by our intercession, three-generation welfare families, continued tinkering with a perfectly lucid founding document, and half a labor force regulating and monitoring the activities of the other half. Whether New Deal liberal or revisionist libertarian, we have overdone it. We always do.

But we still can have the independence of our grandparents without strapping guns to our hips. We can choose where we make our homes. We can slow down, simplify, cherish our spontaneity. We can stop waiting. We can live life to its end.

Further Reading

Bainbridge, John. *Another Way of Living*. New York: Holt, Rinehart & Winston, 1968.

Brand, Stewart, ed. *Last Whole Earth Catalog*. New York: Penguin Books, 1975.

Brooks, Patricia and Lester. *How to Buy Property Abroad*. Garden City, N.Y.: Doubleday & Co., 1974.

Business Plan for Small Manufacturers. Small Business Administration: Washington, D.C., n.d.

Cherry, Mary Spooner. *Would You Like to Live in England?* New York: Quadrangle/The New York Times Book Co., 1974.

Coyne, John. *By Hand: A Guide to Schools and Careers in Crafts*. New York: E. P. Dutton & Co., 1974.

Franke, David and Holly. *Safe Places: East of the Mississippi; Safe Places: West of the Mississippi*. New York: Warner Books, 1973.

Genfan, Herb, and Lyn Taetzch. *How to Start Your Own Craft Business*. New York: Watson-Guptill Publications, 1974.

Gross, Henry. *Financing for Small and Medium-Sized Businesses*. Englewood Cliffs, N.J.: Prentice-Hall, Inc., 1969.

Hunt, Bernice and Morton. *Prime Time*. New York: Stein & Day, 1975.

Jessup, Claudia, and Genie Chipps. *The Woman's Guide to Starting a Business*. New York: Holt, Rinehart & Winston, 1976.

Lanier, Alison Raymond. *Living in Europe*. New York: Charles Scribner's Sons, 1973.

O'Neill, Nena and George. *Shifting Gears*. New York: Avon Books, 1975.

Paulsen, Kathryn, and Ryan A. Kuhn (eds.). *Woman's Almanac.* Philadelphia and New York: J. B. Lippincott Co., 1976.

Price, Irving. *Buying Country Property.* New York: Pyramid Books, 1973.

Putt, William D. *How to Start Your Own Small Business.* 4 vols. New York: Drake Pubs., 1973–75.

Sheehy, Gail. *Passages.* New York: E. P. Dutton & Co., 1976.

Simon, Julian L. *How to Start and Operate a Mail Order Business.* 2nd ed. New York: McGraw-Hill Book Co., 1976.

Wouk, Herman. *Don't Stop the Carnival.* Garden City, N.Y.: Doubleday & Co., 1965.